ReFocus: The Films of Antoinetta Angelidi

ReFocus: The International Directors Series

Series Editors: Robert Singer, Stefanie Van de Peer and Gary D. Rhodes

Board of advisors:
Lizelle Bisschoff (Glasgow University)
Stephanie Hemelryck Donald (University of Lincoln)
Anna Misiak (Falmouth University)
Des O'Rawe (Queen's University Belfast)

ReFocus is a series of contemporary methodological and theoretical approaches to the interdisciplinary analyses and interpretations of international film directors, from the celebrated to the ignored, in direct relationship to their respective culture – its myths, values, and historical precepts – and the broader parameters of international film history and theory.

Titles in the series include:

Susanne Bier Edited by Missy Molloy, Mimi Nielsen and Meryl Shriver-Rice

Francis Veber Keith Corson

Jia Zhangke Maureen Turim

Xavier Dolan Edited by Andrée Lafontaine

Pedro Costa Nuno Barradas Jorge

Sohrab Shahid Saless Edited by Azadeh Fatehrad

Pablo Larraín Edited by Laura Hatry

Michel Gondry Edited by Marcelline Block and Jennifer Kirby

Rachid Bouchareb Edited by Michael Gott and Leslie Kealhofer-Kemp

Andrei Tarkovsky Edited by Sergey Toymentsev

Paul Leni Edited by Erica Tortolani and Martin F. Norden

Rakhshan Banietemad Edited by Maryam Ghorbankarimi

Jocelyn Saab Edited by Mathilde Rouxel and Stefanie Van de Peer

François Ozon Edited by Loïc Bourdeau

Teuvo Tulio Henry Bacon, Kimmo Laine and Jaakko Seppälä

João Pedro Rodrigues and João Rui Guerra da Mata Edited by José Duarte and Filipa Rosário

Lucrecia Martel Edited by Natalia Christofoletti Barrenha, Julia Kratje and Paul Merchant

Shyam Benegal Edited by Sneha Kar Chaudhuri and Ramit Samaddar

Denis Villeneuve Edited by Jeri English and Marie Pascal

Antoinetta Angelidi Edited by Penny Bouska and Sotiris Petridis

edinburghuniversitypress.com/series/refocint

ReFocus:
The Films of Antoinetta Angelidi

Edited by Penny Bouska and Sotiris Petridis

EDINBURGH
University Press

Edinburgh University Press is one of the leading university presses in the UK. We publish academic books and journals in our selected subject areas across the humanities and social sciences, combining cutting-edge scholarship with high editorial and production values to produce academic works of lasting importance. For more information visit our website: edinburghuniversitypress.com

© editorial matter and organisation Penny Bouska and Sotiris Petridis, 2023, 2024
© the chapters their several authors, 2023, 2024

Edinburgh University Press Ltd
The Tun – Holyrood Road
12 (2f) Jackson's Entry
Edinburgh EH8 8PJ

First published in hardback by Edinburgh University Press 2023

Typeset in 11/13 Ehrhardt MT by
IDSUK (DataConnection) Ltd
A CIP record for this book is available from the British Library

ISBN 978 1 4744 9370 3 (hardback)
ISBN 978 1 4744 9371 0 (paperback)
ISBN 978 1 4744 9372 7 (webready PDF)
ISBN 978 1 4744 9373 4 (epub)

The right of Penny Bouska and Sotiris Petridis to be identified as editors of this work has been asserted in accordance with the Copyright, Designs and Patents Act 1988 and the Copyright and Related Rights Regulations 2003 (SI No. 2498).

Contents

List of Figures vii
Notes on Contributors ix
Acknowledgements xii

    Prolegomenon 1
    Penny Bouska

Part 1 Feminism and the Avant-Garde
1 Weird Mothers: The Feminist Uncanniness of Antoinetta
  Angelidi's *Topos* 15
  Rea Walldén
2 'Every Element in a Film Narrates': The Complex Language of
  Heterogeneity in *Idées Fixes / Dies Irae* as a (Feminist) Critique to
  the Practice of Methodological Categorisation in Avant-garde
  Film History 45
  Fil Ieropoulos

Part 2 Concepts and Interpretations
3 *Thief or Reality*: Visual Dialectics on Death Instincts 67
  Penny Bouska
4 Childhood, Desire and Identity in *The Hours* 91
  Christina Adamou
5 Erased Ghost: The Derridean Spectrality of Angelidi's Signs in
  Idées Fixes / Dies Irae 106
  Ioannis Mazarakis
6 The Cinematic Sublime in Antoinetta Angelidi's *Thief or Reality* 124
  Evdokia Stefanopoulou

Part 3 Means and Media

7 From Orchestrated Noise to Elaborated Silence:
 The Audiovisuality of Antoinetta Angelidi's Films 143
 Electra Venaki

8 Dreyer, Magritte and Other Obsessions: Figural Invention in
 Antoinetta Angelidi's *Idées Fixes / Dies Irae – Variations on
 the Same Subject* 164
 Kyriakos Dionysopoulos

9 Antoinetta Angelidi: The Visual Gaze 186
 Calliope (Pepy) Rigopoulou

Interview with Antoinetta Angelidi

Giving Birth to her Films: Wandering with Antoinetta Angelidi 199
Rea Walldén

Appendix: Visual Material Selected by Antoinetta Angelidi 222
Index 233

Figures

1.1	Still, Angelidi, *Topos* (1985)	31
3.1	Still, Angelidi, *Thief or Reality* (2001)	76
3.2	Still, Angelidi, *Thief or Reality* (2001)	82
5.1	Still, Angelidi, *Idées Fixes / Dies Irae* (1977)	115
5.2	Still, Angelidi, *Idées Fixes / Dies Irae* (1977)	117
5.3	Still, Angelidi, *Idées Fixes / Dies Irae* (1977)	119
5.4	Still, Angelidi, *Idées Fixes / Dies Irae* (1977)	121
8.1	Still, Angelidi, *Idées Fixes / Dies Irae* (1977)	169
8.2	Still, Angelidi, *Idées Fixes / Dies Irae* (1977)	170
8.3	Still, Angelidi, *Idées Fixes / Dies Irae* (1977)	174
A.1	Angelidi directing. From the shooting of the film *Topos* at the Gazi Factory, 1984	222
A.2	Still, Angelidi, *Topos* (1985)	223
A.3	Still, Angelidi, *Topos* (1985)	223
A.4	Still, Angelidi, *Topos* (1985)	224
A.5	Angelidi at the Gazi Factory. Portrait by Maria Stefosi, 1988	224
A.6	Angelidi, preparatory sketch for the film *The Hours – A Square Film*, 1989	225
A.7	Angelidi, preparatory sketch for the installation *Boat–Matrix*, 1990	225
A.8	Angelidi, *Screen–Matrix*, installation (Epikentro, Patras, 1991)	226
A.9	Still, Angelidi, *The Hours – A Square Film* (1995)	226
A.10	Still, Angelidi, *The Hours – A Square Film* (1995)	227
A.11	Still, Angelidi, *The Hours – A Square Film* (1995)	227
A.12	Still, Angelidi, *Thief or Reality* (2001)	228

A.13 Still, Angelidi and Walldén, *121280 Ritual* (2008). Original material shot in 1980 228
A.14 Angelidi, *Father, Chair*, installation ('Stranger in a Strange Land', ReMap 3, Athens, 2011) 229
A.15 Angelidi, 'Stitches Without Thread', environment 229

Notes on Contributors

Christina Adamou is Assistant Professor in Film Theory and History at Aristotle University of Thessaloniki, Greece. Her PhD thesis focused on Samuel Beckett's plays for television and film. Her previous appointment was as a Lecturer in Television Studies at the Department of Film, Theatre and Television, University of Reading, UK. She has published in Greece and abroad on television history, acting in superhero and action films, translation and dubbing practices and gender representations. Her current research interests focus on media representations of the economic crisis in Greece, while she is also involved in theoretical and practical research documenting the crisis in everyday life.

Penny Bouska is an Adjunct Professor of Film Direction at Aristotle University of Thessaloniki, Greece. Her research interests focus on experimental cinema, psychoanalysis, and film aesthetics. She has a Masters in Cinema obtained from New Sorbonne University (Université Sorbonne Nouvelle – Paris 3). Her postgraduate studies in Paris were conducted with the financial support of IKY (Greek State Scholarships Foundation). She completed her PhD studies in the department of Film Studies of Aristotle University under the supervision of Antoinetta Angelidi, also financed by IKY. She has directed several short films and a full-length feature, *Common Ground* (2017).

Kyriakos Dionysopoulos received his doctorate in Philosophy at Aristotle University of Thessaloniki, Greece. His main research interests focus on film-philosophy, theories of visuality and psychoanalysis. He has contributed articles on film criticism for various journals.

Fil Ieropoulos studied film at London Metropolitan University and Media Arts at University of Westminster. In 2010 he completed his PhD on the 'Film Poem' at the University of Kent. Since 2003 he has worked at Buckinghamshire New University, teaching video art, theory and animation. He has participated in exhibitions, festivals and conferences all over Europe. He is one half of the art duo FYTA and has collaborated with, among others, the GNO, Onassis Foundation, Neuköllner Oper, Athens Festival, Athens Biennale and Lux Cinema. His film, *ORFEAS2021*, participated in the competition section of the 62nd Thessaloniki Film Festival and was nominated for the Iris Awards.

Ioannis Mazarakis is a PhD candidate in Film Studies, at Aristotle University of Thessaloniki, Greece. He is at the final stages of writing his PhD dissertation, which focuses on the semiological system of what he defines as the post-myth. He received his MA in History of Philosophy in 2015. His research interests include philosophy of language, postmodernism, posthumanism, mythology, film and new media semiotics.

Sotiris Petridis is a Postdoctoral Researcher at Aristotle University of Thessaloniki, Greece. He holds a PhD in Film Studies (Aristotle University) and Master's degrees in Art, Law and Economy (International Hellenic University) and in Film Studies (Aristotle University). His research interests are film and television genres, horror and slasher films, screenwriting theory and practice, audiovisual rights and copyright laws, viral marketing, and the new developments in film and television promotion. He is a member of the European Film Academy and the Hellenic Film Academy.

Calliope (Pepy) Rigopoulou is an Art Historian, and Professor Emerita at the National and Kapodistrian University of Athens. She studied Art History and Theory at Sorbonne I in Paris, from where she also gained her MA on 'Paul Klee: Masques and Marionettes' and her PhD on 'Paul Klee and the Stage'. She has taught at several academic institutions and published several books on art, culture, myth and psychoanalysis. She has organised and participated in numerous international congresses and exhibitions, and directed the theatre group of the Media and Communication Department of the National and Kapodistrian University of Athens. She has also directed art programmes for radio and television and been a columnist in the daily Greek press since 1994.

Evdokia Stefanopoulou received her PhD in Film Studies from Aristotle University of Thessaloniki, Greece. Her research is funded by the General Secretariat for Research and Technology (GSRT) and the Hellenic Foundation for Research and Innovation (HFRI). The topic of her thesis is the American science fiction film in the twenty-first century. Her research interests include film theory, fantastic film genres and semiotics.

Electra Venaki is a researcher and lecturer, former chief editor of the cinema section of <www.in.gr>, and a film editor. She holds a Masters in Cinema and a BA in Cinema Studies from University Paris 1 Panthéon – Sorbonne (1990). She teaches the course in Moving Image as part of the Masters programme of Aristotle University and for two years taught the Sound and Image Editing course, also at Aristotle University (2005–7). She is a long-time collaborator of the University of Thessaly (Greece), and teaches Editing and Sound Design in private colleges and schools in Athens (New York College, AKMI).

Rea Walldén is a film theorist and filmmaker, and holds a PhD in philosophy. Her research focuses on avant-garde and experimental cinema with a semiotic, epistemological and feminist approach. She has taught at Athens School of Fine Arts, National Kapodistrian University of Athens, Aristotle University of Thessaloniki and elsewhere. She has been on the Board of Directors of the Greek Film Centre and the European Network for Avant-Garde and Modernism Studies; and has been President of Women in Film and Television Greece. She has collaborated with Antoinetta Angelidi on several projects, including *Thief or Reality* (feature fiction, 2001, screenplay) and *Obsessive Hours at the Topos of Reality* (feature documentary, 2022, direction).

Acknowledgements

This book would have a totally different form without the inspirational conversations and exchanges, around her films and thoughts, with Antoinetta Angelidi. We would like to thank her for her generosity to share her archives with us and for the permission she granted to reproduce images from this copyright material.

We would also like to express our deepest appreciation to all the contributors for their participation and their commitment to this project that has successfully come to completion.

We gratefully acknowledge the ReFocus series editors, Gary D. Rhodes, Robert Singer and Stefanie Van de Peer, for their valuable assistance with the editing throughout this challenging process. Also, we would like to thank the editorial staff at Edinburgh University Press and particularly the publisher Gillian Leslie, and assistant commissioning editor, Sam Johnson, who have provided excellent support and guidance throughout all stages of the volume.

We would also like to thank the anonymous peer-reviewers for their generous and incisive comments, as well as the editors Amy Tzimoula, Julie Carter and Vaso Zisi for their English language suggestions.

I would like to thank my friends and family for their strong support and encouragement through this tough period of preparing the volume. More specifically, I would like to thank Manolis Kapnopoulos and Tania Nanavraki for all their patience and support, my mother, Maria Petridou, and my little niece, Maria Mastoridou, who was a strong psychological support without even knowing it.

Sotiris Petridis

I would like to thank Maria Laftsidou for all the enlightening discussions we had, during the three years of the preparation of the volume, and the genuine confidence she showed in me. I would also like to thank Stathis Vergidis for his assistance in working with the index as well as for the innovative ideas he shared. I am much obliged to the academics Dafni Papadatou and Ioulia Pipinia, for sharing their valuable editing experiences and for providing helpful advice. I would also like to thank the people working in 'Defacto', for keeping me company while writing. During the long process of writing and editing of this volume, I had the emotional support and trust from my mother Kleio and my father Sotiris Bouskas and I thank them for that. I would like to express my special appreciation to Dr Nikos Polyhroniadis for being an unwearied listener who never stopped expressing his faith to my abilities. Finally, I would like to thank Thodoros Kyrloglou, my lifelong partner, for almost everything but mostly for his love and care.

Penny Bouska

Prolegomenon

Penny Bouska

Unadjusted, unassimilated, misfit. Experimental cinema is more than an artistic practice of expression, more than a technical method of cinema. It exceeds regulations and limitations, searching to renew cinematic language, being in a constant reconfiguration. It is a way of living and contemplating life. This is the distinctive and exceptional filmmaking that Antoinetta Anglelidi introduced to Greek cinema. One of the few women in a particularly male-dominated area of film production, she managed to be acknowledged by the Greek public and screened at international film festivals and contemporary art museums, such as the Centre Pompidou in Paris and the Museum of Modern Art (MoMA) in New York.[1] Angelidi's oeuvre has inspired the current volume to present, through a wide range of academic interpretations, the particularity of her methods and the mentality behind her experimentations in cinema.

Stella Theodoraki, another Greek experimental filmmaker, notes that Angelidi brought 'that which was missing from Greek reality: the contact with a global artistic language of a *different* cinema'.[2] Indeed, at the time of Angelidi's return from Paris, New Greek Cinema[3] was beginning to explore its artistic potential, with most of the Greek filmmakers being directly involved with *political film*.[4] Apart from some exceptions,[5] most of Angelidi's colleagues were making narrative films with historical references, something that, during the seven-year period of military junta (1967–74), came to an abrupt halt, as rigid censorship and cultural repression was imposed by the authoritarian regime. After the fall of the dictatorship, and during a period called *Metapolitefsi*,[6] artists 'turned directly to political subjects and to taboo topics like the Greek civil war and its consequences'.[7] Angelidi immerses herself in the current climate with a different approach. In accordance with Aglaia Mitropoulou's definition of political cinema, which 'is based on a concept and structured according to a certain political criterion',[8] she proposes an interpretation of Greek reality through feminist and Marxist views. In a totally personal and innovative style imbued with pictorial and literary elements, her cinema expands the very notion of political film. In Greece, orthodox Marxism had oriented filmmakers to interpret reality as narrowed down into economic factors and working-class issues. In Paris, the revolt of May '68 had had major political and cultural implications, which had reformed French society. The 'sixty-eighters' had realised that 'with the advent of consumer society, the scope of commodification had transcended the workplace and had begun to encompass almost every aspect of social life'.[9] Closely related to this wider and renewed political view, Angelidi poses political questions that reach an existential point of political thinking, related to gender, feminism and queer identities; a way of thinking that was quite ahead of its time and the socio-political conditions in Greece at the time. This very exceptional and very different form of cinema, born in a historical moment when 'everything seemed possible',[10] went beyond the accepted norm. Pushing the boundaries of standard culture, the reception of her work incited conflicting viewpoints. She remarks that 'by the mid-1980s, populism had made suspect every form of artistic avant-garde, while the advent of neo-liberalism in the 1990s turned the very notion of avant-garde into anathema'.[11]

Private conversations, interviews and Angelidi's personal archives and memories throw an interesting light on the particular events that formed and marked her artistic identity. Angelidi's family background exercised a decisive influence on her political consciousness. Both her parents had origins in the Greek diaspora: her mother Emilia came from Russia and the Black Sea, and her father Orestis came from Madagascar, born of a semi-Malgache mother named Antoinetta. Traced back to the first-wave feminist demands for women's equality, her mother's political views on feminity and feminism had a great influence on Angelidi. Years later, the latter would broaden her feminist ideas to include a wider range of inequalities such as gender discrimination, sexuality and domestic gender roles, aligned to the second-wave's feminist antipatriarchical ideology. A chemical engineer and translator of Russian literature,[12] she also introduced her daughter to the radical thinking of the avant-garde poets of post-revolutionary Russia. If her mother had a political impact on her identity, her father reinforced her love for fine art. He used to bring her art books as presents, feeding her imagination. She remembers dwelling in those illustrated books of art. On Sundays, he used to take her with him on his visits to the factories where he worked as a chemical engineer. Wandering around, Angelidi developed the aesthetics of deserted industrial spaces that would later dominate her cinematic world.

Painting was Angelidi's first love. She was a talented painter herself and as a student of Vaso Katraki's and Panos Sarafianos's workshop,[13] and later of Nikos

Engonopoulos, she was encouraged by her teachers to continue in this direction. She used to spend hours drawing the reflection of her face on the library's window, or sketching the naked body of her mother. 'At school, during the breaks', she says, 'I used to make very fine and detailed drawings of dry leaves and spiders' webs.'[14] She gradually disengaged from representation in search of more abstract painting expressions. This search reaches a turning point when Angelidi recognises a clear connection between the static two-dimensional representation of pictorial art and timing, which will be of major importance for her filmmaking. However, following the family tradition of engineering, she studied architecture at the National Technical University of Athens (Εθνικό Μετσόβιο Πολυτεχνείο), from where she graduated in 1973. Though she would never practice this profession, she would apply the knowledge gained about working with structures in her filmmaking. In 1972, she had a dream about one of René Magritte's paintings, in which she conceived for the first time a sense of timing into the two-dimensional space, in an imperceptible slow motion within the painting. This dream, along with an experience of revelation that she felt on her visit to the exhibition Documenta '72 in Kassel, led Angelidi to cinema.

Her decision to go to Paris was an enforced one, due to the political turmoil in her country. Actively involved in the anti-dictatorial resistance, as a member of the Central Bureau of the Euro-communist youth 'Rigas Fereos', she was forced to leave Greece under secrecy to avoid arrest. Recalling that day, she remembers that she was heading to the airport when the police entered her parents' home to arrest her. Most of the other members of the Central Bureau were arrested, imprisoned and tortured by the authoritarian military regime. Paris for her was more than the city of revolt and cinema; it was also a place of refuge. Angelidi stayed in Paris from 1973 until 1978 and studied cinema at the prestigious Institut des Hautes Études Cinématographiques (IDHEC),[15] where she was admitted with a full scholarship. There she made her first short films, *L'histoirécrite* (1975) and *L'eau* (1976), as well as her first full-length film, *Idées Fixes / Dies Irae* (1977). Angelidi has directed, in total, four full-length films and nine short films. She has also made several artworks, performances and video installations as a visual artist. Her second full-length film was *Topos* (1985), followed by *The Hours – A Square Film* (1995), and *Thief or Reality* (2001). Less known and seldomly screened are her short films,[16] called 'art-happenings' by Vrasidas Karalis,[17] as a reference to their spontaneous and performative character. Unfortunately, almost half of these short films are lost or destroyed. In this volume, we have tried to include some information about them. Working in a complex matrix of heterogeneous elements, Angelidi gradually shaped her cinematic method. 'My method appeared through the making of my films',[18] she confirms, alluding to the slow process of creation.

As a film student, Angelidi was fortunate to have as teachers some of the most prestigious French film theorists – Christian Metz, Noël Burch and Thierry Kuntzel. Motivated by a confluence of theories, such as semiotics, psychoanalysis and art history, she exhibits a multi-levelled structure of representation. A film, for Angelidi, is the result of a certain type of articulation, composed of heterogenous elements in dialectic juxtaposition. 'The central theme of her work', as Karalis notes, 'is the process of constructing images – her cinema is the ultimate model of "structural film-making".'[19] She would make detailed drawings of the films, similar to musical scores. In a Cartesian coordinate system, she would mount elements of sounds, images and graphics on the vertical axis, presented against time on the horizontal axis. Formal combinations can also be seen within the frame. Angelidi remembers, while viewing the film *Faust* (1926) by F. W. Murnau, moving the *pellicule* repeatedly back and forth, until she noticed that the body of Mephistopheles was aligned with the Gothic bell tower. For Angelidi, this was an important revelation; for the first time, she comprehended that the perspectives of film were similar to those of drawing. Her drawing skills would be applied henceforth to her film canvas; a creative interrelation between architecture and cinema. Along with the sense of timing, the graphical drawings would be her first tools in filmmaking.

In addition to being a filmmaker and artist, Angelidi is an important intellectual, having produced many theoretical texts on cinema theory. Most significant among her essays is 'Play with the Uncanny – A Poetics of Cinema' (2005), where she presents her thoughts on the similarities between the formalist mechanism of *defamiliarisation* and the psychical mechanism of the *uncanny*.[20] In reference to formalist Viktor Shklovsky's definition, she acknowledges that 'the technique of art is to make an object "unfamiliar", to make forms difficult, to increase the difficulty and length of perception because the process of perception is an aesthetic end in itself and must be prolonged'.[21] In correlation with the Freudian theory on dream-work, she uses the method of defamiliarisation to create a cinematic atmosphere of unease and anxiety. Also, she manages to objectify abstract elements such as time, space, sound and light, representing them as parts of the material world. A light can be cut through with a knife and a sound can take the form of a *banderole*,[22] as in medieval paintings. Louis Marcorelles notes about Angelidi's first film that 'occasionally, cinema can work exclusively with relations of lines, of shadows and lights or with actors' movements'.[23] Angelidi extends this approach even further to more abstract concepts such as dream, femininity, sexuality, politics and language. The contents of her films become illustrations of abstract ideas, as Angelidi depicts the abstract with body movements, scene sets, dialogues and colour compositions.

Another important essay of hers is 'Dream and Cinema: Three Cinematic Approaches of Life as Dream' (2012).[24] Keeping track of her dreams, Angelidi uses them as raw material for her films. Sigmund Freud in his magnum opus

Interpretation of Dreams (1900) affirms that 'the task of dream interpretation is to unravel what the dream-work has woven'.[25] From this starting point, Angelidi inverses the procedure by creating elaborate compositions of filmic material. Inspired by a profound study made by her teacher Kuntzel,[26] who juxtaposes the dream-work to film-work, Angelidi develops a semiological system similar to rebus puzzles. Induced into an active role, the spectator of her films is called to unravel the enigma. Angelidi really respects her audience. With her films, more than communicating her personal thoughts and experiences, she sets a stage for interaction.

Behind each of her films lies a story worth telling. Her first full-length film, *Idées Fixes / Dies Irae* (1977), was a tribute to another film. Angelidi has a deep admiration for Carl Dreyer and for his film *Dies Iraes* (in English: *Day of Wrath*, in Danish: *Vredens Dag*, 1943), which she believes to be one of the most feminist films of all times. She keeps the Latin title from Dreyer, and adds another half written in French, *idées fixes*, which means 'obsessive ideas', something that refers to her own way of thinking. Hristos Vacalopoulos asserts, 'the days of wrath (and their images, their sounds) should become obsessive ideas',[27] highlighting the need for the feminist discourse to be more obsessive and dynamic in its demands. The original title was written IDEESDIES/FIXESIRAE, or IDEESFIXES/DIESIRAE, in capital letters and on separate lines, to emphasise the interchangeability of the words. The possibility to read the title in many different ways provided a key to understand the film. During its screening at the 1977 Counter-Festival in Thessaloniki, Angelidi was asked to choose a Greek title and she came up with Παραλλαγές στο ίδιο θέμα (i.e., *Variations on the Same Subject*). A frame from the film made the cover of the journal *Cahiers critiques de la literature*[28] in 1979. The journal's editor, Jean Thibaudeau, was impressed by the film's personal and innovative style. In the Thessaloniki Counter-Festival, the film won the Best New Director Award and the Greek Film Critics Award.

Τόπος (*Topos*, 1985) is Angelidi's second full-length film and the first to be made in Greece. Angelidi left her children with her parents in Athens for a short time and returned to Paris with Clairi Mitsotaki to co-write the script. Pavlos Zannas, a significant Greek intellectual who was president, at the time, of the Greek Film Centre, played a key role in the realisation of the project. Zannas was an open-minded man who strongly supported the avant-garde and its young Greek directors. He accepted Angelidi's proposal for funding, along with the proposals of other young directors, such as Takis Spetsiotis and George Korras. At the Thessaloniki Film Festival in 1985, *Topos* received the Special Jury Award, the Best Soundtrack Award and the Greek Film Critics Award, as well as a Hellenic Ministry of Culture Quality Award. During the same period as the screening of *Topos*, Angelidi presented an art exhibition which featured parts of the film's sets and sizeable multi-material objects. The exhibition was called Έχιδνες (*Echidnas*), in reference to the Greek mythological monsters. The Greek title, Τόπος, means place. However, this promising and brilliant return to her *topos* would prove to be quite challenging.

The following year, Angelidi submitted a new script for funding, based on the horror novella of Henry James, *The Turn of the Screw* (1898). However, after the resignation of Zannas, the Greek Film Centre was suspicious of alternative narrations, and the proposal was rejected. This was the beginning of a series of rejections that Angelidi handled by submitting re-writings of the script. It would take almost ten years for the Greek Film Centre to finally fund her third full-length film, Οι ώρες – Μια τετράγωνη ταινία (*The Hours – A Square Film*, 1995). During that long period of waiting, Angelidi made objects and installations inspired by images from the script. Her works *Screen–Matrix* (1990) and *Page from the Book of Hours* (1994) were made during that period. *The Hours* was eventually made and received the Best Sets Award and the Best Costumes Award at the 1995 Thessaloniki Film Festival, as well as a Hellenic Ministry of Culture Quality Award and the Hellenic Ministry of Culture Sets Award.

Her fourth full-length film was made in 2001, with the title Κλέφτης ή η Πραγματικότητα (*Thief or Reality*). In the publicity material, the title was accompanied by the subtitle Τρεις εκδοχές (*Three Versions*), denoting the separation of the film into three different parts. The special story behind that film is that the script was based on a long-term correspondence, from 1995 to 2000, between Angelidi and her daughter Rea Walldén, when the latter left for studies in another city. From a huge amount of material, a selection of texts formed the final script. This productive collaboration evolved later into many more projects. *Thief or Reality* premiered at the Locarno International Film Festival in 2001. It received a Hellenic Ministry of Culture Quality Award and was nominated for Best European Film at the Méliès d'Or at the Porto International Film Festival in 2001. At the time of writing in 2022, two full-length Angelidi's films are in progress: the fiction film *Medea/Kore* (since 2009) and the autobiographical documentary *Obsessive Hours at the Topos of Reality* (2022).

To present the multi-levelled and multidimensional work of Angelidi is not a straightforward endeavour. As a result, and corresponding to three core features of Angelidi's work model, this volume is divided into three thematical parts: 'Feminism and the Avant-Garde', 'Concepts and Interpretations', and 'Means and Media'. The first part is dedicated to the relation of Angelidi's work with post-structural feminism and the second period of the French avant-garde. It comprises two chapters that both place Angelidi's work in the avant-garde and approach it with regard to gender issues and feminist perspectives. More specifically, the interrelation between Angelidi's feminist ideology and avant-garde strategies of filmmaking gives rise to the contemporary theoretical questions that Rea Walldén explores in the inspiring and multi-levelled chapter 'Weird Mothers: The Feminist Uncanniness of Antoinetta Angelidi's *Topos*'. Walldén goes even further – to an understanding of Angelidi's feminist views as an avant-garde practice of uncanniness, exemplified by the film *Topos* (1988). The innovative character of this text is twofold. Firstly, it reveals a very particular side of feminist aesthetics connected to the practice of the avant-garde, and secondly, it relates this connection to Angelidi's personal method in creating the uncanny. This idea, thoroughly developed in the first chapter, condenses the two separate core features of feminism and the avant-garde into an extended mechanism of subjectivity, uncanniness and experimentation.

In Chapter 2, '"Every Element in a Film Narrates": The Complex Language of Heterogeneity in *Idées Fixes / Dies Irae* as a (Feminist) Critique to the Practice of Methodological Categorisation in Avant-Garde Film History', Fil Ieropoulos discusses the feminist discourse articulated by heterogenous avant-garde methodologies in Angelidi's first film, *Idées Fixes / Dies Irae*. With reference to Adams P. Sitney's seminal book *Visionary Film* (1974), Ieropoulos recognises a convergence of antithetical tendencies, making the film both poetic and structural. The two aesthetical methods, despite contrasting each other's purposes, are brilliantly combined in the film. The poetic style allures the audience into an elusive experience, and at the same time the materialistic structure keeps viewers critical and vigilant. In an elaborate analysis of the film, Ieropoulos reveals how this opposition works by reflecting on Angelidi's structures of the avant-garde.

The second part of the volume, 'Concepts and Interpretations', is a collection of four chapters presenting different aspects of Angelidi's films, through the lens of specific theoretical concepts. With critical and analytical insight, the writers offer profound interpretations, of great interest and inspiration. Applying psychoanalytical theory, and more specifically the concept of death instincts, to the fourth of Angelidi's full-length films, *Thief or Reality*, I undertake a broader reading and interpretation of the film's reference to death and to reflections on death. Far from any type of existential interpretation, in the chapter '*Thief or Reality*: Visual Dialectics on Death Instincts', I examine *Thief or Reality* as the aesthetic representation of an instinctual force which is subtle and 'unseen' by the psyche. Following the dense and discrepant methodology of Freudian theory I interpret the cinematic devises of the film as visual examples of an internal process. Through this approach, Angelidi's cinema is seen as an artistic mechanism of the obscure workings of the psyche.

Chapter 4, 'Childhood, Desire and Identity in *The Hours*', looks at the desires and fears shaping one's identity as the core issue behind the general thematical scheme of the film *The Hours – A Square Film* (1995). In this inspiring chapter, Christina Adamou contemplates Angelidi's cinematic representation of growing up and shaping an identity from childhood to adulthood. With reference to Donald Winnicott's ideas on the subject, she uses the concept of the objectified child, corresponding to the good or bad child, and adults' desire for control, violence and sex. Through her examination of the content of the film, Adamou reaches a point where mothering and nurturing oneself seem to be, in Angelidi's images, the most crucial psychological tasks we can undertake in our lifetime.

For Ioannis Mazarakis, the work of Angelidi is an apt illustration of what Jacques Derrida calls a *writing-under-erasure* scheme. In Chapter 5 'Erased Ghost: The Derridean Spectrality of Angelidi's signs in *Idées Fixes / Dies Irae*', he presents an alternative reading of Angelidi's methods on *defamiliarisation* and the *uncanny*, by relating them to the Derridean concepts of *sous rature* and *spectrality*. The deconstructive method of erasing terms – ~~like this~~ – reveals the instability of their semantics, and at the same time the expansion of their meaning. What is written and crossed out is both present and absent; it is a presence of the absence of meaning. Interpretations that ignore the unlimited nature of signification are doomed to fail and the simultaneity of cinematic signs as present and absent becomes more obvious in an ambiguous ontological state, where Angelidi's aesthetics reflect its spectrality.

In Chapter 6, 'The Cinematic Sublime in Antoinetta Angelidi's *Thief or Reality*', Evdokia Stefanopoulou continues the reflection on Angelidi's uncanny structure, with reference to a totally different philosophical concept, the *sublime*. Stefanopoulou presents an inspiring reading of Angelidi's film *Thief or Reality*, through the paradoxical sentiment of an unmeasurable greatness alongside a powerful feeling of inferiority and submission. Using as theoretical context Edmund Burke's and Immanuel Kant's treatises of the sublime, Stefanopoulou argues that Angelidi's film articulates a unique cinematic sublimity, enabling the expansion and transformation of cinematic vision.

The third part of the book is dedicated to the special role that different media played in Angelidi's oeuvre, as well as the particular way in which she uses them in relation to cinema. Three chapters comprise this part, and explore Angelidi's meeting with media such as sound, the figural and visual arts. Chapter 7, Electra Venaki's 'From Orchestrated Noise to Elaborated Silence: The Audiovisuality of Antoinetta Angelidi's Films', supplements previous approaches to Angelidi's work with an analysis of sound aesthetics. For Angelidi, sound is of equal value to images and that is the reason why she constructs meticulous soundscapes, as if someone might hear the film without the images. By contextualising Angelidi's work in its particular geographical and historical circumstances, that is, Greece from the mid-1970s to 2001, Venaki identifies the social, political and cultural influences upon her sound choices, providing interesting information on the period's cinema production.

Kyriakos Dionysopoulos, in his chapter 'Dreyer, Magritte and Other Obsessions: Figural Invention in Antoinetta Angelidi's *Idées Fixes / Dies Irae* – Variations on the Same Subject', places the emphasis on another medium, expressing with the general term 'figural' both the figural layout of words and drawings as well as figurative art. The correlation between Angelidi's cinema and visual art is, as we have already mentioned, of great importance and Dionysopoulos underlines this perspective. With a highly appealing and concise writing style, he describes how Angelidi reverses the spatial axes, transforming space dimensions and creating paradoxes of 'vertical horizons'. In a very particular way, Angelidi incorporates figural and visual content into her thematic variations, creating exceptional narrative artworks.

In the last chapter of the volume, 'Antoinetta Angelidi: The Visual Gaze', a less well-known aspect of Angelidi's work is presented for the first time. Calliope (Pepy) Rigopolou, in her unique style, presents the parallel and less acknowledged career of Angelidi as a visual artist. Referring to a time period of almost fifty years, Rigopoulou presents the variety of techniques and materials Angelidi has used to make various artworks such as paintings, collages, objects, performances and projection installations. Drawing from archive material, interviews with the artist, as well as her personal memories, Rigopoulou guides the reader through this obscure part of Angelidi's creativity.

The book closes with Angelidi herself, via an exclusive interview with her long-time collaborator and daughter Rea Walldén. The style is more like a conversation which at times becomes interactive, and at other points words and thoughts flow as in an inner monologue. In this interview Angelidi provides important information about her methods, her work with actors, the way she handles music, sound and noise, as well as her personal fantasies, and her 'fixed ideas' which become converted into exceptional images.

As the first and the most influential woman film director of feminist ideology and experimental cinema in Greece, Angelidi has influenced the course of the Greek cinema tradition and created the framework for the next generation. This can be seen in the recent 'Greek Weird Wave' cinema.[29] Yet it took a long time for her work to be appreciated. In 2005, as part of the 46th International Thessaloniki Film Festival, there was a retrospective tribute to her work, and she was presented with the honorary Golden Alexander Award for her unique achievements and her exceptional contribution to Greek cinema. The current volume presents Angelidi's work to a much wider reading audience, both scholars and film lovers. With comprehensive, critical and theoretical approaches to her work, including archival material, visual and other, as well as an unpublished interview with Angelidi, we aspire to contribute to a better understanding of her unique way of making cinema.

NOTES

1. In 1977, Noël Burch presented Angelidi's film *Idées Fixes / Dies Irae* (1977) at the Centre Pompidou. He proposed the film's inclusion in the Centre's permanent collection, which was refused because it was Angelidi's first film. In 1995, her film *Topos* (1985) was also screened at the Centre as part of the retrospective on Greek cinema, under the direction of Michel Demopoulos. The same film was also screened in 1993, at the Museum of Modern Art of New York, as part of *Cinemythology: A Retrospective of Greek Film*.
2. Stella Theodoraki (ed.), *Antoinetta Angelidi* (Athens: Aigokeros, 2005), 13.
3. For further information on New Greek Cinema see Anna Poupou, 'New Greek Cinema 1965–1981: History and Politics', *FILMICON: Journal of Greek Film Studies* 1 (September 2013): 160–6.
4. According to Aglaia Mitropoulou, every film is political, as it is a depiction of its time and place, even if this is not directly shown. However, political film, in a strict sense, is a film based on a concept and structured according to a certain political criterion. See Aglaia Mitropoulou, *Ellinikos Kinimatografos* (Athens: Ekdoseis Papazisis, 2006), 243
5. *Modelo* (1974) by Costas Sfikas and *Black and White* (1973) by Thanasis Retzis.
6. *Metapolitefsi* is the Greek word for the extremely creative and liberal transitional period after the end of the junta in 1974 and until 1980.
7. Mitropoulou, *Ellinikos Kinimatografos*, 245.
8. Ibid., 243.
9. Richard Wolin, 'events of May 1968', Encyclopedia Britannica, 19 September 2017.
10. Antoinetta Angelidi and Rea Walldén, 'The Ethics of Heterogeneity and Experimentation: Teaching Film Direction in the Film School of Aristotle University of Thessaloniki', in *Contemporary Greek Film Cultures from 1990 to the Present*, ed. T. Kazakopoulou and M. Fotiou (Bern: Peter Lang, 2017, 369–92), 4.
11. Ibid.
12. Her mother translated works by Anna Akhmatova, Anton Chekhov, Osip Mandelstam and Marina Tsvetaeva.
13. For more information, see: <https://www.panossarafianos.gr/el/ekpompi-20-hronia-apo-thanato-toy-panoy-sarafianoy>, accessed 30 May 2022.
14. Private conversation with Antoinetta Angelidi for this book.
15. IDHEC was the original name of La Fémis (Fondation Européenne pour les Métiers de l'Image et du Son), one of the most prestigious film schools in the world.
16. Further information on Angelidi's short films can be found in the filmography given at the end of the book.
17. Vrasidas Karalis, 'The Feminine Gaze in Antoinetta Angelidi's Cinema of Imaginative Cathedrals', in *Realism in Greek Cinema: From the Post-War Period to the Present* (I. B. Tauris, 2017, 191–214), 191.
18. Angelidi and Walldén, 'The Ethics of Heterogeneity and Experimentation', 4.
19. Karalis, 'The Feminine Gaze', 192.
20. Antoinetta Angelidi, «Το παιχνίδι με το ανοίκειο – μια ποιητική του κινηματογράφου» [Play with the Uncanny – A Poetics of Cinema]. In Angelidi, *Γραφές για τον κινηματογράφο – Διεπιστημονικές προσεγγίσεις* [*Writings on Cinema – Interdisciplinary Approaches*] (Athens: Nefeli, 2005), 11–35.
21. Viktor Shklovsky, 'Art as Technique', in *Russian Formalist Criticism: Four Essays*, ed. Lee T. Lemon and Marion J. Reiss (Lincoln: University of Nebraska Press, 1965), 3–24, 12.
22. The *banderoles* or *speech scrolls* were illustrations denoting titles and speeches in painting mostly produced during the medieval period.

23. Louis Marcorelles, 'Un défi du cinéma grec au pouvoir conservateur', *Le Monde*, 3 November 1977.
24. Antoinetta Angelidi, «Όνειρο και κινηματογράφος: Τρεις κινηματογραφικές προσεγγίσεις της ζωής ως όνειρο» [Dream and Cinema: Three Cinematic Approaches of Life as Dream]. *Annals for Aesthetics* 46 (2012): 363–73.
25. Sigmund Freud, 'The Interpretation of Dreams', Volume IV (1900), in *The Standard Edition of the Complete Psychological Works of Sigmund Freud*.
26. Thierry Kuntzel, ' Le travail du film', in *Communications 19*, 1972, *Le texte: de la théorie à la recherche*, 25–39.
27. Theodoraki, *Antoinetta Angelidi*, 37.
28. *Cahiers critiques de la literature*, September No 1–2, 1979.
29. The Greek Weird Wave appeared in the aftermath of Greece's economic crisis of 2009. Distinguished by a very particular style, *mise-en-scène* and performance, it was introduced to the public with the film *Dogtooth* by George Lanthimos. For more information see Dimitris Papanikolaou, *Greek Weird Wave: A Cinema of Biopolitics* (Edinburgh: Edinburgh University Press, 2021). Moreover, Walldén analyses Angelidi's influence on the Greek Weird Wave in her article 'The Spatio-Temporality of the Avant-Gardes: Feminist Avant-Garde U-Topoi in Greek Cinema from Transition to Crisis', in *Contemporary Greek Film Cultures from 1990 to the Present*, ed. Tonia Kazakopoulou and Mikela Fotiou. Bern: Peter Lang, 2017, 71–99.

BIBLIOGRAPHY

Angelidi, Antoinetta. 'Όνειρο και Κινηματογράφος: Τρεις κινηματογραφικές προσεγγίσεις της ζωής ως όνειρο' (Dream and Cinema: Three Cinematic Approaches of Life as Dream). *Annals for Aesthetics* 46 (2012): 363–732.
Angelidi, Antoinetta. «Το παιχνίδι με το ανοίκειο – μια ποιητική του κινηματογράφου» [Play with the Uncanny – A Poetics of Cinema]. In *Grafes gia ton kinimatografo – Diepistimonikes prosegisis [Writings on Cinema – Interdisciplinary Approaches]*. Athens: Nefeli, 2005, 11–35.
Angelidi, Antoinetta and Rea Walldén. 'The Ethics of Heterogeneity and Experimentation: Teaching Film Direction in the Film School of Aristotle University of Thessaloniki', *Contemporary Greek Film Cultures from 1990 to the Present*, ed. Tonia Kazakopoulou and Mikela Fotiou. Bern: Peter Lang, 2017, 369–92.
Freud, Sigmund. 'Interpretation of Dreams', Volume IV, (1900), in *The Standard Edition of the Complete Psychological Works of Sigmund Freud*, ed. and trans. by James Strachey, coll. Anna Freud, assist. Alix Strachey and Alan Tyson, (London: The Hogarth Press and the Institute of Psycho-Analysis, Volumes I–XXIV (1886–1939), (1981).
Karalis, Vrasidas. 'The Feminine Gaze in Antoinetta Angelidi's Cinema of Imaginative Cathedrals', in *Realism in Greek Cinema: From the Post-War Period to the Present*. London: Bloomsbury Publishing, 2017, 191–214.
Kuntzel, Thierry. 'Le travail du film'. *Communications, 19, Le texte: de la théorie à la recherche*, 25–39.
Marcorelles, Louis. 'Un défi du cinéma grec au pouvoir conservateur'. *Le Monde*, 3 November 1977.
Mitropoulou, Aglaia. *Ellinikos Kinimatografos*. Athens: Ekdoseis Papazisis, 2006.
Poupou, Anna. 'New Greek Cinema 1965–1981: History and Politics'. *FilmIcon: Journal of Greek Film Studies* 1 (September 2013): 160–6. <http://filmiconjournal.com/journal/article/2013/1/9>, accessed 30 May 2022.
Papanikolaou, Dimitris. *Greek Weird Wave: A Cinema of Biopolitics*. Edinburgh: Edinburgh University Press, 2021.

Shklovsky, Viktor. 'Art as Technique,' in *Russian Formalist Criticism: Four Essays*, ed. Lee T. Lemon and Marion J. Reiss. Lincoln: University of Nebraska Press, 1965, 3–24.
Theodoraki, Stella (ed.), *Antoinetta Angelidi*. Athens: Ekdoseis Aigokeros, 2005.
Thibaudeau, Jean. *Cahiers critiques de la literature* 1–2, 1979.
Walldén, Rea. 'The Spatio-Temporality of the Avant-Gardes: Feminist Avant-Garde U-Topoi in Greek Cinema from Transition to Crisis', in *Contemporary Greek Film Cultures from 1990 to the Present*, ed. Tonia Kazakopoulou and Mikela Fotiou. London: Bloomsbury Publishing, 2017, 71–99.
Wolin, Richard. 'events of May 1968'. *Encyclopedia Britannica*, 19 September 2017. <https://www.britannica.com/event/events-of-May-1968>, accessed 30 May 2022.

PART I

Feminism and the Avant-Garde

CHAPTER 1

Weird Mothers: The Feminist Uncanniness of Antoinetta Angelidi's *Topos*

Rea Walldén

'If filmic practice [. . .] is an inscription of the look on the body of the mother, we must now begin to consider the possibilities and consequences of the mother returning the look.'

Constance Penley, 1977

'Native land is not the topos *(place) where we were born. Native land can be just a stain.'*

Topos (Antoinetta Angelidi, 1985)

This chapter is an approach to Antoinetta Angelidi's work in general, and *Topos* in particular, through the interpretive concept of uncanniness, viewed as a feminist avant-garde strategy. It maintains that Angelidi's *Topos* exemplifies both avant-garde and feminist filmmaking, constituting an argument for their close interconnection, while it also traces the distinctiveness of Angelidi's poetics. The figure of the uncanny mother is used as a multifaced simile for an unconventional structuring of women's subjectivity, which resists and refutes patriarchal tropes. The chapter starts by mapping possible relations between filmmaking strategies and feminist politics, as these were investigated by the second-wave feminist film theorists. This leads to the question of the films' situating of the subject, and furthermore, their play with the subject's very constitution. The chapter then proceeds to decode Angelidi's cinematic poetics, as described in her own texts, focusing on the articulation between a strategic uncanniness and her feminist politics. The rest of the chapter analyses Angelidi's 1985 film *Topos*, as the turning point in her work, where her poetics of feminist uncanniness reaches its full maturity in her distinctive style. The film is approached in its questioning and renewing of gender subjectivity and representation, as both deep and surface structures, in their spatial and temporal aspects. I argue that Angelidi's *Topos* is a feminist manifesto, even more than her outspoken *Idées Fixes / Dies Irae* (1977) or her autobiographical *The Hours* (1995). *Topos* opens up new *topoi* for women's subjectivities.

THE POLITICAL POETICS OF WEIRD MOTHERS

Antoinetta Angelidi's films give a unique answer to the question of the connection between avant-garde filmmaking strategies and feminist politics. The historical (almost) simultaneity of the second avant-gardes in the arts with the second wave of the feminist movement meant that this question has been posed and answered many times, in many ways, in the 1970s and 1980s, by feminist film theorists and feminist avant-garde filmmakers. This was also the topic of the 1977 seminal article by Constance Penley, 'The Avant-Garde and Its Imaginary',[1] the closing suggestion of which inspired in a way the present text: 'if filmic practice [. . .] is an inscription of the look on the body of the mother, we must now begin to consider the possibilities and consequences of the mother returning the look'.[2] When I re-read it recently, it sounded to me like a demand or an open call, which Angelidi's *Topos* has answered.

Although the question of the relation between art practice and politics is definitional for the artistic avant-gardes, it is by no means exclusive to them. It goes back to Plato's distrust of the poets in the *Republic*,[3] way before the birth of the concept of 'art' as we know it. Whether defined as magic or worship, as knowledge or fakery, as imitation or creation, art practice has always been political. It has been political even when defined as a completely independent realm, as was the case after the Enlightenment, following Immanuel Kant's 'disinterested' beauty;[4] or, maybe, it was then that it became even more so. There is no doubt that the metaphorical use of the military term 'avant-garde' is part of the semantic universe of the political concept of 'revolution'. It was first applied to an intellectual movement in the late eighteenth century in the context of the French Revolution and was introduced into the field of art by utopian socialists in the nineteenth century. By the early twentieth century, the function of avant-garde was claimed by both political parties and artistic movements; and, in the context of art, it has since become a historical determination. The art avant-gardes to which we now refer are a specific twentieth-century phenomenon. However, it is interesting to observe that the independence of art, and its revolutionary duty, are both children of the Enlightenment. The questions regarding art avant-gardes multiply when reflected in the mirror of politics: what is revolution, is this the only way to change the world, does it need an avant-garde, is it an event or an endless process? And, then again, come the complicated relations between artistic avant-gardes and the various political avant-gardes and their demands. Yet this is not the crucial defining question for artistic avant-gardes. What is important is that while avant-garde art is always revolutionary, not every revolutionary art is avant-garde. What is it, then, that differentiates avant-garde art from, let us say, Romanticism or Realism, which also claimed some form of revolutionary function? Avant-garde art strives not just to be *revolutionary*, but to be *revolution*.

Avant-garde art sets a peculiar and very high standard for consistency. This stems from the belief in the interdependence between form and content, which in turn is part of a general and constitutive questioning of established categorical divisions, such as 'art vs life', 'theory vs practice', 'object vs process'. It follows that a radical content cannot exist without a radical form; it may also be implied that a radical form constitutes by itself a radical content. So, avant-garde art cannot be defined by either its semantic content or its perceptual forms, visual or other, but rather by the way in which it articulates their relation. 'Avant-garde' is a structural approach to art, not a style, and therefore a structural description is needed to comprehend it. This explains why it denotes a wide range of extremely dissimilar art movements and artworks. Moreover, it explains why its agents perform a constant conceptual slippage between the definition of art as avant-garde and avant-garde as a kind of art; from an avant-garde artist's point of view, there is no other kind. To this difficulty must be added the general questioning of the existence of the category of art as such. It is the retrospective meta-definitions of art theory that allow one to see avant-garde art as an overall phenomenon. In this meta-definitional level, a late twentieth-century theoretical debate concerns whether avant-garde art should be defined in terms of form experimentation[5] or with regard to its social function.[6] However, if one chooses a structural interpretation,[7] then the form-oriented and the social-function-oriented definitions of avant-garde are revealed to be indissolubly connected. Structural innovation at the level of the signifier and the destabilisation of the institution of art describe the same structural move: an act of rupture with an existing structure and, possibly, the founding of a new one; in other words, revolution. The link was conscious and obvious to those who theorised the avant-gardes from a closer vantage point. The formalist Viktor Shklovsky, writing his essay 'Art as Technique'[8] in Russia in 1917, obviously modelled art's definitional device of 'defamiliarisation' on a revolutionary reference. Post-structuralist Julia Kristeva is even more outspoken about what, in her 1974 homonymous text, she terms 'the revolution of poetic language'.[9] 'Revolution', 'art' and 'avant-garde art' seem to share the same structure. Through a game between isomorphism and synecdoche, they become almost synonymous.

Avant-garde art and feminism in the twentieth century bear multi-levelled similarities, which suggests that their connection may be more than a historical contingency. On the one hand, avant-garde art was part of the epistemological shift which shaped the twentieth century. It has radically changed the definition of art founded by the Renaissance and the Enlightenment, while following the latter's liberating call. The philosophical background of the avant-garde's questioning of Western categorical bipolarities, within which the interdependence between content and form is framed, is the triple origin of this epistemological shift: Saussurean semiotics, Marxian political philosophy and Freudian psychoanalysis. And it is with them that avant-garde art shares the very high structural demand for consistency. Similarly, feminism is the heiress of the liberating project and critical demand of the Enlightenment, while also dismantling one of the fundamental categorical barriers of Western thought, the one between the public and the private, by introducing gender and the private sphere into politics. Second-wave feminism put it into words in its slogan: 'The personal is political'. Thus, feminism sets an unusually high standard for consistency when it demands that revolution starts in private relationships and at home. On the other hand, the two peak periods of the avant-garde art movements are the 'historical' or 'first' avant-gardes of the early twentieth century up to the 1930s and the 'neo' or 'second' avant-gardes, during the 1960s, 1970s and early 1980s.[10] The dates roughly coincide with the first and second feminist waves. The double peaks of the two periodisations obviously relate to the fertile intellectual environment around the two revolutionary moments of the twentieth century, the 1917 Revolution and May 1968, and are separated by the trauma of the Second World War. In both cases, the second peak is a critical re-iteration and expansion of the first. So, it is both for conceptual and historical reasons that much of the art practice of the second feminist wave belongs to the second avant-gardes; and also that it enters into a dialogue with deconstruction, Althusserian philosophy and Lacanian psychoanalysis.

The 'Chronology'[11] of the Camera Obscura Collective, published in their journal in 1979, describes how the collective gradually arrived at the conclusion that feminist filmmaking could not but use avant-garde strategies. It effectively summarises the arguments with regard to what constitutes feminist filmmaking. It is also particularly relevant to the present study, as Angelidi was in Paris between 1973 and 1977 and followed Christian Metz's seminar, as did the members of the collective. It is obvious that a film made by a woman is not necessarily feminist, although revealing the contribution of women to film history and promoting the rights of women as film professionals are important feminist objectives. At the time, an additional question was posed: whether it was possible to develop a theory of women film directors – which was soon abandoned as 'ill-conceived'. This was probably a misinterpretation of Hélène Cixous's concept of 'écriture féminine' [feminine writing],[12] which has little to do with the way biological women write (create), but rather refers to a kind of 'writing' that doesn't conform to patriarchal rules. Common approaches of feminism to film were either proposing positive female role models or presenting depictions of women's problems, both as part of feminist 'consciousness-raising'. However, the collective started questioning both approaches as relying on identification with the institution of cinema, which, they had started to realise, not only reflects but produces women's oppressive representations. Therefore, for a film to be feminist, feminist subject matter is not enough. So, then, they turned their attention to films' 'signifying production': their 'form' or more precisely 'cinematic codes and narrative structure'.[13] Filmmaking had to be subverting at these levels, in other words, it had to be avant-garde, in order to be feminist. Yet, while one has to be 'careful about making formal concerns "speak" a political message',[14] not all avant-garde filmmaking is feminist.

Constance Penley in her 1977 article 'The Avant-Garde and Its Imaginary' investigates precisely 'the relation of avant-garde strategies to a feminist filmmaking practice'.[15] She argues that structuralist/materialist avant-garde filmmaking fails to break free from the structure of identification and the power of the image, while her contemporary feminist filmmakers may be starting to find a way to do just that. She chooses as her object of critical analysis the London Film-makers' Co-op, and particularly Malcolm Le Grice[16] and Peter Gidal[17], for their explicit combination of political and formal avant-garde intentions. In a textbook avant-garde approach to cinema, they argue for a drawing of attention towards the material aspect of the film, and they are highly suspicious of the ideological aspects of representation and narration. Penley draws on the metapsychological contributions to film theory by Metz[18], Thierry Kuntzel[19], Jean-Louis Baudry[20] and Raymond Bellour[21] to hypothesise that, in a way, all relations to the image are imaginary and all films are narrative, irrespective of their intentional denunciation of representation or story. Metz in his 'Le signifiant imaginaire' [imaginary signifier] claims that what is characteristic in cinema is 'not the imaginary that it may happen to represent but the imaginary that it is'[22] and poses different kinds of spectator identification, the primary among them being with the subject's own activity of looking; practically, the camera. Baudry in his 'Le dispositif' [apparatus] argues that 'the cinema "machine" [. . .] includes not only the instrumental base (camera, lens, projector, etc.) but also the subject, most importantly the subject of the unconscious'[23] and the spectator comes to identify with the entirety of the cinema apparatus. So, Penley comes to the conclusion that the structuralist/materialist avant-garde filmmaking strategies, instead of subverting the deep structures of the institution of cinema, inadvertently re-enforce them. By contrast, several (then) recent women filmmakers manage to be more subversive through 'the construction of another subject-relation to the screen'.[24] In other words, she argues that *feminist* avant-garde filmmaking is more avant-garde that others; she even implies that it may be the only effective one.

I would probably argue for a wider arsenal of strategies, as I argue for a more inclusive definition of avant-garde art. Penley falls into the 'sin' of many avant-gardists and avant-garde theorisers of closing the field too much. Moreover, I would question a certain quasi-metaphysics of vision. However, I believe it is a valid observation that the subject's relation to the film is also constituted by the film itself and the signifying structures that support it – and a consistent questioning of cinema should include this relation. The proposition of the subject's constitution by the film by no means denies the empirical subjects' extra-filmic independent existence. It is rather part of the ways in which a film constructs its relations to its outside; the way it situates its others in itself. Whether the empirical subjects accept this positioning, and to what degree, is a different issue.

Penley's views on avant-garde cinema, as well as the metapsychological film theories on which they are based, rely heavily on psychoanalytic theory, as is also the case with most feminist critical analyses of the dominant cinema at the time, such as the work by Laura Mulvey,[25] Tania Modleski[26] Mary Ann Doane[27] and Teresa de Laurentis.[28] So, their predicament is that they have to struggle with the unresolved issues of the initial psychoanalytic theories on which they rely and particularly their (not so) latent patriarchal biases. Most psychoanalytically oriented film theory converses with Sigmund Freud's Oedipal trajectory[29] and/or Jacques Lacan's Mirror Stage,[30] both of which are part of theories of subject formation. One cannot really re-establish the subject's relation to the screen if one does not question the structuring of the subject itself. And, as this structuring appears to have a very prominent and imbalanced gendered component, its questioning becomes particularly important to a feminist approach. As a matter of fact, this questioning leads one to a re-emergence from film theory to feminist politics in general, facing a crucial and most difficult demand, the ultimate step of a feminist (or any) revolution: a new subjectivity.

For feminist theory, the approach of psychoanalysis to subjectivity is both its greatest contribution and its greatest trap. On the one hand, its discovery of the unconscious and its study of the unconscious structures, mechanisms and functions is one of the great epistemological revolutions of the twentieth century; it is a different subject that emerges, no longer the unified *cogito* of the Enlightenment. Moreover, psychoanalysis contributed greatly to a re-evaluation of sexuality that has had wide-ranging effects too. In these aspects, it has been – and still is – an invaluable tool for feminist thought and practice. On the other hand, its theory of subject formation, that is, the tale of Oedipus, is very much determined by a patriarchal epistemology and is completely dated. To put it simply, the subject of psychoanalysis is a heterosexual man; the formation of the heterosexual woman[31] is theorised as an afterthought and only as a . . . supplement[32] to the man's formation. And the theory does not even begin to address the possibility of gender beyond a binary conception.[33] This kind of contradiction is not uncommon in meaningful theories. Even highly productive theories have blind spots, and these tend to be very useful in understanding them. Yet, as theories are interconnected structures, it is not easy to isolate their mistakes from their productive advancements. It is part of the strenuous process of proofs and refutations that constitutes the scientific path to knowledge.[34] I believe that one can very well endorse psychoanalysis's discovery of the unconscious and its functions without accepting as natural and universal the particular scenarios of subject formation and its pathologies, which are formed by specific social conditions; similar to the way in which Saussurian linguistics clearly distinguishes between the universal human ability to create languages and the specific languages created, which are social constructions. But, of course, the crucial duality that underlies every discussion on gender is precisely the nature/culture opposition. And psychoanalysis is simultaneously one of the main denaturalising theories of the twentieth century and yet one of the deepest naturalising ideologies. Its lack of self-awareness with regard to its second function is even more glaring in the case of Lacanian psychoanalysis that moves its field from the body to language yet keeps all the naturalised connotations of gender. And there is no clearer demarcation of ideology that attributing social structuring to nature.[35]

Feminists who refer to psychoanalysis, including women psychoanalysts, have tried to deal with the contradiction in different ways.[36] Intellectual subjects, mothers of their discourses and works (or should they accept to be called 'fathers'?), some of them mothers of children, were offered the position of the monster. Some of them accepted it, others tried to re-position themselves differently, others tried to re-evaluate the positions, and some even tried to break and/or re-make the system. One of the strategies was to focus on the pre-Oedipal phase of girls, which Freud himself avowed not to have studied or understood enough. For their part, Lacanians chose to focus on women's 'jouissance'.[37] The two feminist philosophers to whom Angelidi most often refers in texts and interviews, Cixous[38] and Luce Irigaray[39], offer some of the most radical critiques and effective counter-propositions to patriarchal ideologies, including psychoanalytical theory. Cixous deconstructs the founding dualities of gender and posits the possibility of 'feminine writing'; Irigaray opens up the Freudian text, revealing its blind points and their – not so hidden – implications, and the possibility of a gender and subject formation different to Oedipus.

Whether in Freudian psychoanalysis or in its Lacanian variation, Mother is a most controversial figure. Her ambiguity is densely interwoven with the impossibilities of the positioning of women as subjects. Mother is considered the paradigm for female sexuality, as the other for her son or for her husband who sees in her his own mother, and who can give her what her father can't, a penis. She is never considered in an interactive sexual relation with a man or woman, or in relation to a daughter or her own mother, or even less as the subject of sexual desire or pleasure or the author(ess) of children of the flesh or the spirit. In Irigaray's words, which Angelidi references to the letter in *Idées Fixes / Dies Irae*, mother-woman is:

> Womb – earth, factory, bank – where the semen-capital is entrusted so that it germinates, manufactures, bears fruit, without the woman being able to claim its property or even its usufruct, being only 'passively' submitted to reproduction. She herself is possessed as a medium of (re-)production.[40]

Let us make a simplifying summary of the Oedipus tale, focusing on the points of gendered unbalance, with the help of Irigaray's close reading. The little boy discovers pleasure in his own sex (penis), desires his mother and wants to replace his father; later he finds out that women don't have a penis and assumes they are castrated; out of fear that his father will castrate him, he learns to control his impulses and enters into civil society; growing up, he transfers the desire for his mother to another woman, who will ultimately give birth to his son(s), taking the place of his mother, while – finally – he takes the place of his father. The little girl discovers pleasure in her own sex (clitoris), desires her mother and wants to replace her father; later finds out that boys have bigger sexes (penises), assumes she is castrated, and starts envying the ones who possess penises; finds out that her mother too doesn't have a penis, gets angry with her for not being able to give her a penis, and abandons her as object of desire; she turns her desire to her father and his penis; growing up, she transfers her desire from her father to her husband, she takes the place of her husband's mother, she changes her place of pleasure from clitoris to vagina and her position of pleasure from subject to object, and – finally – she is given a penis in the form of her penis-possessing son. If she has a daughter, so much the worse for both of them, while her own mother is forever left forgotten in the depths of a silent past. In other words, women begin their lives as little boys who, at some point, have to accept that they are castrated in order to mature into women, their ultimate purpose and desire being to give birth to sons. Can one seriously argue today that this tale is one of women's 'nature' and not the dominant demand of patriarchal societies?

So, as Irigaray observes, in this very unbalanced Freudian tale, the only sexuality is male; and normal female sexuality is a submission to loss. A normal woman should first hate and then forget her origin, her mother and herself. A normal woman does not desire pleasure but possession, and cannot have pleasure except by pleasuring another. A normal woman exists only as the mother of a son. Lacan, in his pseudo-denaturalisation of the Freudian tale, keeps quite distinct and traditionally gendered the positions of Father and Mother, the subject in front of the mirror is still and always a boy, and the much-venerated 'master-signifier' is still the/a penis, despite its linguistic sanctification through archaisation as 'phallus'. Mother is still the speechless Imaginary before entrance into the realm of the Symbolic by the Name of the Father; and her forbidden sex is the forever un-named and un-seen, the abjected, death, the Real. Woman may experience an anarchic and unlimited pleasure (jouissance) unknown to men, but can never be the subject of her desire, her pleasure and her discourse. Woman is defined as 'other' to subject, to culture, to agency. In Irigaray's words, 'woman takes the position of the negative in a phallocentric dialectics'[41] which, while including the psychoanalytic discourse, is much older and wider, and has deep roots in Western metaphysics. In this male-dominated economy of representation, woman's supposedly castrated sex – and by displacement woman in general – holds the position of unspeakable primitive terror, or more particularly, of the 'uncanny' *par excellence*. Nevertheless, feminists like Irigaray[42] and Cixous[43] have suggested that what is really unacceptable to the system, the real source of the uncanny, is precisely the fact that women's sex is *not* castrated.

In his homonymous 1919 text, Freud concludes his collection of examples of the uncanny with 'his [a man's] mother's genitals or her body', as 'the entrance to the former home of all human beings'.[44] He starts his study by asking which intrinsic characteristics cause this peculiar feeling, which he classes as a subset of terror.[45] He observes that the uncanny is 'a hidden, familiar thing that has undergone repression and then emerged from it'[46] as strange and unfamiliar. Not any re-emerging repressed, however, fulfils the description, but only 'infantile complexes' and abandoned 'primitive beliefs'.[47] In this frame, of course, the mother's genitals or her body are more than a random example. A castrating maternal vulva, either penis-possessing or castrated herself, a toothed wound that will take him back to the inexistence from which she brought him forth – there is a whole net of images rooted in infantile complexes and primitive beliefs to terrorise a man.[48] In this context, the mother's genitals (and her body) is Medusa,[49] whose deadly look turns men to stone, and Penley's 'mother returning the look'[50] is (the) uncanny.

Cixous states the (long-unacknowledged) obvious in her declarational 'Medusa's Laughter', when she writes that 'woman is not castrated'[51] and there is 'no reason to align woman to the negative'.[52] What would really happen if we turned and saw her looking is that we would find out that 'she is not deadly. She laughs and she is beautiful!'[53] Of course, we all owe awe to the person who carried us in her body and brought us to life. Yet, the remembrance of the omnipotence of our mother when we first came to be, and this intimacy with her body that is now different to ours, need not cause us terror. What is conceptualised as terrifying is the subversive potentiality of this remembrance that refutes and destabilises patriarchal metaphysics. Moreover, a correspondingly fundamental fear is caused by women who do not conform to the patriarchal system and act as reminders that the system is neither natural nor eternal. A woman need not be a mother, but we all have one. There is nothing terrible in women to be repressed other than their own oppression. This is the secret. Women who destabilise the system are perceived as strange. Feminists should embrace this strangeness, as they embraced the persecuted witches. There is no greater scandal than a woman who loves herself and exists, as a subject. From this starting point a river of weird women flow, threatening to patriarchy but not to men: women who desire but don't need men, or women; who may become mothers but don't need to be; who don't desire to be their lovers' mothers; who when becoming mothers don't cease to be subjects; who search for their own origins and love their mothers; who love their daughters as much as their sons; who claim the authorship of their words and their works; and who, by doing all these so very subverting things, re-define what subjectivity and authorship may be. One may think of this new subject as a weird mother. She does not need to have human children; and if she has them, she is not consumed in them. She is the mother of her desire, her perspective, her speech and her works.

ANTOINETTA ANGELIDI'S EMBRACING OF UNCANNINESS

Antoinetta Angelidi's poetics is characterised by a multi-levelled uncanniness, a particular kind of strangeness that fuses the formalist defamiliarisation strategy and the Freudian structure of the uncanny. The connection between these two kinds of 'making-strange-being-strange' is proposed by the filmmaker herself, most significantly in her theoretical text 'Play with the Uncanny – A Poetics of Cinema'.[54] I choose to call it 'uncanniness' in order to avoid using either of the two terms, to differentiate it from them and stress its novelty. The elements comprising the poetics sustaining Angelidi's dense universe have been pointed out and analysed many times, by the filmmaker herself, as well as by the writer of this chapter:[55] heterogeneity, experimentation, the dream-mechanism, and a combination of defamiliarisation with the uncanny. I think that this latter, 'uncanniness' as I called it, may be the thread that interweaves her avant-garde poetics with her feminist politics, while also offering a name for the specificity of her style. It is both a structure and an effect, and appears in her work as a political position, a poetic strategy, a textual technique and a visual form.

To start with, it is definitely appropriate to classify Angelidi as an avant-gardist, based both on her work and her claims. Although she has not used the term 'avant-garde' to designate her poetics until very recently in retrospective meta-discourses, which is quite understandable given the heaviness of the concept and the second avant-gardes' critique of the certainties of the first avant-gardes, the way she describes her practice reveals a clearly avant-gardist perception of art. Most importantly, since the very beginning of her career, she explicitly subscribes to the avant-garde demand for a structural connection between form and content, poetics and politics, practice and theory, life and art. For example, in an interview she gave after the screening of her first feature-length film *Idées Fixes / Dies Irae* in the 1977 Filmmakers' Counter-Festival in Thessaloniki, she describes her writing – where 'writing', in the semiotically aware terminology that she uses, denotes all kinds of expression, in this case her filmmaking – as follows:

> I try for [my] political views to be embodied in [my] writing. The fact that I write in this way and no other is a political act. The ideal would be for those two not to be distinguished at all.[56]

In this context, it makes sense to study her films as theoretical arguments and her theoretical discourse as artwork, or more accurately, to study them all as an ongoing dialogue of and on the theory and practice of art.

Moreover, there is no doubt that the central component of her politics is feminism. In the previously mentioned interview, among other things, she describes the conflicts and need to combine her left-wing and feminist engagement, as well as her politics and her writing, and denounces dogmatism in all its forms. She goes on to speak of 'a relation of politics with [her] personal life',[57] which alludes to the 'personal is political' principle. It should be noted here that Angelidi did not shy away from political action when it was needed, even putting her life on the line.[58] Feminist active engagement in different forms has never ceased to be a part of her life. The same goes for feminist discourse. Already her two very first short films[59] deal with rape and gendered stereotypes, and her first feature-length film, *Idées Fixes/ Dies Irae*, is an elaborate essay on the oppression of women, which makes its argument by addressing the representation of women's bodies in modern and contemporary art. There, included in a very complicated, heterogeneous and contrapuntal cinematic collage of references, are some word-for-word excerpts from Irigaray. The reference to Irigaray appears also very centrally in her 1979 theoretical analysis[60] of Carl Dreyer's *Dies Irae* (1943). In the same year, in self-presentation, she links the multiplicity and diversity of women's writing to women's orgasm in an obvious reference to Cixous, and denounces 'foreign myths of our bodies and colonies in our collective unconscious'.[61] All her films and other visual works are feminist discourses. Her creative collaborations with Claire Mitsotaki[62] and Rea Walldén[63] are also good examples of feminist solidarity and experiments in co-creation. She says it in film and word, she enacts it in her life, theoretical discourse and film practice: hers is a feminist avant-garde poetics.

I argue that the uncanniness principle embodies the connection between the avant-gardist and the feminist elements of Angelidi's poetics. Making things strange in art has an avant-garde history one cannot avoid, of course. Formalist 'defamiliarisation' is a strategy which Angelidi uses throughout her creative path.[64] She is also aware of Bertolt Brecht's version of it as 'alienation effect,'[65] as it is quite obvious in her early films. Moreover, the notion of a conscious and critical spectatorship, opposed to a lulling and manipulating identification, continues to be central to her views.[66] However, Angelidi's defamiliarisation has a more complicated and ambiguous character, which progressively becomes richer and with a stronger element of the uncanny. This element of the uncanny, which is clearly recognisable at least since *Topos*,[67] Angelidi describes in her 2005 text 'The Play with the Uncanny – A Poetics of Cinema'[68] in a conscious comparison and merging with the strategy of defamiliarisation. It modifies her strategy of defamiliarisation and may provide the key to her distinctive, recognisable aesthetics. There is a mystery in Angelidi's films, a peculiar strangeness, an element of an unfamiliar-familiar, an unsettling of certainties, which moves deeply and yet is neither terrible nor terrifying, and makes you see the world anew. If the defamiliarisation strategy links her to the avant-garde and feminist revolutions, her uncanniness is specifically hers.

How are the elements of Angelidi's poetics – experimentation, heterogeneity and the dream-work mechanisms – interwoven with each other and with her peculiar uncanniness? One has first of all to observe that these elements belong to different orders, which explains how when viewed from different pertinences, each of them appears central. Experimentation is an attitude to the filmmaking process rather than a characteristic of the final work. Avant-garde art practice and art experimentation intersect to the point of co-extension, particularly as avant-garde artworks tend to incorporate their creation process and destabilise the duality between process and work. On their part, heterogeneity[69] and the dream-work[70] mechanisms are structural characteristics of cinematic expression and expression in general. Their purposeful use is drawing attention to materiality, and therefore belongs to a strategy of defamiliarisation.[71] The conscious use of cinematic heterogeneity is central to Angelidi's films since her very first short films, where the different channels of expressive substance are placed in critical counterpoint. In *Topos*, this counterpoint becomes more sensual, gaining a sense of synaesthesia, of melting and merging of the senses, where 'light can be sound and a word can be light'.[72] Correspondingly, if the mechanisms of dream-work – visualisation, displacement, condensation – govern the structural poetics of the entirety of Angelidi's filmography, since *Topos* a dream-feeling becomes part of her films' uncanniness. It is then that her obsession with dreams starts, and it is then, in *Topos*, that the figures of her films start swimming in darkness, immerged in and emerging from it, like dreams. Therefore, uncanniness is both more general and more particular that the other elements of Angelidi's poetics. On the one hand, it is a general principle for approaching art, which also goes beyond art (and cinema), as it proposes a new relation with the world, a new subjectivity – a question of perception but also of active change. On the other, it describes Angelidi's aesthetics. As she explains,[73] hers is a method which could be used by anyone and which she teaches to her students, and yet everyone using it would make different films. What makes the difference, what is the ghost in the machine? Angelidi gives us the answer: the personal viewpoint, how one looks and what one carries with oneself, which includes personal experiences and references, the unconscious and the body of the filmmaker. It is this, in the last instance, which is remains untranslatable; that particular uncanniness that cannot be reduced to a description.

In this context, the structure of a weird motherhood becomes a poetic and political principle. It regards the subjectivity that it constructs and for which it opens up a space. The subject that is author(ess) of her own look and discourse, without excluding the other and accepting the other in herself. The subject that does not repress her relation to her own origin and does not fear it. A subject that gives birth to and nurtures herself. Weird motherhood is also her own relation to her films. Weird motherhood is the way in which she posits herself as author of her films, producer of her discourse. Angelidi's poetics includes subversive structural moves and the questioning of subject position, deconstructs heavily representation and narration but does not deny them, undermines a uniform identification and yet offers enchantment, opens up a path of freedom and a way to see anew. The structure of a weird motherhood underlies all Angelidi's films; in *Topos*, however, it becomes the central thematic concern and narrative structure, while the figure of the weird mother appears also as a character. Moreover, while all her films enact a merging of formal play and lived experience, *Topos* is a moment of balance between the two. *Topos* is the film in which her recognisable style matures.

'Native land is not the topos (place) where we were born', *Topos* claims contradictorily, and most consistently. When the film appeared in Greece in 1985, like a comet in the midst of a general search for an elusive Greekness, it was accused of being '*Topos* without topos. A film with no fatherland'.[74] Angelidi, quite properly, appropriated the accusation and chose to bear it as a badge of honour. The accuser was more accurate than he could have imagined; this is precisely the point: *Topos* has no fatherland; it is against fatherlands. It is a film against the dominant, patriarchal definition of origin; yet it is not without origins. It is about the quest for another origin, another's origin, the other's origin, another kind of origin.

BREATHING *TOPOI* AND EXTRAVAGANT WOMEN

'*Topos*' in Greek has a sense both more specific and more general than *space*. In a mathematical-philosophical context, it indicates a relational spatiality without dimensions; in everyday speech, this relationality denotes localisation (locus, place, region) and often comes to mean people's place of origin. Thus, *topoi* are either arche-forms or lived places; while in the singular, in colloquial speech, they almost always resonate of origin, native land. Significantly for the present argument, *topos* then becomes synonymous with '*patris*', literally 'fatherland'. In Greek (as in Latin and most European languages), the place of origin is (the land of the) father(s). Not Angelidi's *Topos*, though. Angelidi's *Topos* reminds us that before the patriarchal usurpation, the literal origin is maternal. *Topos* is a place of birth, and death, a world of mothers and daughters, where no father figure appears, and the word 'father' is never heard. *Topos* is a women's world.

Yet, «Γενέθλια γη δεν είναι ο τόπος που γεννηθήκαμε. Γενέθλια γη μπορεί να είναι μονάχα μια κηλίδα» [Native land (place of birth) is not the *topos* (place) where we were born; native land may be just a stain (blot, spot)]. It is the only moment in the film that the word 'topos' is heard. It is the voice of the film herself that makes the pronouncement towards the end of the film, which sounds rather like its arriving point. The verse obviously resonates with a reference to Lacan's *objet petit a*[75], the origin of the look. It is the (m)other's look, and her breast, the blind spot of the look, and of theory. And again, quite literally, our origin is our mother's body, not a blind spot, but a repressed one; '*the origin of the world*',[76] as Courbet would have it, diminishing the mother to her sex, the absolute uncanny, the not-to-be-named, the vulva. Simultaneously, it is the grain of materiality, the tain of the mirror, the ink blot of writing, the brush stroke in the paining, the spot of light in the screening. Art, that makes its own medium meaningful, becomes a self-constructed origin. And more, a clot of blood, and a stain. Back again, the abjected Real; once again, for psychoanalysis, the mother. Such a close weave of homologies and displacements. Derrida would argue that there is no origin; origin is a transcendental signifier, ideology. But what if we didn't turn our real birthplace into a blind spot? What if mother is not the absolute other? What if you are (a) woman? Lacan would argue that there is no woman. Derrida would counter-argue that we are all women. Yet some of us have vulvas, and some don't – and do take a moment here to think how rarely you see the word 'vulva' in theoretical texts, as opposed to 'penis'. What if you have in your own body the mythical origin, a part of you, not a wound but the place of your own pleasure? The ambiguous stain that travels through the film *Topos*, 'spreads like oil', to be finally recognised as origin, terrible and familiar. A *topos* of abstract forms and blood. Women's blood, blood of menstruation and birth. 'She loses blood' are the first Greek words spoken in the film, practically the first words the audience fully understands.[77] Blood lost in birth-giving, not in the battlefield. The opposition was stressed in one of the first feminist manifestos in Western history, one that Euripides[78] put in the mouth of the terrifying foreign woman, Medea. *Topos* reminds us of the blotted origin of meanings before their usurpation by patriarchal ideology. *Topos* is a women's world.

Topos deals with representation; both literally as a spatial issue and metaphorically as a philosophical one. In both senses, the Western way of representation was decisively formed during the Renaissance. It is Renaissance painting that cinema in general and *Topos* in particular both continue and burst open. The central perspective and the illusion of a third dimension are both inherited and potentially destabilised by the moving image. On the one hand, *Topos* re-iterates the Renaissance tradition. Its settings have clear geometric forms, its compositions are often centrally symmetrical and emerge from darkness as if enclosed in a dark box, while its deep blacks, rich colours, and imagery are often immediately referencing Renaissance paintings. On the other hand, *Topos* consciously uses the introduction of movement into the image as a revealing and questioning strategy. For example, sometimes the camera enters spaces in unexpected ways, changing their perspective and destabilising the cinematic illusion; other times, it is the lighting of a scene that changes, revealing or hiding part of the image, and thus transforming our sense of space; other times again, the settings are made like architectural models cut open, showing simultaneously inside and outside space, a view that would never be possible in 'real' life; or the entire scene 'enters' the black frame of the screen as if coming down from the sky. The frame becomes visible, the blackness has flesh, the volume is voided, the camera builds and breaks illusions in front of our enchanted and waking eyes. The *camera obscura* [black chamber] is opened up, multiplied, put in movement. The patriarchal voyeuristic objectifying central gaze is dethroned. Offering a new way to look, *Topos* is a women's world.

Topos offers a magical cosmos of living paintings of acute strangeness. And yet, this is a strangeness that does not create distance. It is a strangeness of freedom and closeness, of freedom in closeness. The references are woven into a newly seen world; no longer a collage, no matter how elaborate, but a new world. They are recognisable, and yet transformed. The source of references is the history of Western art; mostly Early Renaissance and Surrealism, but not only these. De Chirico's little girl with a hoop[79] leads the way; following her, we visit hidden places in paintings that we always wondered about, we turn at the forever denied corners. Fini's armoured woman[80] is courted by a Fra Angelico angel[81] in a Carpaccio room;[82] the women of an Uccello birthing[83] cool down opening their dresses in Balthus poses,[84] De Chirico's solid water[85] floods the floors, Pontormo's painted bodies[86] merge with Ingre's odalisques.[87] Is the princess the dragon, or is she the knight, or both?[88] Nothing is as it was. This film neither venerates nor kills its ancestors; *Topos* is a women's world.

The events taking place in *Topos* are all women's moments and rituals, collective and intimate: giving birth, dying, resting, mourning, bathing, singing. Young and mature women, old women and little girls, populate the film. They help each other in labour and folding drapes and wearing their armour(!); they exchange questions and memories and secret recipes. Crucial moments and everyday tasks follow each other, all performed as equally sacred and familiar; a mystical everydayness and an easiness of the sacred. Moreover, the viewing position moves constantly between a woman in labour who dissolves into the women around her, and her daughter who traverses the film at different ages, witnessing and posing questions. The entire film can be interpreted as an internal space: a space inside a woman's (or two women's – mother and daughter) consciousness, maybe even inside her (their) body. This is intensified by the fact that most characters in the film – female and male – speak with the same woman's voice[89] (is it the mother's voice or the daughter's or the film's?), while all the non-dialogic soundtrack of the film is also produced by another woman's voice.[90] There is a simultaneous unity and multiplicity of voices and points of view; an internalisation of the other and an externalisation of the multiplicity of the self. Weaving multiple women's points of view, internal and external, *Topos* is a women's world.

Topos is a women's world; and yet, this is a strange womanhood. Angelidi describes the kinesiology of the women of *Topos* as 'not conventionally women's'[91] and traces her inspiration to animals and birds of prey, and the paintings of Balthus. These women radiate power. They stand firmly, bare-footed, on the earth, as if channelling its energy; their legs apart, their backs straight, their chests open. They rest with a confident sensuality; they move fluently and yet sharply, with an equally confident purposefulness. They pass abruptly from rest to movement, like wild cats. Among the most memorable scenes of the film are the birthing, where all the women around the one in labour move and breathe rhythmically like one body; the shots of women stretching around the fire in different degrees of onanistic pleasure; and the sequence of the two women laughing and playing with each other on all fours (Figure 1.1). Inspired by Fini's armoured women,[92] Carrington's woman with hyena[93] and a merging of the princess, the knight and the dragon of Uccello's Saint George,[94] women in *Topos* wear their Renaissance dresses completed with metallic breastplates,[95] and their hair in elaborate styles or in anti-gravity wildness. They wear their heavy costumes lightly and their nakedness carelessly.

Topos is a women's world. The most significant interpersonal relationship appearing in the film is the mother–daughter connection. It should be noted that the direction of the relationship is mainly daughter to mother, as it is the relation to the past-origin that is mainly thematised and not the experience of motherhood. It is the stories and memories and ghosts of mothers, and even mothers themselves, that return and visit the women of the film. The other omnipresent relationship in the film, one which is however never put into words, is inter-women friendship. All the female characters of the film, primary and secondary, appear always in couples, an omnipresent and unacknowledged duality of women's intimate friendships. Such are, for example, the fluent bodily intimacy between the young women Maria (Jany Gastaldi)

Figure 1.1 Still, Angelidi, *Topos* (1985).

and Phoebe (Arietta Moutousi); the antagonistic complicity between the mature women Anna (Anitta Santorineou) and Eleni (Maya Liberopoulou); the wise conversing between the old women Manio (Zoi Voudouri) and Vassiliki (Iro Kyriakaki). These couples might be interpreted erotically or not; but they are certainly more than that. Conversely, the only acknowledged romantic relationships in the film are between women and men; but these appear more as parts of stories than of experiences.

Topos is a women's world, where men are outsiders. Mostly, men appear as a group that comes from the outside or passes through the space of women, not belonging there. They carry things, are dressed in muddy colours and speak little or not at all. There is only one sequence of predominantly male discourse, as a wedge inserted in the body of the film, a 'foreign body'. There, the men sit around a table, discussing the moon and telling the tale of 'the woman who was lost'. The women sit on the fences around them, making cryptic comments and watching like birds of prey. Only the little girl (Clairi Mirtseki) joins them. The men exchange pseudo-scientific theories and commonplace wisdom with excessive seriousness. Their ignorance and mistaken certainty about the nature of the moon, which they think is hollow and which they call 'foreign body', mirrors their ignorance with regard to Woman, to whom they are equally foreign. Elsewhere in the film, two men appear as the other part of a romantic relationship; the silent angel (Takis Moschos) who keeps vigil under the window of a beloved woman with whom he has never exchanged a word, and the screeching juggler (Stefanos Kotsikos) who proclaims his undying love over the body of his long-dead wife. Both are stories that seem to come out of the pages of the most poetic of romances, and yet something unnerving, even ridiculous, is revealed in them. I am not sure if the audience gets it always; I have heard *Topos* being interpreted as a film about romantic love. But how can one ignore that in these two great romances, there is no communication whatsoever between the lovers? Interestingly enough, the only time that a woman claims to be in love in the film, she does not clarify with whom, if anyone. It seems that romantic love is rather a lonely occupation. Finally, another man that makes his peripheral appearance in *Topos* is the 'annoying old man', played by the Greek avant-garde filmmaker Stavros Tornes. Like the caricature of a cynic philosopher, he breaks open walnuts, keeps the shells and throws away the nuts. I wonder whether this was a friendly sarcasm on the part of Angelidi, addressed to the male avant-garde. Men are voiceless in *Topos*, with the exception of the dinner sequence. The story of the silent lover is told by a woman, while the juggler tells his own story in a woman's voice, possibly as part of a woman's memory. Inversing Western perspective, men are the others.

Topos is a women's world, where bodies and objects breathe in the rhythm of the woman who gives birth, and speak with her voice;[96] it is dark, earthy and warm, where even external scenes feel as if enclosed in a womb, and the forms emerge from the darkness. This is a world that destabilises the certainties of Western thought, transgresses categories and bursts oppositional dualities. At the deepest structural level, a kind of synaesthesia commands the expressive medium. The border between the living and the inanimate is denied, as objects breathe and cry and scream just as humans do, and yet all these bodies are 'said' by their voices that are not really theirs, and pass through them,[97] like spirits. The causal link is broken. Neither is life and death so clearly demarcated; the entirety of the film takes place in that one moment in which a life goes and another comes, entrance and exit merged, a momentary and elongated in-between. And are we awake or asleep? Is it a lucid dream or a somnambulistic existence? 'From now on, I will dream that I am awake', says the adult daughter (Maria) towards the end of the film, which closes with the announcement 'The dawn breaks. The stars shine bright.' The internal position explains the inversion. A film that is inside; inside a (or two or many) consciousness(es) and/or body(ies); and yet outside them, a projection, as all films are. Everything is very intimate and yet nothing is homey. The main shooting location is the Gazi [Gas] factory in Athens that was founded in 1857 and closed down in 1984, just before the shooting of the film. The huge machinery of the factory was still in place and became part of the settings of the film. Furniture, like sofas and tables, is implanted in the industrial setting. It is the definitional distinction between subject and object that is broken apart: multiple points of view, fragmentation of the look, alive objects, inversion of hierarchies and causalities.

Topos is a women's world. It is also a woman's: Antoinetta Angelidi's. She inscribes herself in the film, enacting the avant-garde and feminist demand of breaking the barrier between the author and the work, breaking the illusion of objectivity and distance.[98] The *auctor*, or rather the *auctix*, is not just an intention but a body. In *Topos*, we see some very close-up shots of her eye and her wet tongue, uncanny in their size and intimacy, reminders of the material support of the metaphors of gaze and speech. We also hear the auctix's voice, posing questions through the body of the little girl who walks through the film and sees everything. If the entire film in a way is Angelidi's speech, it is significant that her literal voice only poses questions. As she put it in the 1977 poster of her previous film, once again in the form of a question: 'Is there a women's writing and how does it relate to the inscription of the body?'[99]

THE QUEST FOR AND ARRIVAL OF THE LOST MOTHER

Topos questions representation not only in its spatial sense but also in its temporal – because subjectivity is not only about positions and viewpoints, but also about the quests we choose, the paths we travel and the stories we tell about ourselves. *Topos* has a double narrative structure. On the one hand, a woman gives birth and dies; in this extended moment, she is scattered and enters the bodies of the women around her. On the other, we follow the quest of her daughter to reconstruct her mother's story. Simultaneously, as is the case for all Angelidi's films, it has the form of an initiation journey; one where time denies conventional causality. Moreover, stories are said and shown, sometimes both. Despite and because of this multiplicity and complexity of viewpoints and paths, *Topos* is decisively a women's quest.

The film's plot exemplifies women's forbidden relation to their origin, that is, their own mother. It is not by chance that the characters of mother and daughter are named correspondingly Anna and Maria. St Anne and the Virgin Mary are the only mother-daughter couple that appears centrally in the Christian religion,[100] which sanctifies the relations primarily of father-son and mother-son, and secondarily of father-daughter. Like the ancient Greek Mysteries couple of Demetra and Kore, Anna and Maria personify the dangerous relation that, as Irigaray observes, is excluded from psychoanalytic theory and the exemplary oedipal story. Irigaray shows how establishing the relation of a woman to her mother opens up the possibility for a different kind of subjectivity. So, *Topos* is not just *a* women's quest, it is about *the* women's quest.

The film is divided into four (prelude + 3) parts/stages of a journey of initiation; the temporality inside each of them is different and resists a linear reading. The film opens with a recitation of a fragment of Canto I of Dante's 'Hell',[101] which marks the film as an immersion into the unconscious, the world of dreams and memory, and into cinema. This is followed by the extended moment of almost simultaneous birth and death, where the two extremities of life meet. Time somehow expands into scattered pieces of experience, images and speeches, held together by the rhythmic sound of birthing. Mourning follows. Here time is suspended. The daughter's search for fragmented stories and the rituals of mourning follow each other without causal or temporal link, while the story is shaped like a Möbius strip, resisting even an a posteriori reconstruction. In the final part of the film a certain flow is regained, yet this flow is by no means a linear narration. It is basically effected by the fact that the sound is organised into a continuous chanting, which offers a consistent internal monologue, reminiscent of Cixous's 'mother's song'.[102] All the characters co-exist, finally liberated from their restricting armour, headgear and passions. The woman's voice concludes: 'The dawn breaks. The stars shine bright.' This counter-intuitive temporality is confirmed by the last shot of the film: a semi-spherical ceiling with perforated stars; while the day breaks outside, the stars shine brighter and brighter, and the rest fades into darkness. The shot draws attention simultaneously to the inverted temporality and the internal point of view, while also marking the re-emergence from the unconscious and the film. The film is the journey, the subject and the object of the quest. It is the film who understands and finds herself, and along with her, so do the spectatrix and the spectator, who follow in the film's steps, and those of the auctrix. In Angelidi's words, the film is 'a progression both on the level of narrating an experience and on the level of narrating its self-construction'.[103] *Topos* is a women's quest.

Topos is a women's quest, and yet no one character bears the narrative. The distinct un-reducibility of the point of view is a decisive narrative choice. The filmmaker's description, that accompanied the film to all its screenings, reads: 'A woman gives birth and dies. At the moment of death, her face disintegrates and assumes the aspects of those who stand by her bed.' This text determines the dying mother as the point of departure for the entire film. She is probably the one that later appears in her own memories, or her daughter's, as Anna. Anna who takes part in her own mourning rituals, who returns to set her daughter free. The images we see as film may be the mother's fragmented memories at the moment of her death, a kaleidoscope of projections of her inside world outside or introjections in the opposite direction. This extended moment of merging of the inside and the outside is the end of her journey in life, and may be the beginning of another one. In a way the film is her, the inside of her consciousness and her body, an enclosed cosmos and a gate passing in between. It is she who looks back at us; it is, as Penley predicted, 'the mother returning the look'.

And yet, *Topos* as *the* women's quest is primarily the daughter's, Maria's, quest. The daughter searching for her mother and her mother's story, the woman searching for her origin, is Maria. The film opens and closes with Maria. It is through her body that we hear Dante's Canto about the one who was lost and was led by a poet. Moreover, she is the only character that we see at different ages. As a little girl, she leads us from scene to scene, watching and listening to the deeds of the adults; we often see through her eyes, from her height, or we follow her steps. The very few times that she speaks as a child, she poses questions, and her voice is Angelidi's own. As a grown young woman, Maria is the one who changes and matures during the film. In the final part of the film, she takes off her armour and wears a grown-up version of her childhood dress, signifying her acceptance of her own self and her liberation. She chooses art as her way: she gives the symbolic ball, with which she played as a child, to the woman musician who, clad in male costume, plays a stringless cello. Either as a child or as a young woman, this character is always present on screen – her continuous presence alone making her very significant in watching the film, like a leading and unifying thread between its magic images. The film is as much about her search and her maturing through it as it is about the story of her mother. Is she our Dante or our Virgil, or both?

Topos is a women's quest: a daughter's and her mother's, and yet there is another narrative line, not fully in accord with these two. It is the story of the lost woman or of the woman who went missing; because in Greek «η γυναίκα που χάθηκε» bears both senses. This woman who is and is not Anna, who is and is not the woman who gives birth, who is and is not Maria's mother. This ambiguity is born from the non-linearity of time, a spiral reflection between generations. 'The film records two 24-hour cycles [. . .], recounting events that may span 20 years [. . .] or 40 days.'[104] So, the dying woman and the little girl may be ghosts of many generations past, the little girl may be Maria's grandmother, Anna may be the dying woman's daughter or her ghost; the pieces of the puzzle can never properly fit. 'Tell me the story of the woman who went missing?' asks the little girl in the auctrix's voice at the dinner table. She is told that the woman 'wore her hat and was never seen again', which means that she left on purpose. What was the story and the journey of this woman? We will never know. Men hypothesise about her despite their ignorance. We identify her with Anna, when later Eleni accuses Anna of returning after a long unexplained absence and asks her to pretend that she never left. Anna replies sarcastically that she will say that she was kept prisoner in the house. One cannot avoid hearing a series of echoes over this strange story: Is she the Woman that goes missing and is lost in patriarchal theories? Is she the repressed Mother of whose return psychoanalysis is so much afraid? In any case, she returns and nothing horrible happens. She returns from her not-to-be-spoken-of absence and also, maybe, she returns from the dead as a ghost; or is it the same thing? She returns and, by the end of the film, she is ready to leave again. She may be Anna who concludes her journey of self-awareness leaving behind her living self and setting free her daughter who no longer needs her; or she may be Maria who concludes her journey to maturity, finding her mother at last and then setting her free.

WEIRDING THE SUBJECT: MATERNAL INSCRIPTIONS

In the context of Western metaphysics, where the possibility of a woman to be the subject of her own gaze and her own discourse is structurally denied, the woman-subject and 'the mother who looks back' may represent the uncanny. In this context, a re-defined uncanniness can become a conscious subverting strategy, re-imagining subjectivity. I argue that Angelidi's work precisely re-imagines women's subjectivity through a poetics of intimate strangeness, which *Topos* exemplifies. The film poses questions on literal and political positionality; on perspective, both in the philosophical and the body-centred sense; on representation, both in terms of spatiality and temporality. Moreover, it offers an unconventional approach to gender in iconography and kinesiology, while also narrativising women's search for their identity and their own origin, in their relation to their mothers. In this chapter, under the figure of weird motherhood, we have investigated this different kind of subjectivity, as well as the different relations to authorship and inheritance it implies. Studying *Topos*, we have come to see what happens when filmic practice, more than the inscriptions *on* the mother, incorporates the inscriptions *of* the mother.

A complicated play of self-referentiality and intertextuality opens up beyond the limits of Angelidi's films. As she acknowledges and transcends her weird mothers and deep roots in feminism and the avant-garde, but also in art history and the collective unconscious of the world, she has become a root and a weird mother of others. The theatre directors Theodoros Terzopoulos and Michael Marmarinos, and the chorographer Dimitris Papaioannou, have been in dialogue with her work since the late 1980s. The avant-garde documentarist Eva Stefani calls Angelidi 'the fairy queen of Greek Cinema'; while the leading representative of the recent Greek Weird Wave, Athina Rachel Tsangari, acknowledges that 'you are the teacher of us all' [meaning the Weird Wave filmmakers]. Moreover, a newer generation of filmmakers continues her legacy, many of whom were her students in the Film School at Aristotle University of Thessaloniki, where she taught for many years. Weird mother of this text, I am also Angelidi's very weird daughter.

Answering the call of her weird mothers and sisters, weird mother herself, Angelidi opens up the way for the weird daughters of today and tomorrow, weird mothers of ourselves, to claim the weird motherhood of our gaze and our discourse. Her *Topos* can be interpreted as 'the mother returning the look', and she is beautiful!

NOTES

1. Constance Penley, 'The Avant-Garde and Its Imaginary', *Camera Obscura: A Journal of Feminism and Film Theory* 2 (Fall 1977): 3–33. A short version of the paper was first presented in 1976.
2. Penley, 'The Avant-Garde and Its Imaginary', 26.
3. Plato, *Republic* [375 BC], trans. Robin Waterfield (Oxford: Oxford University Press, 1994).
4. Immanuel Kant, *Critique of the Power of Judgement* [1790], trans. Paul Guyer and Eric Matthews (Cambridge: Cambridge University Press, 2000).
5. Renato Poggioli, *The Theory of the Avant-Garde* [1968], trans. Gerald Fitzgerald (Cambridge, MA: Harvard University Press, 1981).
6. Peter Bürger, *Theory of the Avant-Garde* [1974], trans. Michael Shaw (Minneapolis: Minnesota University Press, 1984).
7. Jacques Derrida, *De la grammatologie* (Paris: Minuit, 1967); Julia Kristeva, *La révolution du langage poétique* (Paris: Seuil, 1974).
8. Victor Shklovsky, 'Art As Technique' [1917], in *The Critical Tradition: Classic Texts and Contemporary Trends*, ed. David Richter, 3rd edition (Boston, MA: Bedford, 2006).
9. Kristeva, *La révolution du langage poétique*.
10. Bürger, *Theory of the Avant-Garde*.
11. Camera Obscura Collective, 'Chronology', *Camera Obscura: A Journal of Feminism and Film Theory* 3–4 (Summer 1979): 5–13.
12. Hélène Cixous, 'Le rire de la Méduse' [1975] and 'Sorties' [1975], in Cixous, *Le Rire de la Méduse et autres ironies* (Paris: Galilée, 2010), 35–68 and 69–197.
13. Camera Obscura Collective, 'Chronology', 8.
14. Ibid., 11.
15. Penley, 'The Avant-Garde and Its Imaginary', 3.
16. Malcolm Le Grice, *Abstract Film and Beyond* (England: Studio Vista, 1977).
17. Peter Gidal, *Structural Film Anthology* (British Film Institute, 1976).
18. Christian Metz, 'Le signifiant imaginaire', *Communications* 23 (1975): 3–55.
19. Thierry Kuntzel, 'Le travail du film', *Communications* 19 (1972): 33–5 ; 'Le travail du film, 2', *Communications* 23 (1975): 136–89.
20. Jean-Louis Baudry, 'Le dispositif: approches métapsychologiques de l'impression de réalité', *Communications* 23 (1975): 56–72.
21. Penley refers to Bellour's then unpublished work presented in his seminar at the Centre Universitaire Américain du Cinéma in Paris, spring 1977. It has been published since as: Raymond Bellour, *L'analyse du film* (Paris: Albatros, 1979).
22. As cited by Penley in 'The Avant-Garde and Its Imaginary', 10.
23. As cited by Penley in 'The Avant-Garde and Its Imaginary', 14.
24. Penley, 'The Avant-Garde and Its Imaginary', 25.
25. Laura Mulvey, 'Visual Pleasure and Narrative Cinema', *Screen* 16, 3 (1975): 6–18; see also 'Afterthoughts on "Visual Pleasure and Narrative Cinema", inspired by King Vidor's *Duel in the Sun* (King Vidor, 1946)', *Framework* 15/17 (Summer 1981): 12–15.
26. Tania Modleski, 'Never to be Thirty-Six Years Old: *Rebecca* as Female Oedipal Drama', *Wide Angle* 5, no. 1 (1982): 34–41.
27. Mary Ann Doane, 'Film and the Masquerade: Theorising the Female Spectator', *Screen* 23, 3–4 (September–October 1982): 74–87; 'Masquerade Reconsidered: Further Thoughts on the Female Spectator', in Doane, *Femmes Fatales: Feminism, Film Theory, Psychoanalysis* (London: Routledge, 1991).

28. Teresa de Laurentis, *Alice Doesn't: Feminism, Semiotics, Cinema* (Bloomington: Indiana University Press, 1984).
29. Sigmund Freud introduced the concept of the 'Oedipus complex' in his 'The Interpretation of Dreams' [1900], see *The Standard Edition of the Complete Psychological Works of Sigmund Freud*, Volumes IV & V (London: Hogarth Press).
30. Jacques Lacan, 'Le stade du miroir comme formateur de la fonction du Je, telle qu'elle nous est révélée dans l'expérience psychanalytique' [1949], in Lacan, *Écrits* (Paris: Minuit, 1966).
31. Freud's main texts regarding female sexuality are 'Some Psychological Consequences of the Anatomical Distinction between the Sexes' [1925] and 'Female Sexuality' [1931], and the posthumously published 'Lecture XXIII: Femininity' [1933]. *The Standard Edition of the Complete Psychological Works of Sigmund Freud* (London: Hogarth Press, 1953–74).
32. For the deconstructive function of the concept of 'supplement', see Derrida, *De la grammatologie*.
33. To be more exact, the subject of psychoanalysis is a white heterosexual cis man.
34. See Imre Lakatos, *Proofs and Refutations* (Cambridge: Cambridge University Press, 1976); *The Methodology of Scientific Research Programmes* (Cambridge: Cambridge University Press, 1978).
35. See Louis Althusser, 'Idéologie et appareils idéologiques de l'état Notes pour une recherche', *La Pensée* 151 (June 1970).
36. Luce Irigaray makes a critical overview of such positions in her essay 'Retour sur la théorie psychanalytique', first published in 1973 as an entry in *Encyclopédie médico-chirurgicale*; and republished as a chapter in *Ce sexe qui n'en est pas un* (Paris: Minuit, 1977). She references Karen Horney, Melanie Klein, Jeanne Lampl de Groot, Helene Deutsch, Ruth Mack Brunswick, Marie Bonaparte and Françoise Dolto.
37. Lacan, *Le Seminaire, Livre XX, Encore* [1972–3] (Paris: Seuil, 1975).
38. Cixous, *Le Rire de la Méduse*.
39. Irigaray, *Speculum: de l'autre femme* (Paris: Minuit, 1974) and *Ce sexe qui n'en est pas un*.
40. Irigaray, *Speculum*, 16.
41. Ibid., 60.
42. Ibid., 58
43. Cixous, *Le Rire de la Méduse*, 54
44. Freud, 'The Uncanny' [1919], *The Standard Edition of the Complete Psychological Works of Sigmund Freud*, Volume XVII (London: Hogarth Press, 1953–74), 245.
45. Freud, 'The Uncanny', 219.
46. Ibid., 245.
47. Ibid., 248–9.
48. Woman as castrator in horror films is analysed by Barbara Creed in *The Monstrous-Feminine: Film, Feminism, Psychoanalysis* (London: Routledge, 1993).
49. Freud, 'Medusa's Head' [1922], *The Standard Edition of the Complete Psychological Works of Sigmund Freud*, Volume XVIII (London: Hogarth Press, 1953–74).
50. Penley, 'The Avant-Garde and Its Imaginary', 26.
51. Cixous, *Le Rire de la Méduse*, 54.
52. Ibid., 53.
53. Ibid., 54.
54. Antoinetta Angelidi, «Το παιχνίδι με το ανοίκειο – μια ποιητική του κινηματογράφου» [Play with the Uncanny – A Poetics of Cinema] in *Γραφές για τον κινηματογράφο – Διεπιστημονικές προσεγγίσεις* [Writings on Cinema – Interdisciplinary Approaches] (Athens: Nefeli, 2005), 11–35.
55. For example, Antoinetta Angelidi, «Ο ποιητικός κινηματογράφος και ο μηχανισμός του ονείρου» [Poetic Cinema and the Dream-Mechanism], *Κινηματογράφος και Επικοινωνία* 7 (2001): 7–11; «Η φιλμική γραφή και ο μηχανισμός του ονείρου» [Filmic Writing and Dream-Mechanism],

in *Το Πάσχον Σώμα – Οι πολιτισμικές σπουδές σήμερα και αύριο* [The Body in Pain – Cultural Studies Today and Tomorrow], ed. Pepi Regopoulou (University of Athens, 2004), 46–9; «Το παιχνίδι με το ανοίκειο – μια ποιητική του κινηματογράφου» (2005); «Όνειρο και κινηματογράφος: Τρεις κινηματογραφικές προσεγγίσεις της ζωής ως όνειρο» [Dream and Cinema: Three Cinematic Approaches of Life As Dream], *Annals for Aesthetics* 46 (2012): 363–73. Antoinetta Angelidi and Rea Walldén, 'The Ethics of Heterogeneity and Experimentation: Teaching Film Direction in the Film School of Aristotle University of Thessaloniki', in *Contemporary Greek Film Cultures from 1990 to the Present*, ed. Tonia Kazakopoulou and Mikela Fotiou (Bern: Peter Lang, 2017), 369–92. Rea Walldén, «Το Παιχνίδι» [Play], in *Αντουανέττα Αγγελίδη* [Antoinetta Angelidi], ed. Stella Theodorakis (Athens: Aigokeros, 2005): 20–3; «Ποιήματα ή Δοκίμια; Οι ταινίες της Αντουανέττας Αγγελίδη» [Poems or Essays? The films by Antoinetta Angelidi], in *Αντουανέττα Αγγελίδη*, ibid. 78–81; 'Conversing with Dreams: An Encounter with Antoinetta Angelidi', *FilmIcon: Journal of Greek Film Studies* 4 (December 2017): 184–94; 'The Spatio-Temporality of the Avant-Gardes: Feminist Avant-Garde U-Topoi in Greek Cinema from Transition to Crisis', in *Contemporary Greek Film Cultures from 1990 to the Present*, ed. Tonia Kazakopoulou and Mikela Fotiou (Bern: Peter Lang, 2017): 71–99.
56. Antoinetta Angelidi and Frida Liappa, interview by Christos Vakalopoulos and Michel Dimopoulos, *Σύγχρονος Κινηματογράφος* 17/18 (May–June 1978): 98.
57. Ibid., 98.
58. During the Colonel's Junta in Greece, Angelidi was in the resistance, even becoming a member of the Central Bureau of the underground communist youth organisation 'EKON Rigas Fereos'. When she arrived in Paris in 1973, it was as a political refugee, to avoid arrest. It is in Paris that she comes in contact with the feminist second wave and enters the IDHEC Film School. It is not without significance that she gives birth to her first child while studying in the Film School, or that she divorces and becomes a single mother of two just before shooting her *Topos*.
59. *L'histoire écrite* (1975); *L'eau* (1976).
60. Antoinetta Angelidi, 'Δυο κληρονομιές; (Dies Irae)' [Two Inheritances? (Dies Irae)], *Σύγχρονος Κινηματογράφος* 21/22 (July–October 1979): 93.
61. Antoinetta Angelidi, [Self-Presentation], *Φιλμ* 17, Special Issue: Women & Cinema (1979): 172.
62. Claire Mitsotaki is the co-writer of *Topos*, and of a few uncompleted projects prior to the film.
63. Rea Walldén is the co-writer of *Thief or Reality* (2001), and in a creative partnership with Angelidi since the mid-1990s.
64. She says in an interview after a screening of *Topos*, '[The] common objective of artists is to reveal the known world as if seen for the first time', and later, 'to dissolve the going-without-saying, the without-thought relation with the world'. See Angelidi, «Η επανάληψη της πορείας για την οργάνωση του χάους» [The Repetition of the Progression in order to Organise Chaos], interview by Katerina Evangelakou, *Κάμερα για τον Κινηματογράφο* 4–5 (December 1985–January 1986).
65. Bertolt Brecht introduced the concept of 'alienation effect' in 1936 in his 'Alienation Effects in Chinese Acting'. See *Brecht on Theatre*, ed. and trans. John Willett (London: Methuen Drama, 2001).
66. For example, Antoinetta Angelidi, «Ο πόθος της επούλωσης και το δικαίωμα του αόρατου» [The Desire of Healing the Scar and the Right of the Invisible], in *Megacities: Από την πραγματική στη φανταστική πόλη* [Megacities: From the Real to the Imaginary City] (Thessaloniki Film Festival, 2000), 83; and «Υπερβαίνοντας το προφανές: Ο χρόνος στον κινηματογράφο» [Transcending the Obvious: Time in Cinema], *Σύναψις* 11, 4 (October – November – December 2008): 98–105.

67. 'A fascinating place of strangeness and familiarity', writes Jocelyne Poirier in '*Topos* (Lieu) par Antoinetta Angelidi', *Les Cahiers de la Femme* (Spring–Summer 1986).
68. Angelidi, «Το παιχνίδι με το ανοίκειο – μια ποιητική του κινηματογράφου».
69. Metz, 'Le cinéma: langue ou langage', *Communications* 4 (1964): 52–90; *Langage et cinéma*, Paris: Larousse, 1971; 'Sémiologie audio-visuelle et linguistique générative' [1973], *Essais sémiotiques* (Paris: Klincksiek, 1977), 109–28.
70. Freud, 'Interpretation of Dreams'.
71. Rea Walldén, 'Matter-Reality in Cinema: Realism, Counter-Realism and the Avant-Gardes', *Gramma: Journal of Theory and Criticism* 20, special issue on semiotics, ed. A-Ph. Lagopoulos and K. Boklund (2012): 187–203; 'Beware! Construction! A Semiotic Methodology for Approaching Avant-Garde Cinema', *Punctum: International Journal of Semiotics* 3, 2 (2017): 111–35.
72. Antoinetta Angelidi, «Το φως μπορεί να είναι ήχος και μια λέξη να είναι φως» [Light Can Be Sound and A Word Can Be Light], interview by Eleni Machaira, *Αυγή* (Athens: Sunday 3 July 1988).
73. Antoinetta Angelidi, «Η γεννέθλια γη του προσωπικού βλέμματος» [The Birthplace of the Personal Viewpoint], in *50 – Why Cinema Now?*, ed. Despoina Mouzaki (Thessaloniki Film Festival, 2009), 26–9; 'Letter to a Young Filmmaker', contribution to the 1st International Conference of the Hellenic Film Academy, *Cinema Speaking . . . The Importance of Audiovisual Education* (Athens: November 2010). Angelidi and Walldén, 'The Ethics of Heterogeneity and Experimentation'.
74. Dimitris Danikas [review of *Topos*], *Ριζοσπάστης* (Athens, 10 November 1985).
75. Jacques Lacan, *Le Séminaire, Livre XI, Les quatre concepts fondamentaux de la psychanalyse* [1964] (Paris: Seuil, 1973).
76. Gustave Courbet, *L'origine du monde* ['The Origin of the World'] (1866).
77. Before this pronouncement, in the prelude to the film, an excerpt of Dante's *Divine Comedy* [1308–20] is recited in the original Italian, without subtitles. The majority of the initial (Greek) audience would not have understood it. A bloody children's song is also intoned.
78. Euripides, *Medea* [431 BC]. For an English translation, see *Medea: A New Translation*, trans. Charles Martin, University of California Press, 2019.
79. Giorgio de Chirico, *Mystery and Melancholy of a Street* (1914).
80. Leonor Fini painted two versions of *Woman in Armour* in 1938, before incorporating the figure in *The Black Room* (1939).
81. Fra Angelico, *Annunciation* (1440–5).
82. Vittore Carpaccio, *The Dream of St Ursula* (1495).
83. Paolo Uccello, *Birth of the Virgin* (1435).
84. Many Balthus paintings offer variations of similar stretching poses; see, e.g., *Drawing Room* (1942); *Drawing Room* (1943), *Nude with Cat* (1949); *The Three Sisters* (1954); *The Room* (1953).
85. A zigzag pattern appearing in many Giorgio de Chirico paintings and engravings. Much referenced in *Topos* is particularly *The Mysterious Swimmer* (1934).
86. Jacopo Pontormo, *The Deposition from the Cross* (1528). In her interview to Evangelakou, Angelidi explains that the principle for the make-up in the film (by Achilleas Charitos) was to work on human skin as if it was a painting surface, in a continuation between the skin and the clothes that cover it; see Angelidi, 'The Repetition of the Progression in order to Organise Chaos'.
87. Jean-Auguste Dominique Ingres, *The Great Odalisque* (1819).
88. Paolo Uccello, *St George and the Dragon* (1470).
89. The actress Anitta Santorineou changes register in order to interpret the different characters.
90. The singer Martine Viard improvises on musical scores by Georges Aperghis.

91. Angelidi, 'The Repetition of the Progression in order to Organise Chaos'.
92. Fini, *Woman in Armour* and *The Black Room*.
93. Leonora Carrington, *Self-portrait* (1936).
94. Uccello, *St George and the Dragon*.
95. The work of Lily Kendaka on the film's costumes is exceptional.
96. 'The space of the film is the body; it sees, it hears', writes Angelidi in 'Introduction to the script' that she published in *Οθόνη: Κινηματογραφικό περιοδικό θεωρίας/κριτικής* 26 (July–September 1986): 69.
97. Angelidi, 'The Repetition of the Progression in order to Organise Chaos'.
98. As Angelidi says in relation to *Idées Fixes / Dies Irae*, 'Positioning myself in all this, as one of the elements that exist in the film, I incur subversions and self-critique [. . .] And this is a political act. It means that I don't take myself out of the picture, I am inscribed as a body in there'; in the interview by Vakalopoulos and Dimopoulos, 98.
99. Poster for *Idées Fixes / Dies Irae*.
100. The woman-woman relation in general and the mother-daughter relation in particular are under-represented in all Abrahamic religions, as they are in psychoanalysis.
101. 'Hell' is the first of the three books of his *Divine Comedy*.
102. Cixous, *Le Rire de la Méduse*.
103. Angelidi, 'Introduction to the script', 69.
104. Ibid., 68.

BIBLIOGRAPHY

Excerpts from texts appearing in this Bibliography in languages other than English have been translated by the author of the chapter.

Althusser, Louis. 'Idéologie et appareils idéologiques de l'état. Notes pour une recherche'. *La Pensée* 151 (June 1970).
Angelidi, Antoinetta. 'Δυο κληρονομιές; (Dies Irae)' [Two Inheritances? (Dies Irae)]. *Σύγχρονος Κινηματογράφος* 21/22 (July–October 1979): 93.
Angelidi, Antoinetta. [Self-Presentation]. *Φιλμ* 17, Special Issue: Women & Cinema (1979): 171–2.
Angelidi, Antoinetta. «Η επανάληψη της πορείας για την οργάνωση του χάους» [The Repetition of the Progression in order to Organise Chaos]. Interview by Katerina Evangelakou. *Κάμερα για τον Κινηματογράφο* 4–5 (December 1985–January 1986).
Angelidi, Antoinetta. 'Introduction to the script'. *Οθόνη: Κινηματογραφικό περιοδικό θεωρίας/κριτικής* 26 (July-September 1986): 68–9.
Angelidi, Antoinetta. «Το φως μπορεί να είναι ήχος και μια λέξη να είναι φως» [Light Can Be Sound and A Word Can Be Light]. Interview by Eleni Machaira. *Αυγή* (Athens: Sunday 3 July 1988).
Angelidi, Antoinetta. «Ο πόθος της επούλωσης και το δικαίωμα του αόρατου» [The Desire of Healing the Scar and the Right of the Invisible]. In *Megacities: Από την πραγματική στη φανταστική πόλη* [Megacities: From the Real to the Imaginary City]. Thessaloniki Film Festival, 2000.
Angelidi, Antoinetta. «Ο ποιητικός κινηματογράφος και ο μηχανισμός του ονείρου» [Poetic Cinema and the Dream-Mechanism]. *Κινηματογράφος και Επικοινωνία* 7 (2001): 7–11
Angelidi, Antoinetta. «Η φιλμική γραφή και ο μηχανισμός του ονείρου» [Filmic Writing and Dream-Mechanism]. In *Το Πάσχον Σώμα – Οι πολιτισμικές σπουδές σήμερα και αύριο* [The Body in Pain – Cultural Studies Today and Tomorrow], ed. Pepi Regopoulou, 46–9. University of Athens, 2004.

Angelidi, Antoinetta. «Το παιχνίδι με το ανοίκειο – μια ποιητική του κινηματογράφου» [Play with the Uncanny – A Poetics of Cinema]. In *Γραφές για τον κινηματογράφο – Διεπιστημονικές προσεγγίσεις* [Writings on Cinema – Interdisciplinary Approaches], 11–35. Athens: Nefeli, 2005.

Angelidi, Antoinetta. «Υπερβαίνοντας το προφανές: Ο χρόνος στον κινηματογράφο» [Transcending the Obvious: Time in Cinema]. *Σύναψις* 11, 4 (October–November–December 2008): 98–105.

Angelidi, Antoinetta. «Η γεννέθλια γη του προσωπικού βλέμματος» [The Birthplace of the Personal Viewpoint]. In *50 – Why Cinema Now?*, ed. Despoina Mouzaki, 26–9. Thessaloniki Film Festival, 2009.

Angelidi, Antoinetta. 'Letter to a Young Filmmaker'. Contribution to the 1st International Conference of the Hellenic Film Academy, *Cinema Speaking . . . The Importance of Audiovisual Education* (Athens: November 2010).

Angelidi, Antoinetta. «Όνειρο και κινηματογράφος: Τρεις κινηματογραφικές προσεγγίσεις της ζωής ως όνειρο» [Dream and Cinema: Three Cinematic Approaches of Life as Dream]. *Annals for Aesthetics* 46 (2012): 363–73.

Angelidi, Antoinetta and Frida Liappa. Interview by Christos Vakalopoulos and Michel Dimopoulos. *Σύγχρονος Κινηματογράφος* 17/18 (May–June1978): 89–98.

Angelidi, Antoinetta and Rea Walldén. 'The Ethics of Heterogeneity and Experimentation: Teaching Film Direction in the Film School of Aristotle University of Thessaloniki', in *Contemporary Greek Film Cultures from 1990 to the Present*, ed. Tonia Kazakopoulou and Mikela Fotiou. Bern: Peter Lang, 2017, 369–92.

Baudry, Jean-Louis. 'Le dispositif: approches métapsychologiques de l'impression de réalité'. *Communications* 23 (1975): 56–72.

Bellour, Raymond. *L'analyse du film*. Paris: Albatros, 1979.

Brecht, Bertolt. 'Alienation Effects in Chinese Acting' [1936]. In *Brecht on Theatre*, ed. and trans. John Willett. London: Methuen Drama, 2001.

Bürger, Peter. *Theory of the Avant-Garde* [1974] trans. Michael Shaw. Minneapolis: Minnesota University Press, 1984.

Camera Obscura Collective [Janet Bergstrom, Elisabeth Lyon, Constance Penley]. 'Chronology'. *Camera Obscura: A Journal of Feminism and Film Theory* 3–4 (Summer 1979): 5–13.

Cixous, Hélène. 'Le rire de la Méduse' [1975]. In *Le Rire de la Méduse et autres ironies*. Paris: Galilée, 2010.

Cixous, Hélène. 'Sorties' [1975]. In *Le Rire de la Méduse et autres ironies*. Paris: Galilée, 2010.

Creed, Barbara. *The Monstrous-Feminine: Film, Feminism, Psychoanalysis*. London: Routledge, 1993.

Danikas, Dimitris. [review of *Topos*]. *Ριζοσπάστης*. Athens, 10 November 1985.

Dante Alighieri. *Divine Comedy* [1308–1320], trans. Dorothy Sayers. Penguin Classics, 1949–62.

Derrida, Jacques. *De la grammatologie*. Paris: Minuit, 1967.

Doane, Mary Ann. 'Film and the Masquerade: Theorising the Female Spectator', *Screen* 23, 3–4 (September–October 1982): 74–87.

Doane, Mary Ann. 'Masquerade Reconsidered: Further Thoughts on the Female Spectator', in Doane, *Femmes Fatales: Feminism, Film Theory, Psychoanalysis*. London: Routledge, 1991.

Euripides, 'Medea' [431 BC]. In *Medea: A New Translation*, trans. Charles Martin. University of California Press, 2019.

Freud, Sigmund. *The Standard Edition of the Complete Psychological Works of Sigmund Freud*, Volumes I–XXIV (1886–1939). Ed. and trans. James Strachey, coll. Anna Freud, assist.

Alix Strachey and Alan Tyson. London: The Hogarth Press and the Institute of Psycho-Analysis, 1981.
Gidal, Peter. *Structural Film Anthology*. British Film Institute, 1976.
Irigaray, Luce. *Speculum: de l'autre femme*. Paris: Minuit, 1974.
Irigaray, Luce. *Ce sexe qui n'en est pas un*. Paris: Minuit, 1977.
Kant, Immanuel. *Critique of the Power of Judgement* [1790], trans. Paul Guyer and Eric Matthews. Cambridge: Cambridge University Press, 2000.
Kristeva, Julia. *La révolution du langage poétique*. Paris: Seuil, 1974.
Kuntzel, Thierry. 'Le travail du film'. *Communications* 19 (1972): 33–5.
Kuntzel, Thierry. 'Le travail du film, 2'. *Communications* 23 (1975): 136–89.
Lacan, Jacques. 'Le stade du miroir comme formateur de la fonction du Je, telle qu'elle nous est révélée dans l'expérience psychanalytique' [1949]. *Écrits*. Paris: Minuit, 1966.
Lacan, Jacques. *Le Séminaire, Livre XI, Les quatre concepts fondamentaux de la psychanalyse* [1964]. Paris: Seuil, 1973.
Lacan, Jacques. *Le Séminaire, Livre XX, Encore* [1972–3]. Paris: Seuil, 1975.
Lakatos, Imre. *Proofs and Refutations*. Cambridge: Cambridge University Press, 1976.
Lakatos, Imre. *The Methodology of Scientific Research Programmes*. Cambridge: Cambridge University Press, 1978.
Laurentis, Teresa de. *Alice Doesn't: Feminism, Semiotics, Cinema*. Bloomington: Indiana University Press, 1984.
Le Grice, Malcolm. *Abstract Film and Beyond*. England: Studio Vista, 1977.
Metz, Christian. 'Le cinéma: langue ou langage'. *Communications* 4 (1964): 52–90.
Metz, Christian. *Langage et cinéma*. Paris: Larousse, 1971.
Metz, Christian. 'Sémiologie audio-visuelle et linguistique générative' [1973], in Metz, *Essais sémiotiques*. Paris: Klincksiek, 1977.
Metz, Christian. 'Le signifiant imaginaire'. *Communications* 23 (1975): 3–55.
Modleski, Tania. 'Never to be Thirty-Six Years Old: *Rebecca* as Female Oedipal Drama'. *Wide Angle* 5, 1 (1982): 34–41.
Mulvey, Laura. 'Visual Pleasure and Narrative Cinema'. *Screen* 16, 3 (1975): 6–18.
Mulvey, Laura. 'Afterthoughts on "Visual Pleasure and Narrative Cinema", inspired by King Vidor's *Duel in the Sun* (King Vidor, 1946)', *Framework* 15/17 (Summer 1981): 12–15.
Penley, Constance. 'The Avant-Garde and Its Imaginary'. *Camera Obscura: A Journal of Feminism and Film Theory* 2 (Fall 1977): 3–33.
Plato. *Republic* [375 BC], trans. Robin Waterfield. Oxford: Oxford University Press, 1994.
Poggioli, Renato. *The Theory of the Avant-Garde* [1968], trans. Gerald Fitzgerald. Cambridge, MA: Harvard University Press, 1981.
Poirier, Jocelyne. '*Topos* (Lieu) par Antoinetta Angelidi'. *Les Cahiers de la Femme* (Spring–Summer 1986).
Shklovsky, Victor. 'Art As Technique' [1917]. In *The Critical Tradition: Classic Texts and Contemporary Trends*, ed. David Richter. Third Edition. Boston, MA: Bedford Books, 2006, 774–84.
Walldén, Rea. «Το Παιχνίδι» [Play]. In *Αντουανέττα Αγγελίδη* [Antoinetta Angelidi], ed. Stella Theodorakis. Athens: Aigokeros, 2005, 20–3.
Walldén, Rea. «Ποιήματα ή Δοκίμια; Οι ταινίες της Αντουανέττας Αγγελίδη» [Poems or Essays? The films by Antoinetta Angelidi], In *Αντουανέττα Αγγελίδη* [Antoinetta Angelidi], ed. Stella Theodorakis. Athens: Aigokeros, 2005, 78–81.
Walldén, Rea. 'Matter-Reality in Cinema: Realism, Counter-Realism and the Avant-Gardes'. *Gramma: Journal of Theory and Criticism* 20, special issue on semiotics, ed. A-Ph. Lagopoulos and K. Boklund (2012): 187–203.

Walldén, Rea. 'Beware! Construction! A Semiotic Methodology for Approaching Avant-Garde Cinema'. *Punctum: International Journal of Semiotics* 3, 2 (2017): 111–35.

Walldén, Rea. 'Conversing with Dreams: An Encounter with Antoinetta Angelidi'. *FilmIcon: Journal of Greek Film Studies* 4 (December 2017): 184–94.

Walldén, Rea. 'The Spatio-Temporality of the Avant-Gardes: Feminist Avant-Garde U-Topoi in Greek Cinema from Transition to Crisis', in *Contemporary Greek Film Cultures from 1990 to the Present*, ed. Tonia Kazakopoulou and Mikela Fotiou. Bern: Peter Lang, 2017, 71–99.

CHAPTER 2

'Every Element in a Film Narrates': The Complex Language of Heterogeneity in *Idées Fixes / Dies Irae* as a (Feminist) Critique to the Practice of Methodological Categorisation in Avant-garde Film History

Fil Ieropoulos

Antoinetta Angelidi's *Idées Fixes / Dies Irae* (1977) occupies a particular place in the history of cinema, not only as it is one of the few examples of experimental/artist film by a Greek auteur in the 1970s, but also as its compositional sensibilities bridge tendencies that historically have been thought of as opposite or contradictory. It is a film that is both poetic and political, wildly visual but also textual, using structural/formal as well as personal/expressionist methodologies. As a member of the second phase (1974–84) of the editorial board of the magazine *Synchronos Kinimatografos* (Contemporary Cinema),[1] but also having previously lived in Paris, Angelidi was aware of the innovations of the international filmic avant-garde and presumably the various polemics of film groups all over the world. Although Greece had no developed experimental film scene, *Idées Fixes / Dies Irae* is a film that was in dialogue with the experimental film innovations of its time[2] and as Angelidi scholar Rea Walldén suggests, it is 'radically avant-garde by any definition of the term'.[3] The question of this definition is of particular interest to this chapter, although I will not deal with the notion of the 'avant-garde' in general, but rather with historical understandings of what avant-garde filmmaking is and more so the various methodological tendencies in the history of experimental cinema. I will argue that on top of its enormous value as a 'milestone of Greek avant-garde cinema',[4] the film is a startling amalgam of filmic strategies that are not frequently combined, resulting in a complex cinematic language, which in the words of Hamalidi, Nikolopoulou and Walldén 'fully exploits the potentialities of cinematic heterogeneity'.[5] I will conclude my case by discussing the film as an example of a feminist work by a female auteur in the male-dominated history of experimental film[6] and consider the possibility of a different herstory of experimental cinema.

Manifestos have been extremely common in the history of experimental cinema. The very birth of the medium coincides with an era in which new manifestos about the purpose of art came to prominence almost every few years (Futurism/1909, Cubism/1912, Vorticism/1914, Dada/1916, Surrealism/1924, and so on). The early twentieth century was a complex time politically; life was moving fast and artists felt the need to communicate revolutionary changes themselves. The extremely influential and prolific Soviet avant-garde has given us some of the most important innovations in cinema, alongside various manifestos about the nature of cinema or cinema and politics, the cinema spectator, etc. In fact, even filmmakers that worked in the same milieu and to an extent the same scene proposed conflicting manifestos, such as the case of Dziga Vertov and Sergei Eisenstein discussed later. A similar tendency towards polemical positions can be found throughout the history of the American avant-garde of the 1960s/1970s; once again filmmakers who often showcased their work at the same venues proposed radically different approaches to the cinematic medium. Considering experimental film's niche existence and a sense that it sometimes feels like a footnote in the history of cinema in terms of exposure, one wonders why there is such a tendency to separate; yet, it is exactly this lack of exposure that often results in polemic language. Hans Richter, Man Ray and Stan Brakhage have all historically used the term 'film poem' to define their work. The term does indeed insinuate a number of methodologies which I will discuss later, but also 'in practice, the film poem label was primarily an emblem of the avant-garde's difference from the commercial narrative film',[7] as James Peterson claims. In Richter's own words: 'The reason I use the word "poetry" is to set it off against the "film novel", which is represented by the entertainment film.'[8] Modernist film artists often felt the need to define themselves against the mainstream and manifestos were a performative expression of this difference. However, for the purposes of this chapter, I will be taking the content of various film schools/tendencies/manifestos at face value, leaving aside the historical context under which they were put forward and their polemical performative gesture of difference.

Not all filmmakers in experimental film history comfortably sat behind manifestos. Antoinetta Angelidi's work is not the only example of a filmic language that does not quite fit into rigid methodological frameworks. Peter Wollen's influential essay from 1975, 'The Two Avant-Gardes', discusses exactly the case of separatisms in experimental film movements in Europe, suggesting instead that cinema should be seen as a multiple system and that 'the search for the specifically cinematic can be deceptively purist and reductive'.[9]

An example he refers to is that of the London Film-makers' Co-op versus the Godard circle, both of which dismiss each other's work for both aesthetic and political reasons. When discussing the avant-garde filmmakers of the 1980s, William C. Wees suggests that 'post-1980s avant-garde filmmakers not only stand in opposition to mainstream, commercial cinema [. . .], but most also oppose, to varying degrees, the aesthetics of modernism that dominated avant-garde film discourse until the 1980s'.[10] It is not my intention to claim that such an opposition was by any means central in Angelidi's film. But her film poetics/politics of 1977 certainly do not align with choosing specific methodologies in the name of structural polemics and she herself states: 'my film poetics relies on a complex use of the potentialities of the cinematic medium' and 'understanding cinematic heterogeneity means realising that every element in a film narrates'.[11] Heterogeneity is seen as key in a text by Hamalidi et al., in which they describe *Idées Fixes / Dies Irae* as an example of a collage work. As they claim, the film creates meaning 'through the juxtaposition of signs' and 'by the synthesis of disaccord between image and sound'.[12] Juxtaposition, heterogeneity, collage, synthesis are all terms that signify combinative methods of working, methods that often bring together seemingly non-compatible strategies. I have separated what I see as these combinative methodologies into three broad sub-categories, though it is important to note that they all interrelate to an extent.

CONTEMPLATIVE SPACES: STRUCTURAL FILM VS PERSONAL EXPRESSION

One of the most important factors that has defined experimental film historically is that, contrary to mainstream industrial cinema which is produced by large studios and many people, it is primarily the work of an (almost always singular) artist. In that respect, a significant part of writings on experimental cinema focuses on the idea that cinema is a medium for personal expression. Writing in 1971, David Curtis claims that: 'the major achievement of the post-war American cinema has been the development of "personal" film-making'.[13] Although this is certainly true, throughout the twentieth century, avant-garde film theory has varied significantly with regard to the extent to which a film ought to be the culmination of personal sensibility. One of the most important divisions in the history of avant-garde film is that between so-called lyrical and structural film. The terms were introduced by one of the major writers on experimental film, Adams P. Sitney. In his seminal book, *Visionary Film*, he states:

> the Lyrical film postulates the film-maker behind the camera as the first-person protagonist of the film. The images of the film are what he sees, filmed in such a way that we never forget his presence and we know how he is reacting to his vision.[14]

His primary example of such methodology is the work of Stan Brakhage, whose films are wildly expressionist and autobiographical and whose work had risen to prominence in the underground film scenes by the mid-1960s. Brakhage has described poetic structures but also expressionist painting as immensely important to his work: 'poetry and painting have alternately proved more growth-engendering sources of inspiration than either the trappings of the stage or the specific continuity limitations of any "making up a story", novelistic tendencies etc."[15] Standing somewhat contrary to such expressionist tendencies, a number of filmmakers in the 1970s proposed a different type of avant-garde cinema, a cinema in which references to the medium itself prevail. Adams P. Sitney termed this 'structural film'.[16] 'The structural film insists on its shape and what content it has is minimal and subsidiary to the outline.'[17] Writing ten (important for its development) years later, Birgit Hein suggests that structural films 'have no narrative or poetic content. The content of structural films refers to the medium itself.'[18]

Based on the definitions given above, one could imagine that Angelidi's work has little to do with the unpoetic tendencies of structural cinema and is rather aligned more easily with the personal/expressionist side. Angelidi has stated on numerous occasions that her work is 'cinema-poetry'[19] and the composition of her shots shows a more integral understanding of the image that does not limit itself to form/content divisions. She has also mentioned that her films are often visual culminations of her dreams, dreams of course being an extremely personal space.[20] However, I would suggest that Angelidi's type of film poetry uses methodologies pioneered by structural filmmakers[21] and that some of the cinematic strategies of *Idées Fixes / Dies Irae* are more frequently connected with structural film than expressionist/personal/lyrical cinema. In his detailed description of the concerns of structural film, Malcolm Le Grice states that two of its characteristics are: 'concern with duration as a concrete dimension' and 'concern with the semantics of image and with the construction of meaning through language systems'.[22] *Idées Fixes / Dies Irae* is absolutely interested in both of these methodologies. I would like to present some examples of parts of the film that suggest so.

The film starts with two long static shots that occupy one quarter of its total duration and also includes another very long shot in the middle. Hamalidi et al. suggest that the film is 'testing our endurance by the extreme length of certain shots'[23] and Walldén adds that the film is 'divided in two by another long static shot, showing the word "Défense" implying the spectator's resistance to cinema'.[24] While I agree that there is a certain aspect of anti-art 'endurance test' to these shots,[25] I would be inclined to suggest that they move further than that and into the realm of the minimalist static-camera tendencies of structural cinema. The first two shots particularly are strongly reminiscent of the perspective games played by Ernie Gehr's *Serene Velocity*

(1970) and Michael Snow's *Wavelength* (1967). Similar to Gehr, Angelidi seems to work with perspective to create startling eye illusions. In the first shot, two characters walk side by side and progressively melt into each other, while Angelidi's patient static camera 'allows' perspective to compose the illusion of movement/non-movement. If we go back to Sitney's text, we can see that he suggests that 'in the work of Ernie Gehr or Michael Snow the camera is fixed in mythical contemplation of a portion of space'[26] and I would claim that a similar sense of mythical contemplation takes place in these first two shots of *Idées Fixes / Dies Irae*. The viewer is literally thrown from the start of the film in these contemplative spaces, in which they have to rethink time and space, the relationship between filmmaker and subjects, the audience's position, and so on. As Nicky Hamlyn suggests, any critical cinema must explore 'how the film apparatus [. . .] confronts space – infinite, three-dimensional, continuous, enduring'[27] and I believe that *Idées Fixes / Dies Irae* is in this sense a critical, structural film, even if it is historically mostly connected with poetic film tendencies. It is not surprising, then, that in an early review of a screening of the film in France, critic J. Thibaudeau compares Angelidi's use of space and time to the work of Ernie Gehr.[28]

This notion of the critical cinema that Hamlyn mentions and in general the film's structural tendencies are not limited to its long static shots. Throughout the film there is a sense of self-reflexivity, the film referring to its own self, by showing the film equipment, the filmmaker herself, whereas text – analysed in more detail in the next part of the chapter – comments on what we see. The viewer is at various points reminded that they see a film; they are discouraged from passively experiencing[29] the film for its aesthetic qualities, as might be the case with more expressionist work. Yet, in Angelidi's films, the Brechtian distantiation techniques do not necessarily contradict the film's poetic qualities. In one of the last shots of the film, the filmmaker poses as if Marat in his bathtub with the word 'HORIZON' written across the screen. Hamalidi et al. see in this shot a sense of 'self irony, the death of the author, a woman's naked body under the burden of politics and high art'.[30] In a similar gesture, George Landow, aka Owen Land, another filmmaker strongly connected with the structural film movement, begins and closes his film *Remedial Reading Comprehension* (1970) with a shot of himself running while the words 'THIS IS A FILM ABOUT YOU, NOT ABOUT ITS MAKER' appear across the screen. Both Angelidi and Landow/Land aim at problematising the relationship between filmmaker and audience, yet, Angelidi's self-reflexivity is not a means to its own end; references to the medium are simultaneously mixed with complex poetic imagery and thus the result is semiotically more open-ended and as such less distancing. Fred Camper suggests that 'by distancing the images, Landow denies them primary reality'[31] and that 'Landows's films are structural rather than sensual'.[32] I would suggest that *Idées Fixes / Dies Irae* aims to be at once structural and sensual. The images do have a primary reality and the audience's senses are invited to experience them visually, while the film still refers to its own structures.

Looking at *Idées Fixes / Dies Irae*, it is apparent that Angeldi believed that it is not contradictory to combine structural and personal/expressionist tendencies and the question that remains is to what extent they are indeed contradictory and in a sense relevant today, forty or fifty years after the writing of the theories mentioned above. William C. Wees suggests that the dichotomy between filmmakers such as Michael Snow and Stan Brakhage has been prevalent throughout film criticism. He mentions a number of terms used to describe this dichotomy: 'abstract expressionist versus minimalist, poetic versus philosophical, personal versus impersonal, perceptual versus conceptual, romantic versus modernist, modernist versus postmodernist.'[33] The fact that there have been so many different terms to describe the dichotomy definitely shows that it has indeed been important for practitioners and theoreticians. However, by the same token, this multiplicity of definitions for the dichotomy points to an extent to its non-significance. Throughout film history there have been filmmakers that have combined such tendencies in single films, making interesting methodological hybrids. In that respect, I believe *Idées Fixes / Dies Irae* is both structural and expressionist and similarly both poetic and philosophical, perceptual and conceptual, and so on.

CINÉMA DISCREPANT: MEDIUM-SPECIFICITY VS HYBRIDS; FILM POEMS AND POETRY-FILMS

Another opposing tendency that I would argue is bridged by *Idées Fixes / Dies Irae*, proposing a hybrid mode of operation, is the question of whether films should be image driven or text driven. If we briefly go back to historical avant-garde film texts, we find that experimental filmmakers frequently took fairly polemic approaches against text being used on film and instead called for a completely visual experience. This was part of positioning themselves against mainstream film, strongly connected to narrative and therefore text. Early avant-garde filmmaker Germaine Dulac believed that 'every cinematic drama [. . .] must be visual and not literary',[34] calling for an image-based cinema which does not need text to compose its meaning. She continues, 'a real film can't be able to be told, since it must draw its active and emotive principle from images formed of unique visual tones'.[35] This search for what comprises cinema's 'unique visual tones' has occupied the minds of various experimental filmmakers throughout the twentieth century, with Stan Brakhage taking this to its most extreme form, both in his films and in his writing. In his influential text 'Metaphors on Vision', he states:

Imagine an eye unruled by man-made laws of perspective, an eye unprejudiced by compositional logic, an eye which does not respond to the name of everything but which must know each object encountered in life through an adventure of perception. How many colors are there in a field of grass to the crawling baby unaware of 'Green'? How many rainbows can light create for the untutored eye? How aware of variations in heat waves can that eye be? Imagine a world alive with incomprehensible objects and shimmering with an endless variety of movement and innumerable gradations of color. Imagine a world before the 'beginning was the word'.[36]

In order to understand why some experimental filmmakers had such difficulty with words it is important to contextualise film historically at a time when the concept of medium-specificity was of particular importance. Part of the early twentieth-century tendency to break away from classicism in order for art to achieve an avant-garde revolutionary potential was for artists to search for what is essential in their medium's very essence. Modern art theorist Clement Greenberg writes, 'Painting and sculpture in the hands of the lesser talents . . . become nothing more than ghosts and "stooges" of literature. All emphasis is taken away from the medium and transferred to subject matter.'[37] This idea of film distancing itself from literature in order to find its 'real self' is echoed in the texts of Soviet avant-garde filmmaker Dziga Vertov. He writes in the introduction to his seminal work *The Man with a Movie Camera* (1929):

> This film presents an experiment in the cinematic communication of visible events without the aid of intertitles (a film without intertitles), without the aid of a scenario (a film without a scenario). This experimental work aims at creating a truly international absolute language of cinema based on its total separation from the language of theater and literature.[38]

What is even more interesting is that Vertov himself, as well as Brakhage and other experimental filmmakers, had no hesitation in describing their work as poetic or poetry influenced. Thus, although text is not often seen favourably by experimental filmmakers, there still seems to be something about the notion of poetry that attracts them.

One of the earliest detailed discussions on the relationship between film and poetry was a symposium held by pioneering film society Cinema 16 and organised by Maya Deren in 1953. The symposium introduced the question of the difference between making films in a poetic way (image driven) or with verbal poetry included (text driven). Deren saw poetry as a structural tool for reforming the visual language of cinema:

> The distinction of poetry is its construction and the poetic construct arises from the fact that it is a 'vertical' investigation of a situation, in

that it probes the ramifications of the moment, and is concerned with its qualities and its depth, so that you have poetry concerned in a sense not with what is occurring, but with what it feels like or what it means . . .[39] [just] as the verbal logics of a poem are composed of the relationships established through syntax, assonance, rhyme, and other such verbal methods, so in film there are processes of filmic relationships which derive from the instrument and the elements of its manipulations.[40]

Deren's writing opens up an interesting epistemological problem: although she generally belongs to the medium-specificity/formalist tradition, as she is interested in the language that is unique to the cinematic medium, she nevertheless calls for a cinema which names itself out of a hybrid (a film poem).

Twenty-five years later, *Idées Fixes / Dies Irae* takes this paradox even further. Angelidi's poetics are certainly interested in the medium itself and she does not shy away from calling her work 'poetry cinema', but she also incorporates actual words in her cinematic vocabulary. As she says: 'every element in a film narrates; light and shadows and colours and sounds and body movements, on equal terms with words'.[41] The reason Angelidi here places visual elements on one side and words on the other is to clarify that her films do not prioritise text and that she is devoted to the tiniest visual detail. But what she ultimately proposes is a cinema whose poetics of heterogeneity bridge formal visual and literary tendencies. Contrary to Brakhage's purist attitude, Angelidi firmly believes that words and images can co-exist, without this jeopardising the visual complexity of the work, especially since she uses text which is a) poetic in terms of language, i.e., poetry in itself, and b) complex in its presentation form (typography, spoken word, and so on). Interestingly, even Deren herself was to an extent open to the use of words, suggesting that they

> would be redundant in film if they were used as a further projection from the image. However, if they were brought in on a different level, not issuing from the image which should be complete in itself, but as another dimension relating to it, then it is the two things together that make a poem.[42]

This different level/other dimension is exactly what goes on in Angelidi's film.

Texts are used widely and wildly in *Idées Fixes / Dies Irae*. They are spoken on and off camera, by multiple voices, in different languages and even accents. They are heard in songs and announcements. They are found on street signs, adverts, even the close-up of a razor blade.[43] They are superimposed graphically on top of the cinematic image. They are beautifully projected on performers' bodies. Angelidi's methodologies carefully obscure the border between the visual and the textual. One could argue that even the inclusion of an instrumental version of 'L'Internationale' (discussed in more detail later) is an implied use of text, as it is a tune that comes hand in hand with its politically loaded lyrics. I would argue that Angelidi is interested in the process of internal speech that accompanies the viewing of a film. Soviet film theorist Boris Eikhenbaum claimed in 1927 that 'those who defend cinema from the imitation of literature often forget that [. . .] the thought, i.e., internal speech, is nevertheless present'.[44] Being fully aware of the issue of internal speech, Angelidi plays with it as much as possible, creating a complex system of words and images that continuously subvert meaning, dazzle and disorient the viewer. In a sense, *Idées Fixes / Dies Irae* is one of the precursors of the so-called 'poetry-film' genre, a type of film that was to come to prominence after the 1980s and which largely deals with the hybrid/fusion of the visual and the textual. According to William C. Wees who coined the term,

> while film poems have long been recognized as central to the avant-garde film tradition, poetry-films have received little special attention [. . .] because poetry-films are a kind of hybrid art form and, therefore, seem less 'pure', less essentially cinematic, in the high modernist sense.[45]

An avant-garde tradition that influenced Angelidi while she was staying in Paris in the 1970s[46] and which has strong connections to literature was that of the lettrists. The lettrists only briefly worked with cinema, but as they already came from a visual poetry background, their films were very much of the hybrid type described above. Among others, Isidore Isou's *Traité de Bave et d'Eternité* (1951) and Maurice Lemaître's *Le Film Est Déjà Commencé?* (1951) presented a cinema of disjuncture, where the textual and the visual were juxtaposed. Andrew V. Uroskie suggests that Isou's first film is 'an audiovisual constellation composed out of multiple and divergent modalities of experience', 'generating a multiplicity of disruption within the heart of the work itself'.[47] The lettrists even scratched words on film, a technique that would later influence the American avant-garde makers,[48] and even gave instructions for happenings in the auditorium at the time a film was due to be projected, therefore opening the way for what would later be called 'expanded cinema'.[49] Using spoken text, written text, found footage, animated elements, unlinking/re-linking images and sounds, the lettrists created a cinema that questions its own structures of representation. Isou used the term 'cinéma discrepant' to describe his films, films in which the visual and textual are in continuous disjunction/dialogue. I would suggest that the term can also be applied to the political/poetic methodologies of *Idées Fixes / Dies Irae*.

PUNCTUS CONTRA PUNCTUM: THE POLITICAL AND THE POETIC

A non-negligible part of the history of experimental film involves filmmakers that focus on generally apolitical content, at least apolitical in the sense of not straightforwardly expressing politics. Especially in the area of poetic film, there has frequently been a tendency towards attempting to achieve transcendental experiences that search for an existential essence of human beauty, removed from specific social issues. Brakhage's attempt to imagine an eye untutored by language points towards this tendency. In his article 'Poetry and Film', he narrates an anecdote that he once presented Eisenstein's *Ivan the Terrible* (1944) to an audience out of focus and '80–90% agreed what was a sad passage or an exciting one',[50] thus suggesting in a way that cinematic poetry is about transcending cultural specificity. The very fact that Brakhage is referring to statistics shows that he is interested in some notion of universal experience. The idea of the poetic or the lyrical has often been used in art film writing as synonymous with something that denotes timelessness.[51] In a historical review about women's experimental film, Robin Blaetz has suggested that 'the broad stroke with which the adjective lyrical is applied to women's film becomes symptomatic of either a refusal actually to examine the work or discomfort with the films themselves'.[52] What is therefore suggested here is that the term 'lyrical' can be used to mean that which is not easily analysable or should not be analysed, presumably because it operates in an abstract experiential way. William C. Wees suggests that one of the main oppositions of 1980s experimental filmmakers to the 'traditional' avant-garde is the notion that films should be 'endowed with "universal" and "timeless" (that is, apolitical and ahistorical) significance'.[53]

On the other hand, overtly political filmmakers have not generally been prone to embracing complex poetics when it comes to constructing their films. In an attempt to promote specific ideologies, filmmakers often consider that abstraction gets in the way of expressing a clear message (which it probably does). In an analysis of the relationship between the international left and art cinema, Amos Vogel of Cinema 16 claims that 'many radical filmmakers cast their works in a conventional, often dated, mould, unaware of the far more profound impact of artists attempting to fuse new content with new form'.[54] Yet, the most critical of the political filmmakers believe that radical content cannot be advanced using what is seen as a sort of bourgeois form, even if the definition of which type of form is more bourgeois than others is tricky. Perhaps the question goes back to the type of political content that a filmmaker wants to communicate in the first place. As Rea Walldén claims, Angelidi 'speaks of the close relation between dogmatic writing and dogmatic politics, and comments on the inconsistency of people of apparently progressive politics who are conservative in issues of art form'.[55] *Idées Fixes / Dies Irae* is a film with a complicated political discourse and accordingly a film that develops in an equally complicated film form.

The earliest discussions on the relationship between film form and revolutionary politics go back to the Soviet filmmakers of the 1920s. Sergei Eisenstein, being arguably the most influential of them, developed a large body of texts and films showcasing his cinematic take on Marxist dialectics, mostly through methodologies of editing/montage. Eisenstein's writings, more so than his films, have been influential for Angelidi and, as Walldén suggests, his 'films and writings had been more diffused in the Greek intelligenzia than those of other representatives of the historical avant-gardes, precisely because of his films' overt and easily interpretable political stance'.[56] In practice, I would argue that the editing system of Eisenstein is nowhere near as open-ended – and in fact dialectical – as Angelidi's montage and that her methodology is actually closer to the poetics of parallelism of Dziga Vertov (one of Eisenstein's rivals), whose material was often dismissed by Eisenstein as aimless play.[57] Eisenstein wanted his audience to experience specific pre-determined emotions when viewing his work, or, in David Finch's words, he wanted 'the viewer's experience [to] correspond to the author's intention',[58] seeing the script as a 'prescription that summarises the general projected emotional effect on the audience'. By contrast, Angelidi firmly believes in a more complex interrelation of shots and a certain 'death of the author' when it comes to making sense of her work. Vertov's description of the way in which his film *Three Songs for Lenin* (1934) works is not far from Angelidi's descriptions of some of her own films:

> the contents of *Three Songs* develop in spiral-fashion, now in the sound, now in the image, now in a voice, now in an intertitle, now through facial expression alone [. . .], now through movement within the shot, now in the collision of one group shot with another, now smoothly, now by jolts from dark to light, from slow to fast, from the tired to the vigorous.[59]

Neither Vertov's form nor his politics were favoured by the communist party of the time,[60] as he believed in a complex fusion of politics and poetics. As Anna Lawton suggests, Vertov 'wove in each of his films a subtle net of semantic relationships'.[61] I will return to this notion of weaving later in the chapter.

Just as Vertov's dedication to the political cause is for an emancipated audience, inspired by his friend Vladimir Mayakovski's work, so Angelidi maintains that part of her Marxist vocabulary is to apply a feminist critique of the left of her time. In *Idées Fixes / Dies Irae*, the viewer is constantly bombarded with juxtapositions – of image and sound, of words spoken and words seen, of one frame within the other, of movement and stillness, of constructed and found objects, etc. Angelidi is interested in creating multiple layers of meaning that do not always live in harmony, either politically or aesthetically/formally. A concept that she uses to describe her methods and which summarises beautifully her synthesis of politics and poetics is that of counterpoint. A term that originally comes from music to explain the parallel co-existence of harmonies in a composition, counterpoint is also *counter*-point. It is about points that co-exist with and against each other; it is about meaning moving in various directions with points commenting and subverting each other.[62] A brilliant example of her counterpoint method is the HORIZON scene mentioned earlier. Angelidi herself re-enacts Marat in his bath, a dead revolutionary, but with the words HORIZON written on top. One revolution dies, another (a female one?) starts. The grand anthem 'L'Internationale' is heard, but played as the smallest possible rendition: via a children's music box. A historical re-enactment, the meta-existence of the filmmaker, gender subversion, the bold white superimposed text, the sound of a dripping tap, a communist anthem, a music box: disparate yet also co-existing and interacting elements that compose a dense political and poetic amalgam of meaning.

In *Idées Fixes / Dies Irae*, ideas are never fixed, not even centred around the filmmaker's subjectivity. Filmmaker and spectator are asked to make sense of the film together; despite the film's fragmented quality, there is a continuous sense of calling the viewer to communicate. This is not a work of 'I', of a self-obsessed film poet; it is the work of 'we', of a utopian community of avant-garde film lovers and revolutionaries. Malcolm Le Grice discusses the I/We difference, suggesting that one of the reasons structural filmmakers reacted to the expressionist film poets' subjective project was ethical/political: 'the "we" implies an attempted co-location of film-maker and spectator within the constraints of the discourse',[63] a way to raise the audience's consciousness and counter their passivity. *Idées Fixes / Dies Irae* works very much in this way of consciousness raising, composing a playground of political and poetic elements for the audience to interact with. Angelidi herself stresses the importance of 'we' for her work by mentioning that she forms important and intense collaborations. She also sees her university film teaching as part of her Marxist scholarship; teaching as a two-way learning process.[64]

EXIT

Closing this chapter, I would like to briefly consider *Idées Fixes / Dies Irae* as the work of a female (and feminist) auteur in the context of the male-centred writing of the history of experimental film. It is not an easily classifiable film according to the particular tendencies of the avant-garde; it seems to play with way too many codes and methodologies and to question them too much in order to take the place it deserves in the pantheon of avant-garde film history. Angelidi's work is by far not the only example of women's work to not quite fit due to its hybridity. In the introduction to the essential collection *Women's Experimental Cinema*, Robin Blaetz suggests that women's work 'often cannot be inserted in a coherent way into any pre-existing history of avant-garde film'.[65] Furthermore, she suggests that women's experimental film is often interested in a layering of images and disjunctions between image and sound. Blaetz uses the metaphor of the *weaving* of meaning, the painstaking process of working with physical material, traditionally related to a gendered division of hand crafts and labour. How are women's films meant to belong to the history that they set out to criticise? In that respect, it is not surprising that women's experimental films are frequently filled with 'surreal disassociations between patriarchal culture and women's lives within it'.[66] This is absolutely the case for Angelidi's film as well, which closes with the words 'usine/cuisine'. From the factory to the kitchen; from production to reproduction.

Lis Rhodes's essay 'Whose History?' deals with the problems of history when it comes to the position of women filmmakers. The essay was written in the context of the exhibition *Film as Film* at the Hayward Gallery in 1979, one of the first and most inclusive attempts to present the history of avant-garde film, accompanied by a detailed catalogue. Commenting on the fact that she was (at least initially) the only woman in the exhibition's curatorial team (of eight), Rhodes claims that 'film history defined by men necessarily positions women outside its concerns. Women appear, but on whose terms? With whose definitions?'[67] How do women fit in a history written without them? And should they? Instead of appearing as the expression of a minority in a wider scheme, Rhodes suggests that a women's *her*story of experimental cinema should be written, in which 'seeing "difference" is more important than accepting "sameness"; realising our own histories and understanding their many, possibly divergent, forms'.[68] In that sense, women's experimental film challenges and positions itself outside the mono-dimensional narration of the avant-garde and proposes a re-writing of the history of women's experimental films, using its own language and its own decisions of representation, of what is important and historically worth mentioning.

Throughout the twentieth century, a number of female experimental filmmakers have expressed their unease or at least scepticism towards the historical avant-garde and its historical categorisations. In a 1979 Festival of Avant-Garde Film in London, Margaret Tait declared that 'there's something too limiting about the idea of avant-garde – as if at all costs you must be making innovations'.[69] Writing about the work of Su Friedrich, Scott MacDonald sees a similar tendency:

> By the 1980s, Friedrich was becoming convinced that the rejection of personal filmmaking, structural filmmaking, or other approaches did not 'liberate' cinema in any practical sense; it simply narrowed the options. The issue was not to avoid the personal or the systemic, but to reappropriate and reenergize as many useful dimensions of the previous film-critical practices as possible.[70]

Friedrich combines, as much as rejects, traditions of avant-garde cinema and, as Janet Cutler claims, her films resist simple explication and are instead 'finely woven tapestries of disparate materials'.[71] Angelidi herself similarly inherits and criticises (from a feminist perspective) avant-garde film traditions in *Idées Fixes / Dies Irae*; in the second half of the film, a number of shots refer to Dadaist, Lettrist or Surrealist work.[72] An interesting term applied by Paul Arthur to the work of Joyce Weiland and which I would argue is also appropriate for Angelidi is 'polycentric'. Weiland belongs to an extent to the history of structural filmmakers, however, as Arthur states, she 'challenged or bridged boundary distinctions among independent film factions of her time'.[73] Disinterested in limiting her options, Wieland, just like Friedrich, Tait and Angelidi, created complex form and content constellations.

Idées Fixes / Dies Irae uses structural film techniques, but without limiting its content to the self-referential; it uses spoken and written texts, while at the same time works with the visual qualities unique to the cinema. It is an intensely political film, presenting a dialectical political discourse in an equally complex poetic cinematic vocabulary. *Idées Fixes / Dies Irae* is a hybrid work of disjunction and internal subversion that startles the audience with its multilayered methodologies and its ability to re-invent itself. It is the work of an emancipated filmmaker, calling for an active, emancipated audience. It is at once in dialogue with the international innovations of the avant-garde and in direct criticism of the avant-garde's 'traditions' and categories. 'Not to comply with a convention is, in a way, by itself an emancipatory move',[74] as Walldén suggests. *Idées Fixes / Dies Irae* does not comply or rest. It is revolutionary in the deepest sense of the word; for, how else must a true revolution be envisaged than through a restructuring of its own language and tropes? A true revolution ought to be self-critical and aware of its own existence; it ought to be polycentric, contemplative. But most of all, and just like Antoinetta Angelidi's *Idées Fixes / Dies Irae*, it ought to be the stuff of dreams: wild, brave, luminous.

Author's acknowledgement
I would like to thank Foivos Dousos and Rea Walldén for their valuable comments.

NOTES

1. Elena Hamalidi, Maria Nikolopoulou and Rea Walldén, 'Real Beyond Realism: The Multiple Faces of Collage in Greek Avant-Garde Art in the 60s and 70s', *OEI 53–54: Dokument, Dispositiv, Deskription, Diskurs* (2011): 968. *Synchronos Kinimatografos* was the most important film/cinephile magazine in Greece, published between 1969 and 1984. It facilitated a dialogue between the Greek audience and international discourses on film, following an auteur cinema position, presenting showcases of minor national cinemas of the world and even hosting thinkers such as Roland Barthes and Jacques Lacan.

2. Elena Hamalidi, Maria Nikolopoulou and Rea Walldén, 'Mapping the Greek Avant-Garde: The Function of Transfers between Aesthetic and Political Dualisms', in *Transferts, appropriations et fonctions de l'avant-garde dans l'Europe intermédiaire et du Nord*, ed. Harri Veivo (Paris: L'Harmattan, 2012), 22.
3. Rea Walldén, 'Greek Avant-Garde Cinema and Marx: The Politics of Form in Sfikas's Modelo and Angelidi's Idées Fixes / Dies Irae', *FilmIcon: Journal of Greek Film Studies* 2 (September 2014): 75.
4. Ibid., 72.
5. Elena Hamalidi, Maria Nikolopoulou and Rea Walldén, 'A Second Avant-Garde Without a First: Greek Avant-Garde Artists in the 1960s and 1970s', in *Regarding the Popular – Modernism, the Avant-Garde and High and Low Culture*, ed. Sascha Bru, Laurence van Nuijs, Benedikt Hjartarson, Peter Nicholls, Tania Ørum and Hubert van den Berg (Berlin: De Gruyter, 2012), 440.
6. For the purposes of this chapter, the terms 'film' and 'cinema', as well as 'avant-garde', 'experimental' and 'artist film' will be used interchangeably.
7. James Peterson, *Dreams of Chaos, Visions of Order* (Detroit: Wayne State University Press, 1957), 29.
8. Hans Richter cited in Jonas Mekas, 'Hans Richter on the Nature of Film Poetry', *Film Culture* 15 (December 1957): 6.
9. Peter Wollen, 'The Two Avant-Gardes', in *Art and the Moving Image: A Critical Reader*, ed. Tanya Leighton (London: Tate Publishing, 2008), 180.
10. William C. Wees 'Peggy's Playhouse – Contesting the Modernist Paradigm', in *Women's Experimental Cinema: Critical Frameworks*, ed. Robin Blaetz (Durham, NC and London: Duke University Press, 2007), 291. Amos Vogel, *Film as a Subversive Art* (London: Weidenfeld and Nicolson, 1974), 291.
11. Rea Walldén, 'Conversing with Dreams: An Encounter with Antoinetta Angelidi', *FilmIcon: Journal of Greek Film Studies* (December 2017): 189.
12. Hamalidi et al., 'Real Beyond Realism', 969.
13. David Curtis, *Experimental Cinema – A Fifty-year Evolution* (New York: Delta, 1971), 170.
14. Adams P. Sitney, *Visionary Film* (New York: Oxford University Press, 1979), 142.
15. Stan Brakhage, 'On Music, Sound, Color and Film', *Film Culture* 67–68–69 (1979): 130.
16. Structural film had nothing to do with structuralism, as Sitney himself has subsequently stated in a discussion with Malcolm Le Grice.
17. Adams P. Sitney 'The Structural Film', *Film Culture* 47 (Summer 1969), reprinted in Adams P. Sitney, *Film Culture Reader* (New York: Praeger Publishers, 1970), 327.
18. Birgit Hein, 'The Structural Film', in *Film as Film: Formal Experiment in Film*, ed. David Curtis and Richard Francis (London: Arts Council of Britain, 1979), 93.
19. Walldén, 'Conversing with Dreams', 194.
20. The importance of dreams in Angelidi's work is analysed in detailed in Walldén, 'Conversing with Dreams'.
21. Angelidi was aware of structural cinema as mentioned in Hamalidi et al., 'Mapping the Greek Avant-Garde', 23.
22. Malcolm Le Grice, *Experimental Cinema and Beyond* (London: BFI, 2001), 17.
23. Hamalidi et al., 'Mapping the Greek Avant-Garde', 16.
24. Walldén, 'Greek Avant-Garde Cinema and Marx', 77.
25. Nicky Hamlyn uses Godard's long tracking shot as an example of an uninteresting endurance shot in which 'the relationship between camera and subject is not problematised in any way', in Nicky Hamlyn, *Film Art Phenomena* (London: BFI, 2003), 128.
26. Adams P. Sitney 'The Structural Film', *Film Culture*, 47 (Summer 1969), reprinted in Adams P. Sitney, *Film Culture Reader* (New York: Praeger Publishers, 1970), 328.

27. Hamlyn, *Film Art Phenomena*, 121.
28. Jean Thibaudeau, 'Presentation of 'IDEESDIES/FIXESIRAE un film de Antoinetta Angelidi', *Cahiers Critiques de la Littérature* (nouvelle série, 1/2, 1979): 35.
29. Angelidi spoke about the correlation between medium self-reflexivity and an active audience at a talk named 'Trapped and emancipated gaze in the cinema' she gave at the Aristotle University of Thessaloniki in 1998. There is no catalogue for the event or transcript of the presentation. Source: Rea Walldén's personal collection/notes.
30. Hamalidi et al., 'A Second Avant-Garde Without a First', 441.
31. Fred Camper 'Remedial Reading Comprehension' in *Structural Film Anthology*, ed. Peter Gidal (London: BFI, 1976), 124–5.
32. Ibid., 123.
33. William C. Wees, *Light Moving in Time – Studies in the Visual Aesthetics of Avant-Garde Film* (Berkeley, Los Angeles, Oxford: University of California Press, 1992), 154.
34. Dulac, Germaine, 'From Visual and Anti-visual Films', in *The Avant-Garde Film: A Reader of Theory and Criticism*, ed. Adams P. Sitney (New York: Anthology Film Archives, 1987), 31.
35. Ibid., 31.
36. Stan Brakhage, 'Metaphors on Vision', *Film Culture* 30 (Fall 1963), no pagination.
37. Clement Greenberg, 'Towards a Newer Laocoon', in *Clement Greenbeg: The Collected Essays & Criticism Vol 1*, ed. John O'Brian (Chicago: The University of Chicago Press, 1986), 25.
38. Dziga Vertov, *The Man with a Movie Camera* film (introductory manifesto) (USSR, 1929).
39. Maya Deren cited in Willard Maas, 'Poetry & the Film: A Symposium', *Film Culture* 29 (Summer 1963): 56.
40. Maya Deren, 'An Anagram of Ideas on Art, Form and Film' in *Maya Deren & The Avant Garde*, ed. Bill Nichols (London: University of California Press, 2001), appendix, 30.
41. Walldén, 'Conversing with Dreams', 189.
42. Maya Deren cited in Maas, 'Poetry & the Film', 59.
43. The female filmmaker's razor mouth seems to be responding to Bunuel and Dali's razor that cuts a woman's eye in *Un Chien Andalou*.
44. Adams P. Sitney, *Modenist Montage* (New York: Columbia University Press, 1990), 41.
45. William C. Wees, 'Poetry-Films and Film Poems', Lux website, <http://www.lux.org.uk>, accessed 5 March 2005, also quoted in Fil Ieropoulos, *The Film Poem* (PhD), University of Kent, April 2010, 29.
46. Hamalidi et al., 'Mapping the Greek Avant-Garde', 23.
47. Andrew V. Uroskie, 'Beyond the Black Box: The lettrist cinema of disjunction', *OCTOBER Magazine* 135 (Winter 2011): 26.
48. In the 1960s, Stan Brakhage wrote a series of letters to Isidore Isou and Maurice Lemaître, in which he discusses how much these films had influenced himself and those around him, despite the lack of lettrist filmmakers' exposure in the United States. The letters can be found in the appendix of Kaira M. Cabanas, *Off-Screen Cinema – Isidore Isou and the Lettrist Avant-Garde* (Chicago and London: The University of Chicago Press, 2014), 135–9.
49. Expanded Cinema was a term coined in 1970 by film writer Gene Youngblood to describe – among other things – the multimedia/intermedia experiments of 1960s underground filmmakers that pioneered areas that would now be considered part of the notion of installation, where the cinematic experience breaks away from the single-viewing screen and expands in space, encouraging a physically active spectator.
50. Stan Brakhage, *Essential Brakhage – Selected Writings on Filmmaking* (New York: McPherson & Co., 2001), 175.
51. Such is often the case with writings on the videos of Bill Viola or the films of Andrei Tarkovski.
52. Robin Blaetz, 'Introduction', in *Women's Experimental Cinema: Critical Frameworks*, ed. Robin Blaetz (Durham, NC and London: Duke University Press, 2007), 8.

53. Wees 'Peggy's Playhouse', 291.
54. Amos Vogel, *Film as a Subversive Art* (London: Weidenfeld and Nicolson, 1974), 120.
55. Angelidi quoted in Walldén, 'Greek Avant-Garde Cinema and Marx', 86.
56. Ibid., 77.
57. Sergei Eisenstein, *The Film Sense*, trans. Jay Jeyda (London: Faber & Faber, 1986; original Russian edition, 1949), 14.
58. David Finch, 'A Third Something: Montage, Film & Poetry', in *The Undercut Reader*, ed. Nina Danino and Michael Maziere (London: Wallflower Press, 2003), 63.
59. Dziga Vertov, 'Without Words', in *Kino-Eye: The Writings of Dziga Vertov*, ed. Annette Michelson (London: University of California Press, 1984), 118.
60. Dziga Vertov quoted in John MacKay, 'Allegory and Accommodation: Vertov's *Three Songs of Lenin* (1934) as a Stalinist Film', in *Russian Avant-Garde and Radical Modernism: An Introductory Reader*, ed. Dennis Ioffe and Frederick White (Boston MA: Academic Studies Press, 2012), 420.
61. Anna Lawton, 'Rhythmic Montage in the Films of Dziga Vertov: A Poetic Use of the Language of Cinema', *Pacific Coast Philology* 13 (October 1978): 49.
62. Walldén, 'Conversing with Dreams', 189.
63. Le Grice, *Experimental Cinema and Beyond*, 194.
64. Walldén, 'Conversing with Dreams', 193.
65. Robin Blaetz, 'Introduction', 7.
66. Ibid., 15.
67. Liz Rhodes 'Whose History?' in *Film as Film: Formal Experiment in Film*, ed. David Curtis and Richard Francis (London: Arts Council of Britain, 1979), 119.
68. Ibid., 120.
69. Margaret Tait quoted in Peter Todd and Benjamin Cook, *Subjects and Sequences – A Margaret Tait Reader* (London: Lux, 2004), 95.
70. Scott MacDonald, *Avant Garde Film – Motion Studies*, (Cambridge University Press, 1993), 103.
71. Janet Cutler, 'Su Friedrich – Breaking the Rules', in *Women's Experimental Cinema: Critical Frameworks*, ed. Robin Blaetz (Durham, NC and London: Duke University Press, 2007), 312.
72. Hamalidi et al., 'Real Beyond Realism', 969.
73. Paul Arthur, 'Different / Same / Both / Neither – The Polycentric Cinema of Joyce Weiland', in *Women's Experimental Cinema: Critical Frameworks*, ed. Robin Blaetz (Durham, NC and London: Duke University Press, 2007), 47.
74. Walldén, 'Greek Avant-Garde Cinema and Marx', 86.

BIBLIOGRAPHY

Arthur, Paul. 'Different / Same / Both / Neither – The Polycentric Cinema of Joyce Weiland', in *Women's Experimental Cinema: Critical Frameworks*, ed. Robin Blaetz. Durham, NC and London: Duke University Press, 2007.
Blaetz, Robin. 'Introduction', in *Women's Experimental Cinema: Critical Frameworks*, ed. Robin Blaetz. Durham, NC and London: Duke University Press, 2007.
Brakhage, Stan. 'Metaphors on Vision'. *Film Culture* 30 (Fall 1963).
Brakhage, Stan. 'On Music, Sound, Color and Film'. *Film Culture* 67–68–69 (1979).
Brakhage, Stan. *Essential Brakhage – Selected Writings on Filmmaking*. New York: McPherson & Co., 2001.

Cabanas, Kaira M. *Off-Screen Cinema – Isidore Isou and the Lettrist Avant-Garde*. Chicago and London: The University of Chicago, 2014.
Camper, Fred. 'Remedial Reading Comprehension', in *Structural Film Anthology*, ed. Peter Gidal. London: BFI, 1976.
Curtis, David. *Experimental Cinema – A Fifty-year Evolution*. New York: Delta, 1971.
Cutler, Janet. 'Su Friedrich – Breaking the Rules', in *Women's Experimental Cinema: Critical Frameworks*, ed. Robin Blaetz. Durham, NC and London: Duke University Press, 2007.
Deren, Maya. 'An Anagram of Ideas on Art, Form and Film', in *Maya Deren & The Avant Garde*, ed. Bill Nichols. London: University of California Press, 2001.
Dulac, Germaine. 'From Visual and Anti-Visual Films', in *The Avant-Garde Film: A Reader of Theory and Criticism*, ed. Adams P. Sitney. New York: Anthology Film Archives, 1987.
Finch, David. 'A Third Something: Montage, Film & Poetry', in *The Undercut Reader*, ed. Nina Danino and Michael Maziere. London: Wallflower Press, 2003.
Greenberg, Clement. 'Towards a Newer Laocoon', in *Clement Greenberg: The Collected Essays & Criticism Vol 1*, ed. John O'Brian. Chicago: The University of Chicago Press, 1986.
Hamalidi, Elena, Maria Nikolopoulou and Rea Walldén. 'Real Beyond Realism: The Multiple Faces of Collage in Greek Avant-Garde Art in the 60s and 70s'. *OEI 53–54: Dokument, Dispositiv, Deskription, Diskurs* (2011).
Hamalidi, Elena, Maria Nikolopoulou and Rea Walldén. 'A Second Avant-Garde Without a First: Greek Avant-Garde Artists in the 1960s and 1970s', in *Regarding the Popular – Modernism, the Avant-Garde and High and Low Culture*, ed. Sascha Bru, Laurence van Nuijs, Benedikt Hjartarson, Peter Nicholls, Tania Ørum and Hubert van den Berg. Berlin: De Gruyter, 2012.
Hamalidi, Elena, Maria Nikolopoulou and Rea Walldén. 'Mapping the Greek Avant-Garde: The Function of Transfers between Aesthetic and Political Dualisms', in *Transferts, appropriations et fonctions de l'avant-garde dans l'Europe intermédiaire et du Nord*, ed. Harri Veivo. Paris: L'Harmattan, 2012.
Hamlyn, Nicky. *Film Art Phenomena*. London: BFI, 2003.
Hein, Birgit. 'The Structural Film', in *Film as Film: Formal Experiment in Film*, ed. David Curtis and Richard Francis. London: Arts Council of Britain, 1979.
Ieropoulos, Fil. *The Film Poem* (PhD), University of Kent, April 2010.
Lawton, Anna. 'Rhythmic Montage in the Films of Dziga Vertov: A Poetic Use of the Language of Cinema'. *Pacific Coast Philology* 13 (October 1978).
Le Grice, Malcolm. *Experimental Cinema and Beyond*. London: BFI, 2001.
Maas, Willard. 'Poetry & the Film: A Symposium'. *Film Culture* 29 (Summer 1963).
MacDonald, Scott. *Avant Garde Film – Motion Studies*. Cambridge: Cambridge University Press, 1993.
MacKay, John. 'Allegory and Accommodation: Vertov's *Three Songs of Lenin* (1934) as a Stalinist Film', in *Russian Avant-Garde and Radical Modernism: An Introductory Reader*, ed. Dennis Ioffe and Frederick White. Boston MA: Academic Studies Press, 2012.
Mekas, Jonas. 'Hans Richter on the Nature of Film Poetry'. *Film Culture* 15 (December 1957).
Peterson, James. *Dreams of Chaos, Visions of Order*. Detroit: Wayne State University Press, 1957.
Rhodes, Liz. 'Whose History?', in *Film as Film: Formal Experiment in Film*, ed. David Curtis and Richard Francis. London: Arts Council of Britain, 1979.
Sergei Eisenstein. *The Film Sense*, trans. Jay Jeyda. London: Faber & Faber, 1986; original Russian edition, 1949.
Sitney, Adams P. 'The Structural Film', *Film Culture* 47 (Summer 1969), reprinted in Adams P. Sitney, *Film Culture Reader*. New York: Praeger Publishers, 1970.
Sitney, Adams P. *Visionary Film*. New York: Oxford University Press, 1979.

Sitney, Adams P. *Modenist Montage*. New York: Columbia University Press, 1990.
Thibaudeau, Jean. 'Presentation of IDEESDIES/FIXESIRAE un film de Antoinetta Angelidi'. *Cahiers Critiques de la Littérature* (nouvelle série, 1/2, 1979).
Todd, Peter and Benjamin Cook. *Subjects and Sequences – A Margaret Tait Reader*. London: Lux, 2004.
Uroskie, Andrew V. 'Beyond the Black Box: The lettrist cinema of disjunction'. *OCTOBER Magazine* 135 (Winter 2011).
Vertov, Dziga, 'Without Words', in *Kino-Eye: The Writings of Dziga Vertov*, ed. Annette Michelson. London: University of California Press, 1984.
Vogel, Amos. *Film as a Subversive Art*. London: Weidenfeld and Nicolson, 1974.
Walldén, Rea. 'Conversing with Dreams: An Encounter with Antoinetta Angelidi'. *FilmIcon: Journal of Greek Film Studies* 4 (December 2017).
Walldén, Rea, 'Greek Avant-Garde Cinema and Marx: The Politics of Form in Sfikas's Modelo and Angelidi's Idées Fixes / Dies Irae'. *FilmIcon: Journal of Greek Film Studies* 2 (September 2014).
Wees, William C. 'Peggy's Playhouse – Contesting the Modernist Paradigm', in *Women's Experimental Cinema: Critical Frameworks*, ed. Robin Blaetz. Durham, NC and London: Duke University Press, 2007.
Wees, William C. *Light Moving in Time – Studies in the Visual Aesthetics of Avant-Garde Film*. Berkeley, CA and Oxford: University of California Press, 1992.
Wees, William C. 'Poetry-Films and Film Poems', Lux website, <http://www.lux.org.uk>, accessed 5 March 2005.
Wollen, Peter. 'The Two Avant-Gardes', in *Art and the Moving Image: A Critical Reader*, ed. Tanya Leighton. London: Tate Publishing, 2008.

PART 2

Concepts and Interpretations

CHAPTER 3

Thief or Reality: Visual Dialectics on Death Instincts

Penny Bouska

'Since the death instinct exists in the heart of everything that lives, since we suffer from trying to repress it, since everything that lives longs for rest, let us unfasten the ties that bind us to life, let us cultivate our death wish, let us develop it, water it like a plant, let it grow unhindered. Suffering and fear are born from the repression of the death wish.'

Eugène Ionesco, 1967

All the salient features of Antoinetta Angelidi's film *Thief or Reality* (2001) converge on a contemplation of death. The references are abundantly clear in the film: death as a ritual in reference to the afterlife and religion; death as loss of a loving person; death as free will in suicide. However, the controversial concept of the *death instinct*,[1] inaugurated by Sigmund Freud in 'Beyond the Pleasure Principle' *(*1920), indicates a new perspective in the aesthetic analysis of Angelidi's film: death as life, the dynamic of destruction.

From a Freudian point of view, death is more than just a biological outcome antagonistic to life. It is identified as a destructive instinct that 'works subtly as a force inside us',[2] so as to reach an earlier inorganic state of minimum excitation. From this perspective, the death instinct represents a conservative force that opposes change. Furthermore, Freud was compelled to say that as 'inanimate things existed before living ones', then it seems that 'the aim of life is death'.[3] Life 'is regarded as only a circuitous route to death',[4] a type of evolutionary detour. Teresa de Lauretis regards the conception as a paradox. 'In the "circuitous path to death", the human drives to self-preservation, self-assertion and mastery, which appear to us as the guardians of life moving us towards change and progress, actually work in the service of death.'[5] Moreover, Freud goes as far as to declare that 'the pleasure principle seems to serve the death instincts'.[6] It is not easy to unravel the contradictions of this paradox. It amounts to saying that 'only by the concurrent or mutually opposing action of the two primal instincts – Eros and the death instinct – never by one or the other alone, can we explain the rich multiplicity of the phenomena of life'.[7]

Angelidi reflects the ambiguity in images. Freud asserts that 'thinking in pictures [. . .] stands nearer to unconscious processes than does thinking in words'.[8] And Angelidi's visuals strictly adhere to this process, expressing a 'pure culture of death instinct'.[9] Evidence lies in two reasons. The first reason is that the philosophical consideration of death is set aside in favour of a metapsychological interpretation,[10] and the second reason is that the film is construed as visualising the death instinct's most distinctive feature, the phenomenon of *compulsion to repetition*.

Freud places the concept of the death instinct into the new theoretical field he calls 'metapsychology', also introduced in 'Beyond the Pleasure Principle' (1920). It is considered to be Freud's epistemological answer to metaphysics.[11] Metapsychology considers economic, dynamic and topographic factors in the study of psychical processes. The economic view accounts for the evaluation of the stimulation quantities accumulated in the psychical system, the dynamic encompasses their energetic motion, and the topographic is concerned with their place in the psychical mapping. In the film, similar categorisations correspond to the protagonists' affects and behaviours. Angelidi attributes to her characters functions that exclude the pleasure principle, thus resonating strongly with the Freudian supposition of a self-destructive psychical force. This was, among others, a dispute resolution for psychoanalysis on the problem of human aggression, acknowledged not just as a motor discharge to the external world, that is, as violent behaviour, but as 'the primary derivative of death drive',[12] that has an auto-destructive connotation. Multiple cinematic elements in the film support the 'revolutionary thesis that all aggression and destructiveness in human beings is, according to its original nature, self-destructiveness'.[13]

Stepping thereby onto metapsychological grounds, Angelidi reflects on the compulsion to repetition. Alongside traumatic dreams, the film illustrates several compulsive instances, such as the masochistic actions of the Sculptress, the elder sister, which are linked to affects of guilt and punishment; the repetitive mistreatment of the ego in melancholy of the Scientist, the younger sister, after the loss of her child; and the repressed traumatic memories of the Actor, the brother, expressed 'not toward the outside (as aggressivity), but toward the subject'.[14] Angelidi illustrates all these in a sublime dissolution of being, showing that the death instinct 'is radically not a drive to murder, but a drive to suicide or to kill oneself'.[15]

Engaging herself in 'an act of trust in the language of the unconscious',[16] Angelidi goes beyond the conception of death as the ending of life and beyond the existential perspective of its inevitability, placing an unpleasurable emphasis on 'the concept of death that is registered in our psychical reality'.[17] She chooses to depict reality as a Thief, enacted by a non-libidinal figure. According to Angelidi, 'reality robs you of your dreams and you have to rob it in order to dream'. The Thief intrudes in the house of a family of two sisters and a brother to rob them of their dreams, but the characters' dreams are deprived of pleasure and wish fulfilment, altered by a compulsion to repetition. A contradiction is noted: reality deprives you of pleasure and death reclaims it by leading the organism to the ultimate pleasure, zero tension. The Thief becomes a witness of reality and death at the same time. Both pleasurable and painful. The psychical structure is transformed into a narrative system, where people are being tormented by severe psychical agencies, desires and prohibitions of reality. Angelidi envisions a cartographic recording of the death routes circumventing pleasure, not in order to reach it at a later point, as the reality principle usually does, but, in accordance with the Freudian theory, to expose the pain that nests in it.

RE-VISING DEATH IN FREUD'S SECOND THEORY ON INSTINCTS

To begin with, to coherently analyse the link between Freud's instinctual theory and Angelidi's film, it is imperative that we clarify some of the original ideas of that theory. But this is not an easy task. As Ernest Jones notes, 'the train of thought [is] by no means easy to follow',[18] due to its complexity and vagueness. According to Jean Laplanche, this speculative theory marks Freud's doctrine[19] in such depth that, as Jacques Lacan asserts, 'to evade the death instinct in his doctrine is not to know his doctrine at all'.[20]

In 'Beyond the Pleasure Principle' (1920), Freud posits one of the most challenging psychoanalytic concepts, a self-destructive instinct that aims at death. Unable to observe it clinically, Freud, by speculating its existence, provoked 'organizational tensions within the international community of psychoanalysis'[21] as no other of his works had done. The death instinct corresponds to a non-libidinal part of the ego that is in conflict with all the other libidinal parts. Laplanche stresses that the death instinct is 'the soul of conflict. An elemental force of strife', that stands in the forefront of Freud's theoretical formulations.[22]

Freud's view is pre-eminently dualistic. In his first instinctual theory, the ego's instincts, which strain for self-preservation and the satisfaction of internal needs, such as starvation, pain, etc., are opposed to the sexual instincts, which aim at evolution, growth and reproduction. This initial opposition is replaced when, in 'Instincts and their Vicissitudes' (1915), Freud affirms that 'originally, at the very beginning of mental life, the ego is cathected with instincts and is to some extent capable of satisfying them on itself. We call this condition "narcissism" and this way of obtaining satisfaction "auto-erotic"'.[23] So, the primary narcissism indicates that a part of the ego is also invested with sexual instincts. In early infancy, the cathected investments, later oriented to objects of the external world, turn to the inside, and treat the ego as an object. Inevitably, Freud brought libido to the ego itself. This would correspond to the later concept of *Eros*, or life instincts consisting of both ego and sexual urges. However, at this point, it seemed that all psychical processes stemmed only from libidinal conflicts, a one-sided view that took Freud in search of another instinctual force to juxtapose with that of sexual instincts.

Prior to that, in the early text 'Formulations of the Two Procceses of Mental Functioning' (1911), Freud had pointed out that the psychical apparatus works as a homeostatic system regulated by two principles, the pleasure principle and the reality principle. Above all regulations, the primitive mental function of the psyche 'strives towards gaining pleasure' and 'draws back from any event which might arouse unpleasure'.[24] The pleasure principle, which is tantamount to a constancy principle or Nirvana principle,[25] accounts for the extinction or reduction of accumulated excitations coming from the internal or external world. It regulates the quantities of tensions in order to sustain the equilibrium. 'Pleasure is in some way connected with the diminution, reduction or extinction of the amounts of stimulus prevailing in the mental apparatus, and that similarly unpleasure is connected with their increase.'[26] The reality principle is, in a sense, an appraisal of reality. It formulates the psychical capability to evaluate reality and be able to make a distinction between what is agreeable and what is real, 'even if it happened to be disagreeable'.[27] Obviously, it poses obstacles to the purposes of pleasure. But it is not an opponent insofar as the psychical system tolerates the tensions coming from the real world, only to discharge them at a later time. Freud also notes, however, that an increase in sexual tension cannot provide an explanation for the pursuit of constancy. Furthermore, he observed a number of repetitive instances, like the recurrent dreams of patients with traumatic neurosis,[28] the re-dramatisation of painful experiences in children's plays, the negative therapeutic reaction, sadism and masochism, etc., that also challenged the dominance of the pleasure principle regulations. More specifically, people with anxiety dreams were seen to be reproducing a traumatising experience, forcing themselves to relive the traumatic moment. Freud asserts that in such cases the event happened at an abrupt moment and the overwhelmed system was not ready to react properly at the time. This triggered the repetition in order to deal with the event retrospectively. The fact that unpleasure for the one psychic agency might represent satisfaction for another[29] is not relevant in this case. This experience exceeds the dream's purpose for wish fulfilment.[30] Associated with a compulsion for repetition, the dream re-creates a situation that could not in any way be pleasurable. Behind its purpose hides a force with the opposite effects of destabilisation and dissolution. Freud admits that

> we shall no longer be able to adhere to the belief that mental events are exclusively governed by the desire for pleasure. These phenomena are

unmistakable indications of the presence of a power in mental life [. . .] which we trace back to the original death instinct of living matter.[31]

A second observation of compulsory repetition refers to children's play. Freud was familiar with the theory that children are used to transferring all kinds of anxiety and painful experiences to their playing. Watching his grandson, Freud noticed that in his mother's absence, the infant was repetitively throwing away a string bound to a spool, expressing agitation at its disappearance which successively changed to satisfaction when he pulled it back. The repetition was revealing of an effort to master the displeasing sentiments caused by his mother's absence. The child was provoking in himself the unpleasurable feeling with the disappearance of the spool, yelling '*Fort*' ('gone'), and the subsequent pleasure shouting '*Da*' ('there'), on its appearance. This reaction implied an effort to master the painful experience by re-creating it at a conscious level.

During the analytic process, patients seem to display a similar behaviour, constantly expressing their most negative affections, thereby obstructing therapy. Some neurotic patients react negatively to any praise or appreciation of their progress. Freud called these tendencies *negative therapeutic reactions*, which 'explain[ed] the self-inflicted character of all neurotic suffering'.[32] Freud detects that 'we are dealing with what may be called a "moral" factor, a sense of guilt, which is finding its satisfaction in the illness and refuses to give up the punishment of suffering'.[33] All the above are instances of masochistic indications that Freud could not explain with the previous instinctive theory of libidinal conflicts. He was forced to go beyond the pleasure principle to non-libidinal layers, to expose the opponents of the libidinal forces that he was looking for in the workings of the death instincts.

In all those cases, 'the repetition compulsion represented, in effect, a compulsion of the patient to torment his own ego'.[34] The motives behind this could not be sufficiently explained by the masochistic theory as it was. Thus, such cases were interpreted with the function of the bound and unbound[35] state of circulating energies in the psychical apparatus. Freud and Josef Breuer elaborated upon the theory in the very first study on psychoanalysis, *Studies on Hysteria* (1895). According to their findings, the psychical system is charged with energy in two forms, the freely mobile cathexis that is unbound and seeks a discharge, and the quiescent cathexis that is bound and under control. 'It was in terms of unbound versus bound energies that Freud distinguished between the psychically unmastered instinctual forces of the id and the more organized and differentiated processes characteristic of the ego.'[36] The ego is the agency of consciousness and control, while the super ego and id are unconscious agencies that charge the ego with multiple demands or desires. From the economic point of view, the binding is a process of energy change 'from a freely flowing into a quiescent state',[37] and in the topographical and dynamic sense, from the id to the ego. 'The death drive designates the pressure of unbound energies against the limitations of the bound structure of the ego.'[38] A high accumulation of unbound energy, as Anna Potamianou asserts, '[gives] great freedom to destructive functions and to unbound libido'.[39]

The energy that moves freely in the psychical apparatus corresponds to a primary process and its binding to a secondary. Freud declares that the compulsory phenomena, although they seem to overpass the dominance of the pleasure principle, make an effort to bind the unbound energy of the traumatising events and gain control of the experience at a conscious level. In the conversion from primary to secondary, the process might partly serve the pleasure principle. 'The binding of an instinctual impulse would be a preliminary function designed to prepare the excitation for its final elimination in the pleasure of discharge.'[40] Freud projects the binding as a requirement for the pleasure principle to dominate. According to this, 'the death instincts are involved both when it comes to the binding of instinctual impulses as well as in the ensuing release of tension provided by feelings of pleasure, a description which Freud applied to the sexual act'.[41] At this point, death urges yearn for life instincts and their borderlines intertwine.

Freud grounds his reasoning in biology in an effort to make it more epistemological and less speculative. This thinking, however, exceeds the boundaries of what the present article explores. Roughly speaking, death is viewed as an innate urge that operates on a cellular level, aiming at its dissolution. It was along this line of reasoning that Freud recognised a conservative character in the organic instincts that was 'acquired historically'.

> The phenomena of organic development must be attributed to external disturbing and diverting influences [. . .] if conditions remained the same, it would do no more than constantly repeat the same course of life [. . .] Those instincts are therefore bound to give a deceptive appearance of being forces tending towards change and progress, whilst in fact they are merely seeking to reach an ancient goal by paths alike old and new.[42]

In this light, organic life is the outcome of a deviation from the first and most important goal of life, the return to the previous inorganic state. Freud claims that since inanimate things existed before living ones, then the aim of life is death. Disturbing though this statement may sound, it was meant to undergird the interrelation between death and life.

> Eros aims at complicating life and at the same time, of course, at preserving it. Acting in this way, both the instincts would be conservative in the strictest sense of the word, since both would be endeavouring to re-establish a state of things that was disturbed by the emergence of life. The emergence of life would thus be the cause of the continuance of life and also at the same time of the striving towards death; and life itself would be a conflict and compromise between these two trends.[43]

Within the antithesis 'not between ego-instincts and sexual instincts but between life instincts and death instincts',[44] Freud discerns a convergence of their aims. Both death and life have the same goal of reaching the initial state of minimum excitation. In a broader sense, they both aim at death. By this reasoning, Freud posits in death a biological reality, which is a displacement of natural death to the psychical field.

Angelidi's view supports the controversy: 'I sense death with intimacy and love. I do not believe it is something eerie. For me it is not related to grief and abandonment. But to motion and energy.'[45] It is not the absence of fear but rather the substantial understanding of it that makes Angelidi address death this way. The momentum of the most significant experiences in life, like birth and death, is dissociated from positive or negative signs, or any ethical connotations whatsoever. In 'Instincts and their Vicissitudes' (1915), Freud affirms that we understand instincts by their motor factors. What is common to all of them is their 'exercising pressure', a characteristic of their own essence. And he contributes to 'every instinct a piece of activity; if we speak loosely of passive instincts, we can only mean instinct whose *aim* is passive'.[46] The death instinct, mandatory – as already mentioned – in aggression, masochism and libidinal perversions, diverts only a small amount of its activity to the external world; most of it resides in the psychical structure.

Similarly, in *Thief or Reality*, Angelidi expresses an innerness, illustrated, mostly, in spatial and temporal dimensions. There is no 'outside' in the film. There are no external places, realistic sceneries or views of the horizon. There is no daylight or night light. Everything is prefabricated. Time seems episodic, dissected in short, private, and unlinked moments, like vertical aliquots interrupting horizontal orders. Angelidi is like a visual tacker sewing without a thread.[47] Substitutes for narration, a long succession of 'happenings' express diverse options of psychical experiences. Vrasidas Karalis explains that 'viewers feel and understand that something is *happening* – the *happening* itself, the event of visual epiphany, becomes itself the epicentre of her films'.[48] In relation to the death instinct, those events appear in internal conflicts, inner actions pointing to the intertwining of pleasure and discomfort, fear and daring, *philotis* and *neikos*,[49] life and death. More specifically, the elder sister's libidinal needs are bound with punishment, the self-hanging brother performs Antigone, and in the torments of melancholia, the younger sister reunites with her dead child.

Due to the fact that the id ignores death, as with all types of negations, the only agency able to recognise it is the ego. Apart from the biological distress, what is fundamentally challenged by the death instincts is rather, as Richard Boothby annotates, 'the psychological integrity of ego'.[50] Angelidi parcels out the features among the characters, shaping at the same time a peculiar representation. The brother relates to an ego agency. He is under the control of reality, playing roles and taking responsibility for his actions. The ego is the only part that can be tormented by the death instincts and commit suicide. The id personality is identified in the younger sister, who is constantly under the torments of her desires. In search of a discharge, she is overwhelmed by feelings of pain, lust and anger. The elder sister manifests the super ego features, limited by strict and bossy prohibitions with contradictory demands.

In an article entitled 'The Enjoyment of the Artist' (2005),[51] explaining the process of creative labour, Angelidi asserts that what begins as an exfoliating effort to see your face turns into suffering separations.[52] Freud makes a similar hypothesis 'that living substance at the time of its coming to life was torn apart into small particles [. . .] and ever since, [they] endeavored to reunite through the sexual instincts?'[53] Combining the two thoughts, then, the birth of a character seems like a separation which multiplies to other characters and fictional narratives that all refer to the same initial character. And at the end of the film Angelidi envitions a unity of them in one person once again. In a scene of absolute magnitude, she places all the characters in the film around a table. She divides the scene into three levels, placing the blind lady at the top, along with some minor characters, and the Thief at the bottom. In the middle, dead people are sitting on left side of the table and the living on the right. Pomegranate seeds are spread everywhere and at the head of the table, on a higher level, people drink the nectar. The scene recalls purgatory, a state of limbo where death and life meet in an unresolvable situation and where people seem trapped in between two undefinable stages. 'By dying I found myself in a world that I had not imagined. By dying I got the intimacy. The terrible truth', says the Actor in his monologue just before this scene, correlating the state of being dead with familiarity and honesty. The fundamental experience of death coincides with the essence of life. At the end of the scene, the characters freeze into a tableau vivant. The Sculptress recapitulates: 'the only thing that is certain is that we are destined to die', then immediately poses the question: 'Now, can we live?' Angelidi places great emphasis on this scene. The rhetorical question that urges us to action is in contrast with the stillness of the scenery. Action and stillness are tangled together in a similar way to life and death.

THE *EXTRATERRITORIALITY* OF DEATH

The space where Angelidi places her characters is defined by topographical, dynamic and economic tensions, discernible first in the film's division into three chapters. 'The Net', 'The Dice' and 'The Will' adhere to a homologous division expressing different worldviews in life, specifically the belief in fate, chance, and free will.[54] Although interesting existential and philosophical interpretations clarify the meticulous structure, it is from a psychoanalytical point of view that the tensions involved press towards the emergence of a destructive excitation.[55]

As mentioned above, the film world constructs an inner system, and in the theory of psychoanalysis an inside stimulation can become severely traumatic in the same way as if it were external. The sensory organs that perceive a large range of stimuli are able to generate instinctual impulses. But the internal excitement relates to and 'can perceive only the increase and decrease of the tension'.[56] This total lack of representation is filled with the topographic division of the id, super ego and ego that Freud himself presented pictorially, placing the id at the bottom, the super ego at the top and the ego in between the two. Although mapping grounds means placing borders and shaping territories, at the psychical level the three agencies mingle with one another. Similarly, the three siblings, the ego or the Actor, the super ego or the Sculptress, and the id or the Scientist, are tormented by diverse tensions, intertwine, and shape the unity of a closed system.

Analysing *Thief or Reality* in accordance with this psychical apparatus topology, we see that the three chapters correspond to three perceptions of reality. The connotations of the first chapter, entitled 'The Net', spawn a sense of confinement and restriction, as taught by the ethical and moral traditions of Christianity. The super ego is described as the guardian of authority restrictions, religious prohibitions and school textbooks. The elder sister is a sculptress of marble. She is hysterical and strictly religious, surrounded by tombs and burial statues. Black crows and barking dogs attack her in her sleep. Waking up, she finds herself in a similar situation, thus blurring the lines between reality and dream. Dressed head to toe in heavy and dark clothes, she prevents any gaze on her body. The external stimulus is forbidden, stopped, it cannot intrude to incite immoral desires. She literally carries the weight of the family on her shoulders. 'She carries her siblings inside her, and she asks a high price for it', confirms the blind woman at the end of the film. Artistically illustrated in an exemplary scene, the Sculptress holds up a slanted wall with both her hands, preventing its demolition. In a symbolic reference to the nuclear family, Angelidi places a couple and two children inside a frame-cage, at the bottom of a wall, carrying each other's burden. They are naked, and together they create an undefined shape (Figure 3.1). Reality presents itself in a precarious form that transcends symbolism. Within the register of the psychical structure, Freud affirms that 'the super-ego retains the character of the father',[57] with the significant aim of repressing the Oedipus complex. The more powerful the Oedipus complex is, the more dominant and harsher the super ego will be on the ego 'in the form of conscience or perhaps of an unconscious sense of guilt'.[58] Tangled with the compromised ego, the demanding super ego enforces its commands.

Figure 3.1 Still, Angelidi, *Thief or Reality* (2001).

In terms of guilt there are two prevailing aspects in the film, lust and envy. The former is linked to religious prohibitions against sexual desires, while the latter refers to the free will to make life choices that both the Actor and the Scientist enjoy. The repetitive character of guilt expression motivates a compulsory action. Freud notes that the power of this compulsion is strong enough 'to overrule the pleasure principle, lending to certain aspects of the mind their daemonic character'.[59]

There is a scene where the Sculptress carves a female statue with a chisel and a hammer, repeating the phrase 'Lord, give me the force to sort the wheat from the chaff'. Each time she repeats the phrase, she changes the place of one word in the sentence, as if she is playing an articulation game similar to the 'Fort-da' game that Freud's grandson played, to ease a discomfort. The urge of the woman becomes so intense that her voice gets louder in an orgasmic crescendo, like a verbal masturbation. Finally, she lets her body go and she throws herself onto a bed, emotionally discharged and evidently repentant. The verbal, masochistic urge for sexual satisfaction changes from passive to more active in a later scene. 'The supreme pleasure torments me', she says, and starts hitting herself hard with both her hands, injuring and at the same time pleasuring her vulva. Similarly, in another scene, she gets inside a stone tub that is full of water, with her clothes on, and masturbates in the same way. She hits her genitalia with a hard soap and although this looks like a punishment, she is satisfied, experiencing a masochistic pleasure. The water is spread all around as an act of ejaculation. After indulging her desires, she repents and asks for forgiveness for her sins. 'I'm horrified by my words. Thou, supreme darkness', she says.

Jean Laplace, in his revision of Freud's theory, notes that the subject is considered masochistic when the pleasure derives from suffering and not when one system suffers while another does not. There is no 'algebra of pleasures',[60] he notes emphatically. The masochistic pleasure derives from the pain itself and cannot be the price of the suffering. 'This compulsion with a hint of possession by some "daemonic" power',[61] in Freud's words, overwhelms the Sculptress with unpleasure. She turns to religious prejudices, and she is convinced that an evil force has possessed her. In a sense, she diverges from gaining pleasure, following, against her will or consciousness, a possessive, automatic power. The masochistic behaviour is explained at a secondary level as a metaphysical urge, as temptation for a moral and carnal sin, coming from the outside to her. Although the force inside her repeatedly appears at the primary level too, it causes pain that indulges pleasure. It is on the masochistic compulsion that death ascribes its routes, which is what Angelidi emphasises in her representations.

The impulse towards repetition, apart from its masochistic manifestations, is also admitted into the film via recurrent traumatic dreams. Just as the Thief enters the house, the elder sister wakes up from a dream, forced from sleep by disturbing demands. She sleeps with her eyes open. Or she is awake while sleeping, similarly to the super ego's operative functions. Ferocious dogs bark without sound, four archaic reliefs of women engraved in marble come to life, a crow grasps the holy scriptures with its claws. Freud asserts that 'anxiety and punishment dreams are unproblematic, as they fulfil the "wish of the sense of guilt"'.[62] The heroine's dream has the purpose of satisfying a need for punishment. This dream fulfils the super ego's negative wish to punish the ego with guilt and remorse. The stimulus overcomes the sensory defence system and results in interrupting the dream process. At the unconscious level, the affects circulate freely from the one psychical system to the other, penetrating one another. The interrelations among the three psychical parts and similarly among the three siblings intensify the experience of discomfort. And sometimes, as Angelidi notes, the heroes may even enjoy the discomfort.[63]

In a subsequent scene, the younger sister kneels in front of a man and starts to undress herself, saying, 'I took the soap, I put it between my legs. I had some violent orgasms'. She becomes possessed by the acts of her elder sister, making the experience her own. The two agencies mingle. The man slaps her in the face. The super ego is 'fundamentally hostile to the satisfaction of desire',[64] but the id is fundamentally built by the repressed material. She collapses naked in his hands. The restrained and vacillating need for sexual satisfaction is expressed with the intervention of another system, the id, represented by the Scientist.

In the third chapter of *The Interpretation of Dreams* (1895), Freud states that 'there are no dreams other than wish-fulfilment dreams'.[65] This generalisation, although true for anxiety and punishment dreams, is disproved by the dreams of traumatic neurosis. Positioned to explain the recurrent nightmares of patients suffering from traumatic neurosis, Freud affirms that the dreams diverge from their purpose because they are 'helping to carry out another task, which must be accomplished before the dominance of the pleasure principle can even begin'.[66] It is the manifestation of a compulsion to repetition[67] of the unpleasurable traumatic event that evokes those dreams. In some cases, this is a process of binding the unbound moving energy. 'The function of binding energy retrospectively allows "for a certain control over the event (stimuli)". The event "where the sum of excitation surpasses that which the mental apparatus is able to bind"'[68] fails to keep up with the pleasure principle and the tension is discharged mainly through the dreaming process. The death instinct is 'exempted' from the jurisdiction of the dream law for wish fulfilment and the pleasure principle. It is the only exception that weighs heavily upon the traumatic dreams.

The Scientist suffers from a real loss, the death of her child. The boy dies in an accidental fire and the mother is trapped into a compulsive repetition, dreaming the traumatic event with anxiety. At the beginning of the dream, her son blames her for the misfortune. 'Mother, can't you see I'm burning?' Angelidi pictures the woman sleeping in a bed with a man by her side. She suddenly wakes up and runs to save the child. But the child is already dead, the catastrophe has completed, and she collapses on her knees, screaming in anguish in front of the burning cradle. 'Life has already been', she says at a later point. Her action is passive. She cannot contain the damage and she is subjected to an extremely large amount of stimuli. The 'dreams occurring in traumatic neuroses have the characteristic of repeatedly bringing the patient back into the situation of his accident, a situation from which he wakes up in another fright'.[69] When she wakes up, the younger sister is highly melancholic. Freud's approach in this situation acknowledges the role of the death instinct. The gathered energy of psychical pain increases the tension that Freud relates to displeasure. In this version, there is no gain of pleasure whatsoever. The event is shocking, and the repetition of the experience is also horrifying. We are in a territory beyond pleasure where, driven by death instincts, the psychical structure collapses. Unable to even stand on her feet, the younger sister acts vocally and inarticulately, with a scream. The only motor action is a vocal one. Unmastered energies provoke the discomfort. Angelidi, referring to artistic creativity, affirms that 'utter the discomfort, articulate the discomfort, is a way to alter the discomfort. Sometimes you get a sense of pleasure into the discomfort that is going to be altered.'[70] The ego gets prepared no matter how gruesome the outcome, and, in each repetition, is ready for a better reaction to the stimulus. The feeling of powerlessness deepens into a forceful reaction. In a later scene, the younger sister embraces a mound of soil with her hands, as if she is holding her child, saying, 'my soul would have been soothed, if I had reacted then'. In a sense, the 'death drive is thus not seen to operate in an autonomous way, but is mediated by suffering and trauma, especially the trauma of an early lack of affect'.[71]

Angelidi accentuates suffering and discomfort in a sublimating effort to ease them, to let them be discharged, and mostly, to guide them to a higher sense of awareness. The closer to consciousness, mentally or synesthetically, the stronger the understanding at a secondary level. The death force, exiled from the dream world, finds its proper image in the film.

THE LIBIDINAL LAMENTS OF A MELANCHOLIC EGO

To associate the film with the essence of the death instinct's workings, we need to interpret the representations according to the libidinal conversions effectuated in them. From an economic point of view, the libido intermingles with the death instinct in order to control its destructiveness. A part of this 'libidinal' urge for destruction is directed to the outside and to other objects in the form of muscular aggressiveness.[72] Freud explains that

> in this way the instinct itself could be pressed into the service of Eros, in that the organism was destroying some other thing, whether animate or inanimate, instead of destroying its own self. Conversely, any restriction of this aggressiveness directed outwards would be bound to increase the self-destruction, which is in any case proceeding.[73]

Only a small part of the death instincts converts to aggressiveness. The major part 'remains inside the organism and, with the help of the accompanying sexual excitation [. . .] becomes libidinally bound there. It is in this portion that we have to recognize the original, erotogenic masochism.'[74] The figure of the brother in the film corresponds to a melancholic ego. 'I am sad. I let the hours pass. On me. I'm not here,' he says. From a topographic point of view, he is an 'executor of instinctual discharge'.[75] However, the effectuated libidinal processes lead him to a precarious state of unpleasure. In the absence of object relations, his restrained aggressiveness directs the death instinct against himself. The figure of the mother, displaying an arrogant, narcissistic concern for herself, 'understands only what she belittles'. Closely related to the brother, she keeps him close to serve her. Angelidi attributes an aesthetic function to object relations. In a later scene, the pathogenic unity of the mother and brother is formally illustrated with the camera movement, when he emerges from the back of her head at a dinner table. The mother is the proof of his libidinal loss on object cathexis. With her slovenly appearance, long brittle white hair and fixed gaze, the first loving object is repulsive to the brother. She is constantly carping: 'I'm in decay. Look at my body how it has decayed.' He wishes for a father to replace her, but there is a void. There is no contrasting father figure. Suffocated beneath his mother's arms which are hooked upon his back like a vulture, he says, 'I wish you were him'. Angelidi disputes the Oedipus complex, in an inverted version with the male exhibiting an object-tie with the 'absent' father. According to Potamianou, some formulations of the death instinct set a distance between the ego and object relations.[76] Recalling the libido from the object-cathexes, the brother turns to his narcissistic storage and the desexualised Eros.[77] In this way, the displaceable libido is in accordance with the pleasure principle and helps to discharge the energy. However, 'by setting itself up as sole love object, and desexualizing or sublimating the libido of the id, the ego is working in opposition to the purposes of Eros'.[78] The fusion effected inside the brother's psychical system between Eros and the death instincts indicates an unbalanced mixture. Freud confirms that 'defusions would also be liable to occur'.[79]

> The ego's attitude [. . .] gives the death instincts in the id assistance in gaining control over the libido, but in so doing it runs the risk of becoming the object of the death instincts and of itself perishing. [. . .] since the ego's work of sublimation results in a defusion[80] of the instincts and a liberation of the aggressive instincts in the super-ego, its struggle against the libido exposes it to the danger of maltreatment and death.[81]

The destructive urge ignites the introjection of the brother's role as Antigone and soon after he also commits suicide by hanging.[82] Angelidi conceives and stages the performance of Antigone's laments combining Byzantine aesthetics with the theatrical elements of an ancient tragedy. The brother, dressed in a white robe, performs the role of Antigone, spinning repeatedly around a small hole and a hill of dirt, thus shaping the infinity symbol. His movement is hypnotic and ritualistic, accentuated by the monologue of Antigone's laments whose rhythmic and pretentious enunciation resembles songs from the Byzantine hymnography. A displacement of the collision between the instinctual forces of death and life from the psychical to the sound structure has an evocative power. The audience, in the candlelit march to the theatre, sings 'Epitáphios Thrēnos', a chant sung during the Epitaph procession in the evening of the most solemn day of Christianity, Good Friday.

The cross-dressing illustrates the duality of the collision inside the brother. As an actor and as a man, he is a martyr of the unconscious desires of the id and the punishing prohibitions of the super ego that penetrate the ego. 'For Lacan, the traumatic force of the death drive aims not at the biological organism but at the unity of the ego.'[83] The brother says, 'I can't stand myself', for the unity has become a burden to consciousness. But he also dies with a biological death, complying with the greater wish of the id and the fieriest demand of the super ego. The brother 'sees [himself] deserted by all protecting forces and lets [himself] die'.[84]

Furthermore, the decomposition of the drives may result in a predominance of the death drives as illustrated in melancholia, in which, following Freud, we experience the super ego as the purest form of the death drive.[85]

Nevertheless, the brother had strived with all his power to sustain life. Another nuance of libidinal investments, which counterbalances the conflict between needs and demands, is seen in the Actor's relation to the Thief. Even though the tarot cards have augured the imminent death of the Actor, he challenges the Thief to a chess game.[86] The urge comes from the life instincts that want to preserve and evolve life. The Actor calls it 'courage', but the Thief corrects him, saying that this is a stupidity because no man has won this game. Apart from the philosophical connotations referring to human mortality, the balance of the libidinal tensions seems to have intrigued another type of object cathexis. As Benno Rosenberg asserts, the contribution of the death instincts is essential for functional relations between libido and objects.[87] This means that the death instincts interrelate with life from the beginning and an aspect of their mixture aims at resolving and dissociating from over-condensed and suffocating psychical structures, permitting new investments and energy bindings.

Yearning for death itself, the brother conveys the paradox of a psychical organ that works with constant bound and unbound formations linked to the antagonistic forces of death and life,[88] an endless repetition that Angelidi brings to the surface by picturing Friedrich Nietzsche's concept of the *eternal return*. This is a timeless moment in which the human psyche contemplates its own perishing over and over again to eternity.

AN *AD LIBITUM* MEMORY

A reverse movement of white dust floating upwards, and then the Thief climbing out of a window, introduces a scene that deals with the return of a repressed memory in the story. Black walls on both sides of the frame limit the view to a vertical opening. This gives the shape of a door, tempting a symbolic interpretation of a gate to the unconscious. Angelidi's *mise-en-scène*, setting three different levels of action, endows the scene with a specific scenic character. At the first level, the ego-brother stands hidden behind the wall, peeping at his naked sisters. At the second level, the two sisters are having a bath, both inside a concrete bathtub filled with water. They are placed horizontally to the frame, intersecting the vertical opening. At the back, the aged mother sits motionless, leaning over one of her legs (Figure 3.2). The sisters are initially seated back-to-back and when the camera starts smoothly moving in, they begin to act.

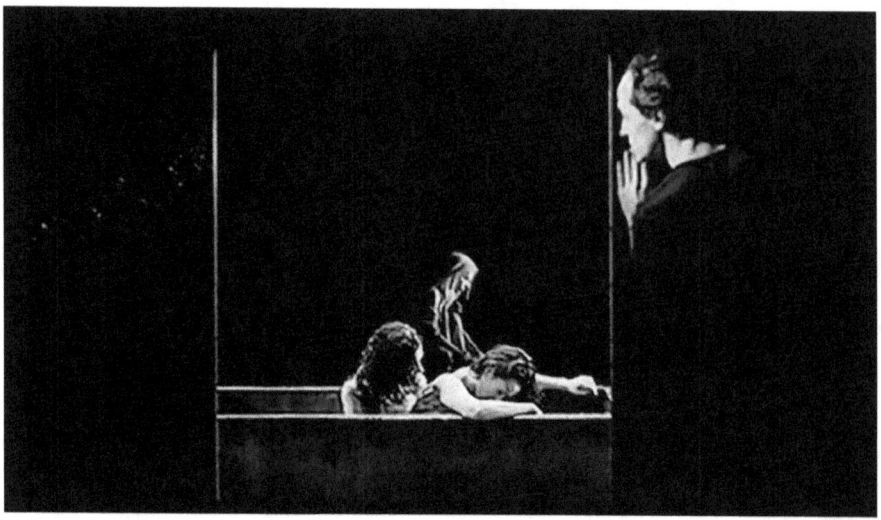

Figure 3.2 Still, Angelidi, *Thief or Reality* (2001).

A brief repeating dialogue pattern takes place: 'I wonder what you could do about these bruises', says the elder sister, and after a short pause she continues, 'I cover'. The other sister responds as if in a word game, changing the word 'cover' to the word 'discover' by saying, 'I always discover your flanks. How beautiful my sister is!' The following line has no causal relation to the previous. 'Do you remember? My calves were swollen and you couldn't walk.' And abruptly they turn again to their initial posture with their backs against each other, initiating a faithful repetition. Exact, similar movements and understated dialogues take place as the camera approaches closer and closer, reaching, finally, the mother at the back of the scene. The repetition is evident of Angelidi's emphasis on the way in which a repressed memory tries to come to light. The stronger the emphasis is visualised, the more indelible the memory.

Freud 'links the compulsion to repeat with the return of the repressed',[89] which is attributed to the workings of the death instincts. Part of what makes death instincts so difficult to cope is with their relation to the ego. Laplanche and Jean-Bertrand Pontalis refer to the unconscious parts of the defensive mechanisms of the ego which, as the subject ignores their aims and structures, are presented in a compulsive and repetitive way.[90] Freud claims that 'the compulsion to repeat, which the treatment tries to bring into its service, is, as it were, drawn over by the ego to its side (clinging as it does to the pleasure principle)'.[91] The scene is built as the ego's effort to bring about a repressed memory. The ego and the death instincts form a partnership even if the compulsion to repeat challenges the ego's stability. And this is because the ego tolerates the repetition insofar as it may be 'a potential source of pleasure'.[92] Freud's clinical observations showed that patients oppose the compromise with a negative therapeutic reaction. They behave with a compulsion to repetition not only against the analyst, but in their everyday life too, struggling to hold the repressed memory at a distance from their consciousness. In some cases, 'the patient does not *remember* anything of what he has forgotten and repressed, but *acts* it out. He reproduces it not as a memory but as an action; he *repeats* it, without, of course, knowing that he is repeating it'.[93] Death workings are enfolded in the unconscious action. The postponement of memories has a *quid pro quo* effect on the compulsion to repeat. An unconscious repetition of an action or behaviour is a way to replace the impulse to remember. Freud explains that this is a way of remembering traumatic or painful experiences from early childhood.[94] The repressed material that comes back to light can be in alliance with the pleasure principle since the ego is partly satisfied by expressing part of the id's desire, even though it has been disintegrated by the traumatic memory. At the same time, the affect that 'recalls from the past experiences which include no possibility of pleasure'[95] cannot be pleasurable. As a result, the compulsion to repeat sorrowful context appears to be agreeable to the ego.

The scene works as a symptom of the compulsion to repeat. It acts out the repressed memory through repetition. In accordance with psychical processes of visualisation in dream-work, Angelidi uses mechanisms of displacement and condensation. She sets at the first level the ego-brother as the only conscious part of the psyche able to observe the scene. As the ego loosens its control over consciousness, the camera moves deeper into the space, deeper into the unconscious and closer to the other psychical parts-siblings. This is a metaphor of the psychoanalytical work. The scene is a view of a common domestic habit of siblings bathing together. However, the grown-up, naked sisters alter the connotations of infant eroticism. The dialogues between them are enunciated in a pretentious and uncommon way, while their thematisation denotes a mild aggressiveness. Primarily inspired by jealousy of the body marks and bruises of the younger sister, this aggressiveness is apparently linked with an active sexuality, and the beauty of the elder sister's body. Their hostility retains a character of caresses. Instead of remembering the ambivalent love and hate emotions, they are acting through repetitive touching and pushing. The repetition also emerges in the language process as a game of altering meaning and blocking communication. An attempt to use words as objects, loosening causal relations, gives an even more playful character to the game. Angelidi asserts that

> discourse is a visual object. It is like a snake getting out of the mouth. Huge tongues burst out and freeze in the air. Like in medieval paintings where spoken words coming from the mouth, are written in a tape enrolled in painting's space.[96]

The Actor will confirm at a later point that 'the discourse can suddenly roll out of the mouth like a long ribbon'.

Moreover, the sisters show an abrupt and automatic movement as if they were tuned to perform well, ordered to act in an autonomous and uncanny way. The mother is like a ghost at the back, pampering herself instead of bathing her children. She is both present and absent, a painful context in the background. It is easier to soothe the negativity of this notion through an image than by conscious thought. The valuable work of the death instincts manifests itself in the repetition of an action of a repressed memory. 'The repetitions are motivated precisely by what lies beyond the pleasure principle and constitutes a violation of it.'[97] It is not the return of the repressed material that awakens the destructive urge, but the unpleasurable context it carries inside. Despite the brother's guilt, the mother's ignorance and the sisters' envy, the conversion manifested in the film exposes an elemental desire for dissolution. 'How can one not conceive that each great instinctual metamorphosis in the life of the individual will once again challenge its delimitation,' asserts Lacan, 'composed as it is of a conjunction of the subject's history and the unthinkable innateness of his desire?'[98]

The dead body of the Actor lying on a wooden table is disjointed from his voice, which continues to perform a farewell monologue – a symbolic act of interjection entrapping the Actor between the two states of being alive and being dead. Angelidi represents the ambiguity of the limits. The verbal context interprets a process of awareness, a type of estimation as somebody would engage in at the end of a long period of psychoanalytical therapy. Abruptly, the Actor understands all the previous complex thoughts, the meaning of the actions and their interrelations, the significance of the innate force that has finally managed to expose itself. He says 'you can't remember something that you have known but all of a sudden everything repeats the same thing [. . .] There, the present becomes, in a flashlight, the past. And now you live in a world in ruins.' The dissolution of the death instinct is an action of deep awareness. Angelidi represents this pure desire for knowing oneself as transcending the death structure. However, 'it still remains to be decided which death, that which is brought by life or that which brings life'.[99]

The compulsion to repetition is inscribed in both the thematic and figural construction of Antoinetta Angelidi's *Thief or Reality*, and the unrepresented force of the death instincts acquires an aesthetic form. Death is not presented as an outcome of life, but as a living psychical pain in constant presence. With the death instincts theory, Freud elaborates on 'problems as the origin of life and the nature of death',[100] which, in a creative and cinematic homology, Angelidi highlights in the images and narrative of *Thief or Reality*.

NOTES

1. Sigmund Freud uses the German word 'Todestrieb' to describe at times the biological instinctual behaviour of animals, and at other times the ambiguous elemental psychical force with a 'daemonic power'. In English the term was translated as 'instinct' or 'drive'.

In this chapter I will use the translation proposed by James Strachey in the preface to *The Standard Edition of the Complete Psychological Works of Sigmund Freud*, Vols. I–XXIV. However, I keep the word 'drive' in some instances, to be consistent with the original text. For more information on the concept, see Jean Laplanche, *Life and Death in Psychoanalysis* (Baltimore: Johns Hopkins University Press, 1976).

2. Anna Potamianou, one of the most important Greek woman psychoanalysts and theorists, notes that Freud's concept meets the order of the *Reel* in Lacan's theory. In a way she asserts a general relation between the death instinct and situations in real life that can not be controlled, such as the perishing of our beloved ones. The death instinct is 'a force that works subtly inside us'. In Anna Potamianou, *Monopatia Thanatou, Stixis kai antistixis* (Athina: Ikaros Press, 2007), 22.
3. Sigmund Freud, 'Beyond the Pleasure Principle', in *The Standard Edition of the Complete Psychological Works of Sigmund Freud*, Volume XVIII (1920–1922), ed. and trans. James Strachey, coll. Anna Freud, assist. Alix Strachey and Alan Tyson (London: The Hogarth Press and the Institute of Psycho-Analysis [1955], 1981), 38.
4. Richard Boothby, *Death and Desire: Psychoanalytical Theory in Lacan's Return to Freud* (New York: Routledge Library Editions: Lacan, First 1991, 2014), 3.
5. Teresa de Lauretis, 'The Stubborn Drive,' *Critical Inquiry* 24, 4 (1998): 877.
6. Freud, 'Beyond the Pleasure Principle', 63.
7. Sigmund Freud, 'Analysis Terminable and Interminable', in *The Standard Edition of the Complete Psychological Works of Sigmund Freud*, Volume XXIII (1937–1939), 243.
8. Sigmund Freud, 'The Ego and the Id', in *The Standard Edition of the Complete Psychological Works of Sigmund Freud*, Volume XIX (1923–1925), 21.
9. Freud, 'The Ego and the Id', 53. Freud associates the super ego with the death instincts. 'What is now holding sway in the super-ego is, as it were, a pure culture of the death instinct, and in fact it often enough succeeds in driving the ego into death, if the latter does not fend off its tyrant in time by the change round into mania.'
10. Freud gives the description in an earlier text, saying that 'when we have succeeded in describing a psychical process in its dynamic, topographical and economic aspects, we should speak of it as a metapsychological presentation', in Sigmund Freud, 'The Unconscious', in *The Standard Edition of the Complete Psychological Works of Sigmund Freud*, Volume XIV (1914–1916), 181.
11. 'It is impossible to overlook the similarity of the terms "metapsychology" and "metaphysics", and indeed Freud very likely intended to draw this analogy. (. . .) he defines metapsychology as a scientific endeavour to redress the constructions of "metaphysics".' Jean Laplanche and Jean-Bertrand Pontalis, *The Language of Psychoanalysis*, trans. Donald Nicolson-Smith, intro. Daniel Lagache (London: Karnac Books [1967], 1988), 249.
12. Victor Blüml, Liana Giorgi and Daru Huppert (eds), *Contemporary Perspectives on the Freudian Death Drive: In Theory, Clinical Practice and Culture* (London: Routledge, 2019) 8.
13. Boothby, *Death and Desire*, 5.
14. Jean Laplanche, *Problématiques IV: L'inconscient et le ça* (Paris: Presses Universitaires de France, 1981), 230.
15. Ibid.
16. Stella Theodoraki (ed.), *Antoinetta Angelidi* (Athens: Aigokeros, 2005), 94.
17. Potamianou, *Monopatia Thanatou*, 25–6. Potamianou notes further that death 'gives us an evidence of what cannot be disproved, the lethal concept registered into our psychical reality and the battle against it'.
18. Ernest Jones, *Sigmund Freud: H Zoi kai to Ergo tou*, Volume I, Syntomeymenh ekdosi, Lionel Trilling και Steven Marcus (Athens: Indiktos 2003), 510 (in English: Ernest Jones, *The Life and Work of Sigmund Freud*, shortened version).

19. Freud was committed to this concept until the end of his life, though it provoked 'organizational tensions within the international community of psychoanalysis' that no other of his work did. In Blüml, 'Contemporary Perspectives on the Freudian Death Drive', p. 74. For Lacan, 'to evade the death instinct in his [Freud's] doctrine is not to know his doctrine at all'. See Lacan, 'The Subversion of the Subject and the Dialectic of Desire in the Freudian Unconscious', in Lacan, *Écrits: The First Complete Edition in English* (New York: W. W. Norton, 2006) (671–702), 679.
20. Insofar as every drive is repetitive and marked by the deathly power of the signifying letter, Lacan will later radicalise Freud's position, suggesting that 'every drive is virtually a death drive'. In Lacan, *Concept and Form: The* Cahiers pour l'Analyse *and Contemporary French Thought*, <http://cahiers.kingston.ac.uk/concepts/drive.html>, accessed 10 November 2022.
21. Blüml et al., *Contemporary Perspectives*, p. 74.
22. Jean Laplanche, *Life and Death in Psychoanalysis*, trans. Jeffrey Mehlman (Baltimore, MD: Johns Hopkins University Press, 1976), 106.
23. Ibid., 56.
24. Sigmund Freud, 'Formulations of the Two Principles of Mental Functioning', in *The Standard Edition of the Complete Psychological Works of Sigmund Freud*, Volume XII (1911–1913), 219.
25. Freud, 'Beyond the Pleasure Principle', Chapter V.
26. Sigmund Freud, Introductory Lectures on Psycho-Analysis, Part III, 'Lecture XXII – Some Thoughts on Development and Regression – Aetiology', in *The Standard Edition of the Complete Psychological Works of Sigmund Freud*, Volume XVI (1916–1917), 356.
27. Freud, 'Formulations of the Two Principles of Mental Functioning', 219.
28. As the Great War had just ended, many patients had war neurosis and repetitive dreams of painful war experiences.
29. Freud asserts that: 'It is clear that the greater part of what is re-experienced under the compulsion to repeat must cause the ego unpleasure, since it brings to light activities of repressed instinctual impulses. That, however, is unpleasure of a kind we have already considered and does not contradict the pleasure principle: unpleasure for one system and simultaneously satisfaction for the other.' In Freud, 'Beyond the Pleasure Principle', 20.
30. Freud will subsequently publish a supplementary revision to his theory on dreams.
31. Freud, 'Analysis Terminable and Interminable', in *The Standard Edition of the Complete Psychological Works of Sigmund Freud*, Volume XXIII (1937–1939), 243.
32. Boothby, *Death and Desire*, 3.
33. Freud, 'The Ego and the Id', 49.
34. Boothby, *Death and Desire*, 73.
35. Translation of the German words *Bindung* and *Entbindung*.
36. Boothby, *Death and Desire*, 81.
37. Freud, 'Beyond the Pleasure Principle', 31.
38. Boothby, *Death and Desire*, 84.
39. Potamianou, *Monopatia Thanatou*, 37.
40. Freud, 'Beyond the Pleasure Principle', 62.
41. Gunnar Karlsson, 'Beyond the Pleasure Principle: The Affirmation of Existence', *The Scandinavian Psychoanalytic Review* 21, 1 (1998): 42.
42. Freud, 'Beyond the Pleasure Principle', 38.
43. Freud,'The Ego and the Id', 41.
44. M. Andrew Holowchak and Michael Lavin, *Repetition, the Compulsion to Repeat, and the Death Drive: An Examination of Freud's Doctrines* (London: Lexington Books, 2018), 70.

According to Freud, 'Our views have from the very first been dualistic, and today they are even more definitely dualistic than before – now that we describe the opposition as being, not between ego-instincts and sexual instincts but between life instincts and death instincts.' In Freud, 'Beyond the Pleasure Principle', 53.
45. Theodoraki, *Antoinetta Angelidi*, 119.
46. Sigmund Freud, 'Instincts and Vicissitudes', in *The Standard Edition of the Complete Psychological Works of Sigmund Freud*, Volume XIV (1914–1916), 122.
47. Antoinetta Angelidi, 'Sewing Dreams in a Ribbon', interview by Giannis Fragoulis, Greek News Blog, <https://greeceactuality.wordpress.com/2012/12/05/%cf%83%cf%85%ce%bd%ce%b5%ce%bd%cf%84%ce%b5%cf%85%ce%be%ce%b7-%ce%b1%ce%bd%cf%84%ce%bf%cf%85%ce%b1%ce%bd%ce%b5%cf%84%cf%84%ce%b1%cf%83-%ce%b1%ce%b3%ce%b3%ce%b5%ce%bb%ce%b9%ce%b4%ce%b7/>, accessed 10 November 2021.
48. Vrasidas Karalis, *Realism in Greek Cinema: From the Post-War Period to the Present*, ed. Julian Ross and Lúcia Nagib (London: I. B. Tauris, 2017) (191–214), 196.
49. Empedocles of Acragas (c. 490–430 BC) was a Greek pre-Socratic philosopher. According to his theory of the cosmic cycle, all there is in the world is structured by four basic elements: fire, water, earth and air. Those elements are in constant mixture and separation by two elemental forces called *Neikos* ('strife') and *Philotis* ('love'). The opposed powers cause the variation between harmony and disharmony in the universe. 'Sometimes by Love all coming together into one, sometimes again each one carried off by the hatred of Strife', in 'Empedocles', *Stanford Encyclopedia of Philosophy*, first published 26 September 2019; substantive revision 7 April 2020, <https://plato.stanford.edu/entries/empedocles/#Cosm>, accessed 10 November 2021.
50. Boothby, *Death and Desire*, 96.
51. This is a speech that Angelidi gave at the symposium 'H Apolaysh sthn Texnh' (i.e., The Enjoyment of the Art), 18 May 2002, Kentro Sygxronhs Eikastikhs Dhmioyrgias, Institouto Mesogiakvn Spoudvn, Rethimno, Crete (Museum of Contemporary Art in Crete). During the conference there was an art exposition entitled 'Anthropoi, Prosvpa, Morfes' (i.e., People, Faces, Forms), which featured some of the works of Angelidi. The text 'The Enjoyment of the Artist' was published in the special volume edited by Stella Theodoraki, *Antoinetta Angelidi* (Athens: Aigokeros, 2005), during the retrospective programme of the 46th International Thessaloniki Film Festival dedicated to Angelidi's oeuvre.
52. Theodoraki, *Antoinetta Angelidi*, 94.
53. Freud, 'Beyond the Pleasure Principle', 58.
54. Theodoraki, *Antoinetta Angelidi*, 114.
55. The 'extraterritoriality of death' is a metaphor for the immunity enjoyed by death in the psychical territory. Jean Baudrillard notes that 'we speak less and less of the dead, we cut ourselves short and fall silent: death is discredited. End of a solemn and detailed "death in the family": we die in hospital, death has become *extraterritorial*', in Baudrillard, *Symbolic Exchange and Death*, trans. Iain Hamilton Grant, intro. Mike Gane (London: Sage Publications [1993], 2000), 182.
56. 'An operating principle of the perception-consciousness system is that, while it is sensitive to a great diversity of qualities originating in the external world, it can only apprehend internal reality in terms of the increase and decrease of tension, as expressed on a single qualitative axis – namely, the pleasure-unpleasure scale'. In Jean Laplanche and Jean-Bertrand Pontalis, *The Language of Psychoanalysis*, trans. Donald Nicolson-Smith, intro. Daniel Lagache (London: Karnac Books [1967] 1988), 323.
57. Freud,'The Ego and the Id', 34.
58. Ibid., 35.

59. Sigmund Freud, 'The Uncanny', in *The Standard Edition of the Complete Psychological Works of Sigmund Freud*, Volume XVII (1917–1919), 238.
60. Jean Laplanche, *Zvh kai Thanatos sthn psycanalysh* (i.e., *Life and Death in Psychoanalysis*), trans. Natalia Papagiannopoulou (Athens: Nefeli [1970] 1988), 197.
61. Freud, 'Beyond the Pleasure Principle', 36.
62. Holowchak and Lavin, *Repetition, the Compulsion to Repeat, and the Death Drive*, 65–6.
63. Theodoraki, *Antoinetta Angelidi*, 94.
64. Brooksby, *Death and Desire*, 167.
65. Sigmund Freud, 'The Interpretation of Dreams', in *The Standard Edition of the Complete Psychological Works of Sigmund Freud*, Volume IV (1900), 134. In the later text, 'Beyond the Pleasure Principle', 32, Freud will admit for the first time an exception to the proposition that dreams are fulfilments of wishes.
66. Holowchak and Lavin, *Repetition, the Compulsion to Repeat, and the Death Drive*, 65–6.
67. Ibid., 64. The phenomenon accounts also for the tendency of patients to obstruct treatment, the repetitive games of children in which a painful loss is symbolically re-experienced, and the case of masochism in which pain intertwines with pleasure.
68. Karlsson, 'Beyond the Pleasure Principle: The Affirmation of Existence', 38.
69. Freud, 'Beyond the Pleasure Principle', 13.
70. Theodoraki, *Antoinetta Angelidi*, 94.
71. Raluca Soreanu,'Something Was Lost in Freud's Beyond the Pleasure Principle: A Ferenczian Reading', *The American Journal of Psychoanalysis* 77, 3 (2017): 223–38, 229.
72. 'The libido has the task of making the destroying instinct innocuous, and it fulfils the task by diverting that instinct to a great extent outward – soon with the help of a special organic system, the muscular apparatus.' In Sigmund Freud, 'The Economic Problem of Masochism', in *The Standard Edition of the Complete Psychological Works of Sigmund Freud*, Volume XIX (1923–1925), 163.
73. Sigmund Freud, 'Civilisation and its Contents', in *The Standard Edition of the Complete Psychological Works of Sigmund Freud*, Volume XXI (1927–1931), 119.
74. Freud, 'The Economic Problem of Masochism', 163.
75. Brooksby, *Death and Desire*, 98.
76. Potamianou, *Monopatia Thanatou*, 36.
77. 'The transformation [of erotic libido] into ego-libido of course involves an abandonment of sexual aims, a desexualization', in Freud, 'The Ego and the Id', 46.
78. Freud, 'The Ego and the Id', 46.
79. Sigmund Freud, 'Two Encyclopaedia Articles (1923 [1922]) (B) The Libido Theory', in *The Standard Edition of the Complete Psychological Works of Sigmund Freud*, Volume XVIII, 258–9.
80. The separation of an emotion-provoking stimulus from the unwanted emotional response as part of a therapeutic process, in the same way as when a bomb is 'defused'.
81. Freud, 'The Ego and the Id', 56.
82. In Sophocles' tragedy, Antigone disobeys Creon's, the King of Thebes, behest and buries her brother Polinices. Creon sentences her to death and Antigone commits suicide by hanging. Similarly, the Actor in Angelidi's film, introjecting his role, dies by hanging against his mother's demands for nursing, against the id's needs for sexual satisfaction through object relations.
83. Brooksby, *Death and Desire*, 71.
84. Freud, 'The Ego and the Id', 58.
85. August Ruhs, 'In the Name of Janus: Do We Need a Dualistic Drive Theory?', in Blüml et al., *Contemporary Perspectives on the Freudian Death Drive*, 127.
86. The scene is a reference to a scene from another film, *The Seventh Seal* (1957) by Ingmar Bergman.

87. Potamianou, *Monopatia Thanatou*, 29.
88. Ibid., 30.
89. Brooksby, *Death and Desire*, 93.
90. Laplanche and Pontalis, *The Language of Psychoanalysis*, paragraph V, 138–9.
91. Brooksby, *Death and Desire*, 93.
92. Ibid.
93. Sigmund Freud, 'Remembering, Repeating and Working-Through (Further Recommendations on the Technique of Psycho-Analysis, II)', in *The Standard Edition of the Complete Psychological Works of Sigmund Freud*, Volume XII (1911–1913), 150.
94. The term in German is *wiederholungszwang*.
95. Freud, 'Beyond the Pleasure Principle', 20.
96. Theodoraki, *Antoinetta Angelidi*, 87.
97. Brooksby, *Death and Desire*, 87.
98. Lacan, *Écrits: A Selection*, trans. Alan Sheridan (New York: W. W. Norton, 1977), 19–20.
99. Lacan, *Écrits: A Selection*, 308.
100. Ernest Jones, *The Life and Work of Sigmund Freud*, Volume III, 'The Last Phase' (1919–1939) (New York: Basic Books, 1957), 266.

BIBLIOGRAPHY

Angelidi, Antoinetta. 'Sewing Dreams in a Ribbon', interview by Giannis Fragoulis, Greek News Blog, <https://greeceactuality.wordpress.com/2012/12/05/%cf%83%cf%85%ce%bd%ce%b5%ce%bd%cf%84%ce%b5%cf%85%ce%be%ce%b7-%ce%b1%ce%bd%cf%84%ce%bf%cf%85%ce%b1%ce%bd%ce%b5%cf%84%cf%84%ce%b1%cf%83-%ce%b1%ce%b3%ce%b3%ce%b5%ce%bb%ce%b9%ce%b4%ce%b7/>, accessed 10 November 2021.

Angelidi, Antoinetta. 'The Enjoyment of the Artist', speech given at the conference 'H Apolaysh sthn Texnh' (i.e., The Enjoyment of the Art), 18 May 2002, Kentro Sygxronhs Eikastikhs Dhmioyrgias, Institouto Mesogiakvn Spoudvn, Rethimno, Crete (Museum of Contemporary Art in Crete).

Baudrillard, Jean. *Symbolic Exchange and Death*, trans. Iain Hamilton Grant, intro. Mike Gane. London: Sage Publications, (1993), 2000.

Boothby, Richard. *Death and Desire, Psychoanalytical Theory in Lacan's Return to Freud*. New York: Routledge Library Editions: Lacan, 1991, 2014.

'Drive, La pulsion', *Concept and Form: The Cahiers pour l'Analyse and Contemporary French Thought*, supp. Kingston University, CRMEP, AHRC, <http://cahiers.kingston.ac.uk/concepts/drive.html>, accessed 10 November 2021.

'Empedocles', *Stanford Encyclopedia of Philosophy*, first published 26 September 2019; substantive revision 7 April 2020, <https://plato.stanford.edu/entries/empedocles/#Cosm>, accessed 10 November 2021.

Freud, Sigmund. *The Standard Edition of the Complete Psychological Works of Sigmund Freud*, Volumes I–XXIV (1886–1939). Ed. and trans. James Strachey, coll. Anna Freud, assist. Alix Strachey and Alan Tyson. London: The Hogarth Press and the Institute of Psycho-Analysis, 1981.

Freud, Sigmund, and Josef Breuer.'Studies on Hysteria', in *The Standard Edition of the Complete Psychological Works of Sigmund Freud*, Volume II (1893–1895). Ed. and trans. James Strachey, coll. Anna Freud, assist. Alix Strachey and Alan Tyson. London: The Hogarth Press and the Institute of Psycho-Analysis, 1981.

Holowchak, M. Andrew, and Michael Lavin. *Repetition, the Compulsion to Repeat, and the Death Drive: An Examination of Freud's doctrines*, London: Lexington Books, 2018.

Jones, Ernest. *The Life and Work of Sigmund Freud*, Volume III, 'The Last Phase', (1919–1939), ed. Lionel Trilling and Steven Marcus. New York: Basic Books, 1957.

Jones, Ernest. *Sigmund Freud: H Zoi kai to Ergo tou* (in English: Jones, Ernest. *The Life and Work of Sigmund Freud*, shortened version), Volume I, 'Ta xronia ths diamorphosis kai oi magales anakalipseis' (i.e., The Formative Years and the Great Discoveries, 1856–1900), trans. Komnhnos Xenofvntas, intro. Xartokollhs Petros. Athens: Indiktos, 2003.

Karalis, Vrasidas. *Realism in Greek Cinema: From the Post-War Period to the Present*, ed. Julian Ross and Lúcia Nagib. London: I. B. Tauris, 2017, 191–214.

Karlsson, Gunnar. 'Beyond the Pleasure Principle: The Affirmation of Existence'. *The Scandinavian Psychoanalytic Review* 21, 1 (1998): 37–52.

Lacan, Jacques. *Écrits: A Selection*, trans. Alan Sheridan. New York: W. W. Norton, [1977] 2006.

Lacan, Jacques. *Écrits: The First Complete Edition in English*. New York: W. W. Norton, 2006, 671–702.

Laplanche, Jean. *Life and Death in Psychoanalysis*, trans. Jeffrey Mehlman. Baltimore: Johns Hopkins University Press, [1976] 1985.

Laplanche, Jean. *Problématiques IV: L'inconscient et le ça*. Paris: Presses Universitaires de France, 1981.

Laplanche, Jean. *Zvh kai Thanatos sthn psycanalysh* (i.e., *Life and Death in Psychoanalysis*), trans. Natalia Papagiannopoulou. Athens: Nefeli [1970] 1988.

Laplanche, Jean and Jean-Bertrand Pontalis. *The Language of Psychoanalysis*, trans. Donald Nicolson-Smith, intro. Daniel Lagache. London: Karnac Books, [1967] 1988.

Lauretis, Teresa de. 'The Stubborn Drive'. *Critical Inquiry* 24, 4 (1998): 851–77, <http://www.jstor.org/stable/1344110>, accessed 1 June 2022.

Potamianou, Anna. *Monopatia Thanatou, Stixis kai antistixis*. Athina: Ikaros Press, 2007.

Soreanu, Raluca. 'Something Was Lost in Freud's Beyond the Pleasure Principle: A Ferenczian reading'. *The American Journal of Psychoanalysis* 77, 3 (2017): 223–38.

Theodoraki, Stella (ed.). *Antoinetta Angelidi*. Athens: Aigokeros, 2005.

Victor Blüml, Liana Giorgi and Daru Huppert (eds). *Contemporary Perspectives on the Freudian Death Drive: In Theory, Clinical Practice and Culture*. London: Routledge, 2019.

CHAPTER 4

Childhood, Desire and Identity in *The Hours*

Christina Adamou

The concepts of desire and identity are of course inherent to psychoanalysis and their development through childhood is quite central in psychoanalytic theories. Desire and identity are also rather central to cinema, as so often – both in commercial and experimental films – our interest and pleasure as viewers rely on who the character is and what (s)he wants. Childhood in films and cultural texts in general has been a difficult issue to broach, both by artists and cultural theory. As children do not partake in the creative process, their representations are created by adults who may project on to them cultural stereotypes, adult desires and fears.[1]

Angelidi's films represent childhood in complex ways and they focus on identity and desire, so psychoanalytic theories seem to be ideal for their analysis. Yet, it is important to think about what particular insights psychoanalytic theories could offer and which psychoanalytic theories would be best suited to analyse experimental films and Angelidi's films in particular. We will examine the most prominent psychoanalytic theories for film as well as turn to Donald W. Winnicott's psychoanalytic theories and argue why they are most pertinent to Angelidi's film *The Hours*.

When selecting methodological tools, one has to set very clearly the aims of the analysis. I do not aim to psychoanalyse the screenwriter and director, Angelidi, nor to psychoanalyse the characters. Rather, I will use psychoanalytic theories to look into the cinematic representations of developmental stages, of the self and of desires that are present in *The Hours*.

When thinking about psychoanalysis and film, Christian Metz's and Jean-Louis Baudry's psychoanalytic film theories are the first to spring to mind, as they are seminal in film studies. They focus mainly on the primary and secondary identification. The viewer, for Metz, experiences a primary identification with the act of perception itself, with the camera as a point of view, placing them as a producer of the image and by extension the producer of meaning(s). The secondary identification is with the main character and more specifically with the character's body.[2] The identification with the body is pivotal in the formation of the ego. Freud first pointed out that 'The ego is first and foremost a body-ego; it is not merely a surface entity, but it is itself a projection of a surface.'[3]

However, Metz's and Baudry's theories are mainly based on Lacan, as Lacan took Freud's thought further by articulating his theory on the Mirror Stage. The secondary identification in cinema is based on or can be seen as a re-enactment of the Lacanian Mirror Stage. Gallop gives this brief definition of it:

> the infant that has not yet mastered the upright posture [. . .] will, upon seeing herself in the mirror, 'jubilantly assume' the upright position. She thus finds in the mirror image 'already there' a mastery that she will actually learn only later.[4]

There is a gap between real capacities to control the body and the environment and the image of unity and control with which the baby identifies that leads to a fascination with that image. Sandy Flitterman-Lewis has underlined the element of fascination in the Mirror Stage and linked it to the cinema spectator, stating that there is a 'correspondence between the infant in front of the "mirror" and the spectator in front of the screen, both being fascinated by and identifying with an imaged ideal, viewed from a distance'.[5]

We could also note the distance mentioned by Flitterman-Lewis, which refers to the conditions of cinema spectatorship. Both the primary and secondary identifications are enabled by the conditions in the cinema theatre, the darkness and stillness of the audience and the projected light, images and sound, that resemble a state of sleeping and dreaming. The conditions of cinema spectatorship thus facilitate a regression to the Lacanian Mirror Stage. 'Although Metz and Baudry do not assert it directly, their theories come close to describing cinematic spectatorship as a private temporality apart from public time or space.'[6] Primary and secondary identification are useful tools, yet they can prove to be quite complex when analysing a film in which there are multiple images of the protagonist simultaneously on screen, as we shall see. Apart from identification, though, both the concept of regression and the idea of private temporality may prove quite useful in the analysis of a film about growing up.

The centrality of the Mirror Stage in Metz's and Baudry's theories is quite telling, as it also constitutes an introduction to the Imaginary and is permeated by Metz's theory on the *Imaginary Signifier*, film images as signifiers of something that was once in front of the camera and is no longer there as a material entity. As Penley also asserts, '[t]he imaginary can only be endlessly played out; its infinite metonymy can only be stopped into *fictions* of materiality, never materiality itself.'[7] The distance from materiality can also be viewed as enabling cinematic signifiers to represent processes of the psyche.

I will be using these ideas and concepts to analyse *The Hours* and the representations or simulacra of the development and processes of the psyche. As Penley points out, there is a difference between Metz's and Baudry's theories. 'For Baudry, the cinema is not an extension or prothesis of the psyche (as it is for Metz) but a faultless technological simulacrum of the systems Ucs [Unconscious] and Pcs – Cs [Pre-Conscious – Conscious) and their interrelations.'[8] I would like to differentiate my methodology from Baudry and Penley at this point and suggest that film could offer images or simulacra of the development of the self or desire through different stages of development, metonymies or metaphors, yet not any form of knowledge of the unconscious per se. A film, as a work of art, cannot offer knowledge of the unconscious, as the very concept of the unconscious defies our knowledge and control. 'For Lacan the unconscious undermines the subject from any position of certainty, from any relation of knowledge to his or her psychic processes and history.'[9] Although both filmmakers and viewers may draw upon metaphors and metonymies of the unconscious, in order to communicate via creating and interpreting films, it is important to remember that we always rely on disguised desires of the unconscious and representations of identity as opposed to true desires and identities.

Experimental films like Angelidi's invite viewers to focus on this play of disguised desires and metaphors of psychic processes by not burdening the narrative with naturalistic details. 'Le Grice cites what can be learned from information theory: by reducing the information within the film to an extreme degree, the spectator's awareness can be focused solely onto his or her own perceptual responses.'[10]

The Hours is not an abstract film, yet both the narrative and the image are far from naturalistic. The film both stresses the absence of materiality of cinematic signifiers and seems to open a dialogue with the Mirror Stage and the development of identity as well expressions of desire. Quite tellingly, the film is characterised in the titles as 'a rectangular film'. The darkness to the left and right on the cinema screen is a constant reminder of what remains hidden, unknown, irrepresentable, and could be seen as a metaphor for the unconscious. Spendo, the main character, states in the first sequence that she is tired of the visible things fighting the invisible, a declaration that could stress the darkness left and right of the cinematic images. The darkness as a cinematic signifier, unknowable and uninterpretable, could be a constant metaphor of the unconscious, particularly as the darkness does not claim to offer a simulacrum or any kind of knowledge of the unconscious.

The very first sequence of the film could be read as a reference to the Mirror Stage. Spendo is looking at her reflection in the water. Yet, it constitutes a different representation to what Lacan describes. As Spendo looks into a cistern of water, then plunges her head in and is surrounded by water, the image could be read as a metonymy for the womb and in relation to water's ability to withhold and embrace any object or person submerged in it. It is not merely a reflection, but a reflection that she dives into – a simulacrum of a futile attempt to either be unified with the reflection or return to the womb. The problematic formation of identity and regression are thus present in the first scene.

The use of water and the narration differentiate Spendo's identity from Lacan's Mirror Stage and Freud's concept of a bodily ego. The differentiation is stressed even further when Spendo states that she is tired of living in a foreign body. The identification with the image of a unified body, described by Freud and Lacan, is here negated in the very first scene. We are therefore required to turn to Winnicott, as, in his view, the integration of the psyche into the body (soma) is not considered automatic as in Freud but dependent upon a healthy environment in early childhood.[11] The mother plays an important role in the formation of a healthy ego. As Winnicott asserts:

> if human babies are to develop eventually into healthy, independent, and society-minded individuals, they absolutely depend on being given a good start, and this good start is assured in nature by the existence of the bond between the baby's mother and the baby, the thing called love.[12]

Meanings in Angelidi's films often remain open, however, both engaging and negating the audience's desire to produce stable meanings. The next scene ascribes a political meaning to the body. Spendo narrates that the political instruction was for her to leave or go underground. Greek viewers assume that the reference is to the Communist party's political instructors during the Civil War (1945–1949) or the Dictatorship (1967–1974) or the restless years in between. Spendo's narration links the two scenes closely as she refers to the need 'for this body to stop being seen'. The wording 'this body' echoes her previous narration of living in a foreign body, and the desire for it to stop being seen echoes Spendo's desire for the fight between the visible and the invisible to cease.

This close link between the formation of the ego – identity – and politics brings to mind the principle that the personal is political. Winnicott's reference to 'society-minded individuals' quoted above also stresses the links between social roles and the psyche. The integration of the psyche into the body, the identification with the body, and the integration into society are all linked and in Spendo's case deeply problematic. The social milieu here is of course also problematic, as Spendo states that she has been forced to choose between going underground and self-exile for being left-wing.

The issue of desire is also introduced in the same scene. Spendo's lover is naked under the covers – though we momentarily get a full frontal – and Spendo (in her dress) initiates their sexual contact and seems to come to orgasm at the end of it. We could just read this scene as oppositional to classical Hollywood, which, in Mulvey's view, represents men as subjects of desire and subjects of the gaze and posits women as silent objects of the (male) gaze and as objects of desire.[13]. Here the man is the silent object of the protagonist's and the viewers' gaze, while Spendo expresses and acts upon her desire, conquering her lover.

However, as her identity and the formation of her ego have already been problematised, it would be an oversimplification to posit Spendo as the subject of desire. The unity of her subjecthood has already been called into question. Her desire is also rendered problematic when she sits up on the bed after the sexual act, looking upset. Through her narration and the male character's words we learn that he is or was her political instructor and this was her first time. Spendo then refers to their copulation as a rape of him and/or herself. The film proceeds to question further the formation of the unified ego, irrespective of circumstances.

When the political instructor leaves, Spendo heads to the bathroom and as she reaches for a glass of water, a rectangular beam of light comes on and her mother's voice is heard, saying, 'This time there will be no play' (07:40–07:43), and we see a little girl on tip-toe. The scene that follows can be seen as a representation of the adult Spendo's regression at a time of crisis – a point that we will return to – as well as a metonymy for Spendo's childhood and relationship with her mother. Summers refers to Bettelheim's 'definition of regression as the simulation of an earlier form of adaptation [. . .] A developmental task that must be overcome in the course of psychological growth is a potential nodal point that can be "regressed to".'[14]

Spendo as a little girl in the film is around three years old. According to Winnicott:

> Children in early years undertake simultaneously three psychological tasks: building a notion of 'self' in relation to reality as they begin to understand it, a capacity for their relationship with the mother and the capacity for a personal relationship with a person other than the mother – usually in nursery school.[15]

Spendo's mother, though, seems unable or unwilling to form a relationship with her. Three shots between the shot of the girl in the bathroom and a shot of the girl at the table signify a shift to a slightly earlier time and a repetition of Spendo being punished for not eating. During these three shots (07:55–08:40) we see the mother's profile from her thighs up to her shoulders, the mother's back and a travelling shot of the table. The absence of the mother's face is palpable and her only interaction with Spendo is her pressing the fork on her cheek and ordering her to chew.

There is a failure in establishing a relationship between the mother and the child – a relationship that is pivotal in forming an ego. Spendo is locked in the bathroom by a young man who seems to be a much older brother. He is played by the same actor as the man with whom we saw the adult Spendo in the first erotic scene. He is also failing to form a relationship with her as 'a person other than the mother'.

If we now turn to the establishment of the relation between the adult Spendo and the three-year-old Spendo, we might note the presence of water. Water serves as a link between the adult Spendo – taking a glass of water – and the three-year-old Spendo who is locked in the bathroom for not eating and plays with the water dripping from the tap. If we carry forth the metaphor of the water as the womb, we could perhaps conclude that the three-year-old is already regressing to an earlier state.

The adult Spendo also seems to regress, as we see the three-year-old spreading toothpaste on the bathroom floor and sketching out a face with her fingers, an act that intersects with and is followed by the adult Spendo spreading toothpaste on the bathroom mirror (09:50–10:40). We are thus introduced to the role of play. We know that the mother will prohibit it – at least while Spendo is locked in the dark bathroom – because we have already heard her say that this time there will be no play and we can deduce that it is a flash forward and that the three-year-old Spendo is locked in the bathroom again. We also see the adult Spendo regressing to playing with the toothpaste and the three-year-old resorting to play. According to Winnicott, play is pivotal in the formation of personality and relation. To sum up his extensive work on play, we could note that Winnicott argues that children play for pleasure, to express aggression, to master anxiety, to gain experience, to make social contacts, to integrate their personality and to communicate with people.[16] The prohibition of play is another problematic element, alongside the relations with the mother and older brother.

Playing with the toothpaste in the dark bathroom forms a bridge between the three-year-old Spendo's reality and her imaginative world. 'The child of two, three, and four is in two worlds at once. The world that we share with the child is also the child's own imaginative world, and so the child is able to experience it intensely.'[17] Spendo experiences the reality of being locked in the bathroom both intensely and imaginatively by spreading the toothpaste and thus turning the bathroom floor into a canvas.

Winnicott is well known for his work on childhood and his ideas have often been used in relation to play as well as transitional objects. The temptation here is to label the toothpaste as a transitional object – just because it seems to be important to the protagonist and because it is linked to her regression. Winnicott, however, differentiates between transitional objects and comforters. Transitional objects are symbolical of some part-object, which is usually the breast, and are similar yet different to the mother.[18] Comforters may comfort a baby or a young child of two or three, but they are not 'more important than the mother, an almost inseparable part of the infant.'[19] In this case, the toothpaste and the act of drawing are comforters, but they do not soothe Spendo.

In fact, after we see her punishment being repeated and the mother depriving her of the toothpaste, which she takes with her before locking Spendo in the bathroom, we see the adult Spendo sketching on a wall. Sketching therefore seems to be an expression that has evolved from play. The black-and-white sketch could connote a play between light and darkness, particularly since the adult Spendo once again refers to all visible fighting the invisible. She is then scolded and told to erase everything by her lover, Sotiris (22:17–22:57), thus ruling out artistic expression through sketching.

The scene of Spendo sketching on the wall, being scolded and erasing it all is intersected with a sequence of Spendo at her school, where her teacher reads an imaginative essay about an adventure in Madagascar, accuses her of lying and tears up the essay and the drawing that Spendo had made (23:22–24:46). The teacher is played by the same actress as the mother, suggesting that even though their role ought to be differentiated, they are essentially the same. To accentuate the resemblance even further, the teacher wears a black dress and its cut is very similar to that of the white dresses that the actress wears as Spendo's mother. She is also particularly stern with Spendo. We are here reminded of Winnicott's stress on the role of a relationship 'with a person other than the mother – usually in nursery school' and the important part that the teacher could play enabling the formation of the ego.

Although we could trace threads of psychoanalytic readings throughout the film, I would like to focus on Spendo's important relationships in her journey towards and through adulthood.

As a young adult, Spendo is physically hurt by her childhood friend Stamatis who coerces her to have sexual intercourse with him (18:00–22:08). The scene rather confusingly ends with Spendo licking his blood and kissing his arm. Since the film goes forth and back in time constantly, we already know that later she had sexual intercourse with her political instructor and this time the man was the unwilling participant. In Spendo's universe, desire seems to objectify and victimise the object of desire.

Both as object and as subject of desire, Spendo seems unable to function as a consenting adult having sexual intercourse with another consenting adult. It is not our job to diagnose the main character of the film, but in reading the film we can draw attention to the close and perplexing link that it establishes between identity and desire: 'By constructing a soul or psyche for itself, the 'civilized body' forms libidinal flows, sensations, experiences, and intensities, into needs, wants, and commodified desires that can gain a calculable gratification.'[20] Spendo's desires are not commodified and therefore not gratified in a culturally acceptable way.

Rose also stresses that libido for Lacan is tied to the Imaginary, as access to the object, and desire of an object, can only be realised through the act of identification with the body image.[21] Desire for the (m)other presupposes the differentiation between the infant and the mother. 'While fulfilling desire liberates and strengthens the self to mature, the reality principle demands that it be accompanied by disappointment because the m/other is ultimately unattainable.'[22] The mother is the first Other, the first object of desire.

There is, however, another layer of meaning in Angelidi's film, as a woman's desire is often forbidden in a patriarchal culture. In a dream-like scene, where Spendo finds herself in front of a wall with many holes and apples in them, she grabs one and is verbally and physically confronted by a man she had previously seen in church (27:10–28:34). The man has long hair and a beard and is dressed in a black shirt and black trousers. Although he does not wear the frock that Greek Orthodox monks wear, his appearance greatly resembles theirs. When confronted by him, Spendo claims that she fell in love and is not ashamed of it and that we need to re-invent rather than remember thought. The symbolic meaning of the apple as sin invokes the ideology of Christianity. In the Greek Orthodox church, patriarchy is especially prominent, as women, for instance, cannot become clergy and do not receive the holy communion during menstruation. The symbolic, the social and cultural laws – based on difference and termed by Lacan the Name of the Father[23] – have ascribed to women the role of objects of desire. In renouncing this role and becoming subjects of desire, women, according to the Greek Orthodox ideology, commit sin.

Sinning and evil obviously play a part in how Spendo is perceived by others. Her mother repeatedly wonders 'how a child could do such things' (see 14:00–14:17). She seems to perceive Spendo through the stereotypes of the innocent-angelic child versus the evil child. The seven-year-old Spendo cannot live up to the innocent child stereotype.

The film moves away from such stereotypes, clearly not adopting the view of the mother, as Spendo at different ages is the main character and the one who narrates her story and shares insights with the audience. The film rather offers representations of the main character's struggles with identity, desire and stages of development.

The four-year-old and even the seven-year-old Spendo seem fixated on the oral stage. The four-year-old bites a baby's – perhaps a sibling's – toes (11:59–12:02), while the seven-year-old bites Stamatis's fingers (17:33). These are representations of early expressions of desire and aggression. According to psychoanalytic theories initially developed by Melanie Klein, the oral stage that a typical baby goes through during the first year of their life is a stage of libidinal development and aims to incorporate the breast and food but is also aggressive towards the breast.[24]

There is also a representation of oral abjection. When the violin teacher sexually harasses the seven-year-old, she runs out and spits (33:30), then returns to the room in order to gather her violin and leave (34:40–34:50). According to Julia Kristeva's views, the process of creating a socially acceptable identity entails the abjection from the body of everything that is considered unclean or improper. The abject, however, can never be fully separated from the subject. It threatens the subject's stable identity and fascinates.[25] Spendo spitting can be read as an abjection, as an effort to constitute a stable identity that would be separate from improper relations with adults.

Although Spendo leaves and seems disgusted by her violin teacher's harassment, she sleeps with the violin in her bed. Music, just like sketching and creative writing, are creative arts, expressions of identity and desires that become forbidden to Spendo. Sophia, the maid, orders Spendo never to put the violin on her bed again. We later see Sophia grabbing Spendo's violin and taking it away (40:45–41:02). Sophia is also played by the same actress as the mother and the teacher. All three roles come to symbolise maternal authority and abuse.

The mother accuses Spendo of lying, slaps her and then complains to the father that she cannot tolerate this child between them. Spendo is not the phallus or an object of desire for the mother (38:19–38:57); she represents an obstacle between her and the father.

The father does not seem interested in Spendo at all. He is absent throughout the film except for the scenes in which the mother complains, resulting in him asking Spendo to come to him to be beaten, and in the scene that follows in the narrative timeline, where he briefly interrupts reading the newspaper to physically punish Spendo (38:59–40:20).

Although we see the father physically punishing Spendo, the order of power in the family is clear and is spelled out by the seven-year-old Spendo who says: 'Thus was the order of things set. Above father, there is mother. Above mother, there is Ms Sophia' (41:10–41:33). In another dream-like sequence, the adult Spendo picks up a baby that is sleeping beside Sophia and runs (44:23–45:20). Her stealing or rescuing the baby could symbolise her effort to also save herself from the phallic and omnipresent mother. She could also be trying to save her own baby from such experiences, from the repetition of an unhappy childhood. The dream-like scene comes after a scene with Spendo as a mother. As she is rocking her baby to sleep, her partner comes in and starts shouting. With decisive movements, she turns him towards her and asks him to keep his voice down (41:58–42:28). Her partner then asks her to suggest to him som reading matter on the feminist movement (42:40). The sarcasm of the film is palpable, as he does not respect his partner or her role as mother.

Although the omnipresent and rather omnipotent mother denies Spendo the love she needs to develop as a subject and she stands in the way of Spendo expressing her self through art, patriarchy also puts up serious obstacles. The father who is only present to punish her, the abusive older sibling, Stamatis who forces her into sexual intercourse, a disrespectful partner, a paedophile, and a monk destined to help her but who – as we will see – initially relates love to sin make up the mosaic of patriarchy and are actively aggressive towards Spendo as a little girl and as an adult, inhibiting the creation of a stable identity and the expression of desire.

The instability of identity is present throughout the film. There are intertitles in the film and, quite tellingly, one of them reads 'I or Not' (47:42). The intertitle is followed by a shot of Spendo buried in the sand – just her face visible – that we also saw at the beginning of the film. The intertitle and the shot of her buried in the sand suggest that it is a reference to Samuel Beckett. One of his short plays is titled *Not I* (1972) and constitutes a Mouth (the only part of a woman visible on stage) telling the story of a woman unloved and unable to speak, while the mouth is unable to utter the word 'I'. There is also a Listener, suggesting that they could be part of the Mouth's fragmented subjectivity. Beckett is also well known for the image of the half-buried woman Winnie in his play *Happy Days* (1961).

The film has a lot in common with Beckett with regard to the representation of identity and the representation of impossibility in terms of unity and stability. The multiple images of self are common in Beckett, for example, in *Come and Go* (1966), *Ohio Impromptu* (1981) and *What Where* (1983). Angelidi also uses multiple images of the self, yet the emphasis here is clearly on the self at different ages. A short while after the intertitle 'I or Not' the viewers see through a camera swinging up and down as if they were on a swing or seesaw (49:00–49:33). Our primary identification is with the camera and it invites regression to childhood as well as strengthens our secondary identification with Spendo, as we then see the seven-year-old Spendo on the seesaw with Stamatis repeatedly reciting 'free-slave' as they go up and down. Desire – for freedom – is linked to Spendo's identity, as the adult Spendo is revealed to be watching them seated on a swing. The initial rocking movement of the camera thus invites a strong identification between the viewer, the seven-year-old Spendo and the adult Spendo. It is, however, a multiple body image of Spendo and thus the viewer is invited to identify with the problematics of identity, rather than with a stable idealised subject. At this point, the duplicate and later multiple images of Spendo start taking over the film. Quite tellingly, they are established with the relation between Spendo as an adult and Spendo as a little girl.

The main character and the film work through the problematics of identity and desire, yet refrain from simplistic solutions. Spendo strengthens and frees herself both through fighting patriarchy and through embracing her self, as we shall see. The issues of identity, desire and childhood are linked in complex ways from the beginning of the film and remain inextricably linked to the end.

In order to be a subject, to claim an ego and be the subject of desire, as a woman, Spendo has to confront patriarchy. We watch the symbolic burial of a man in sand (54:00–54:41) as well as the confrontation of the adult Spendo with her violin teacher who suggests that she should commit suicide in order to add value to her oeuvre (54:41–55:30).

In an ambivalent scene, Spendo seems to baptise herself in love (56:29–58:10), as we see the adult Spendo in front of a cistern that could be the cistern of water that we saw in the opening sequence, as she plunges her head into the water and wrenches it out when she is desperate for air. Although it seems to bring her violently close to drowning herself, she pledges to adhere to her desire. In her interrupted monologue, she repeats: 'I will not make love again without loving' and 'God is not a threat'.

The man she had met in church suggests that committing suicide is pointless. He later takes on the role of a zookeeper (58:20), yet seems to be in a cage himself. The zoo might symbolise both the wild instincts and the imprisonment of these instincts or of the self by religion, society and culture. The zookeeper/monk tells the seven-year-old Spendo that it is time to switch cages. The seven-year-old Spendo seems to address the adult Spendo off-screen in the zoo and to ask her to take her place. Although she replies, 'Good morning' and 'Let's go', we never actually see the adult Spendo. The seven-year-old's invitation to take her place might as well be addressed to the viewer.

We will soon see two versions of Spendo in the same place. The adult Spendo is seated. She is holding a baby boy and the three-year-old Spendo is standing on the armchair and hugs her from behind (01:12:29–01:13:10). The travelling shot lets our gaze explore the image. Spendo claims a different identity to her father, her mother, Apollo and Sophia, addressing each one and saying, 'I am not you'. In that differentiation, she is claiming her own identity, while her past-self is embracing her. The film does not work towards building an ego through identification with the body of the (m)other. It works towards building an identity through love.

In the next shot, the water spills out of the stern like a wave, and the stern in a medium shot resembles a boat. Spendo in voice-over asserts that she interrupted her journey on the ship and turned back. The sequence that immediately follows (01:13:30) shows an exhibitionist, whom the three-year-old and seven-year-old Spendo are looking at. The adult Spendo appears to shield their eyes with her dress and ask him to leave. These two scenes suggest that Spendo has turned bask in time in an inward journey and protects her past selves.

Equally important seems to be the symbolic union with the man she met in church. After collecting his blood in a glass and using it to dye the faces of old men – perhaps from her past – they both undress and stand naked facing each other. His arm on her back and her hand caressing his face could be reminiscent of a tango dance, but the religious hymn in the background reminds the audience of the previous scene with the apples, and thus the image constitutes a reference to images of Adam and Eve (01:15:50–01:16:08).

In becoming the subject of desire and the subject of love, Spendo completes her circle. In the next scene, the seven-year-old Spendo is sleeping on the adult Spendo's lap (01:16:13). She carefully puts her to bed, caresses her hair and kisses her on the forehead. A travelling shot follows the adult Spendo, then moves through darkness to reveal Spendo writing – perhaps in her journal – as she says 'thus, that night I tore down the skeleton of the void'. The travelling shot continues to reveal the seven-year-old Spendo looking directly at the camera. The 'skeleton of the void' is of course a poetic phrase. It connotes an empty body, death, a hard frame; it might remind the audience of references at the beginning of the film to a foreign body and the struggle between the visible and the invisible (the skeleton is usually invisible but may become visible in the void). The return to the seven-year-old Spendo in the travelling shot suggests a continuity achieved through the adult Spendo taking on the role of mothering her past self.

Her assuming the role of the mother of herself is therapeutic. Winnicott locates psychosis, futility, unreality and the false-self personality in early environmental failure. With certain patients only, the emphasis is on changes in technique in the idea of regression to dependence. In the process of analysis, the therapy sessions reproduce early mothering and invite regression, seen here as an organised return to early dependency and the success of primary narcissism.[26]

The film mirrors the psychoanalytic sessions that encourage regression. With no help from the psychoanalyst, Spendo finds the strength to regress to dependence and early mothering by herself.

Apart from the representation of the character's therapeutic regression, the film returns to the maternal and to the feminine in other ways too. Irigaray argues that Western culture has been established on an effacement of the desire for the mother.[27] Desire for the mother in *The Hours* is not encouraged by the mother herself, yet the film foregrounds the desire for mothering and being mothered. As the desire is partially based on confrontation with patriarchal roles and ideologies, the personal once again becomes political.

The urge for a return to the maternal-feminine could also be linked to Kristeva's work. 'Kristeva challenges the Lacanian narrative which assumes cultural meaning requires the repression of that primary relationship to the maternal body.'[28] She links the symbolic to the masculine gender, where closed meanings and rather strictly structured ways of expression, dictated by social and cultural laws, prevail. The feminine is linked to the semiotic, in contrast to the symbolic. 'For Kristeva, the semiotic expresses that original libidinal multiplicity within the very terms of culture, more precisely, within poetic language in which multiple meanings and semantic nonclosure prevail.'[29]

Angelidi's film could of course be read in terms of the symbolic, piecing together the biography of Spendo. However, a strictly symbolic reading would be missing the point, as it is a deeply poetic film, in terms of engaging the viewer in the multiplicity of narrative, multiplicity of subjectivity or identity and of course multiplicity of meaning. The constant back-and-forth movement in narrative time and the multiplicity of self images allow viewers to become actively involved in representation of the psyche and the development of identity and desire. The unconscious remains of course unknowable, yet we get glimpses of the troubled formation of Spendo's identity. We are not invited to identify with Spendo as an ideal image, but to partake in her circular journey and quest of locating the psyche in the body. The film is an open text, largely semantic, in that it is open to different readings. What is perhaps most striking with regard to its semantics is the representation of the central and complex role of childhood for both identity and desire.

NOTES

1. Karin Lesnik-Oberstein, 'Childhood and Textuality: Culture, History, Literature', in Lesnik-Oberstein (ed.), *Children in Culture: Approaches to Childhood* (New York: Palgrave Macmillan, 1998), 2–7.
2. Jacqueline Rose, *Sexuality in the Field of Vision* (London and New York: Verso 1986), 195.
3. Sigmund Freud, *A General Selection from the Works of Sigmund Freud*, ed. John Rickman (New York: Liveright Publishing Corporation 1957), 215–16.
4. Jane Gallop, *Reading Lacan* (Ithaca NY and London: Cornell University Press 1985), 78.
5. Sandy Flitterman-Lewis, 'Psychoanalysis, Film, and Television', in *Channels of Discourse, Television and Contemporary Criticism*, ed. Robert C. Allen (London: Methuen & Co. Ltd, 1987), 184.
6. Anne Friedberg, *Window Shopping: Cinema and the Postmodern* (Berkeley, CA and Oxford: University of California Press, 1993), 132.
7. Constance Penley, *The Future of an Illusion: Film, Feminism, and Psychoanalysis* (London and New York: Routledge 1989), 12.
8. Penley, *Illusion*, 61.
9. Rose, *Sexuality*, 29.
10. Penley, *Illusion*, 8.
11. Lesley Caldwell and Angela Joyce. 'Editors' Introduction to "Mind and its Relation to the Psyche-Soma" (1949)', in *Reading Winnicott*, ed. Lesley Caldwell and Angela Joyce (Sussex, USA and Canada: Routledge, 2011), 83–5.
12. D. W. Winnicott, *The Child and the Family: First Relationships*, ed. Janet Hardenberg. Second Publication (London: Tavistock Publications Ltd, 1962), 5.
13. Laura Mulvey, *Visual and Other Pleasures* (London: Macmillan 1989), 15–20.
14. Frank Summers, 'Self Psychology and Its Place Among Contemporary Psychoanalytic Theories', in *The Annual of Psychoanalysis* Volume XXIV, ed. Jerome A. Winer (Chicago Institute for Psychoanalysis, 1996), 164.
15. Winnicott, D. W. *The Child and the Outside World: Studies in Developing Relationships*, ed. Janet Hardenberg. Second Publication (London: Tavistock Publications Ltd, 1962), 21.
16. Winnicott, *The Child and the Outside World*, 149–52.
17. Winnicott, *The Child and the Family*, 54.
18. D. W. Winnicott, *Playing and Reality* (London and New York: Routledge – Institute of Psychoanalysis, 1999), 6.

19. Winnicott, *Playing and Reality*, 7.
20. Elizabeth Grosz, *Space, Time, and Perversion* (London and New York: Routledge, 1995), 34.
21. Rose, *Sexuality*, 174.
22. D. W. Winnicott, *Donald Winnicott Today*, ed. Jan Abram. The New Library of Psychoanalysis (general editor Alessandra Lemma). (London and New York: Routledge – Institute of Psychoanalysis, 2013), 325.
23. For an analysis of the Name of the Father, see Judith Roof, 'A Verdict on the Paternal Function: Law, the Paternal Metaphor, and Paternity Law', in *Lacan, Politics, Aesthetics*, ed. Willy Apollon and Richard Feldstein (New York: State University of New York Press, 1996), 105–6.
24. See Andrew M. Colman (ed.), *Oxford Dictionary of Psychology* (Oxford: Oxford University Press, 2015), 532.
25. Barbara Creed, 'Dark Desires: Male Masochism in the Horror Film', in *Screening the Male: Exploring Masculinities in the Hollywood Cinema*, ed. Steven Cohan and Ina Rae Hark (London and New York: Routledge, 1993), 121.
26. Lesley Caldwell and Angela Joyce, 'Editors' Introduction to "Meta-Psychological and Clinical Aspects of Regression within the Psycho-Analytic Set-Up' (1954)", in *Reading Winnicott*, 129–30.
27. Luce Irigaray, *The Irigaray Reader*, ed. Margaret Whitford (Oxford and Cambridge, MA: Basil Blackwell, 1991), 35.
28. Judith Butler, *Gender Trouble: Feminism and the Subversion of Identity* (New York, London: Routledge, 1990), 79.
29. Butler, *Gender Trouble*, 79–80.

BIBLIOGRAPHY

Baudry, Jean-Louis. 'The Apparatus: Metapsychological Approaches to the Impression of Reality in the Cinema', in *Narrative, Apparatus, Ideology*, ed. P. Rosen. New York: Columbia University Press, 1986, 299–318.

Butler, Judith. *Gender Trouble: Feminism and the Subversion of Identity*. New York, London: Routledge, 1990.

Caldwell, Lesley, and Angela Joyce. 'Editors' Introduction to "Mind and its Relation to the Psyche-Soma" (1949)' (83–6). 'Editors' Introduction to "Meta-Psychological and Clinical Aspects of Regression within the Psycho-Analytic Set-Up" (1954)' (128–30), in *Reading Winnicott*, ed. Lesley Caldwell and Angela Joyce. Sussex, USA and Canada: Routledge, 2011.

Colman, Andrew M. *Oxford Dictionary of Psychology*. Oxford: Oxford University Press, 2015.

Creed, Barbara. 'Dark Desires: Male Masochism in the Horror Film', in *Screening the Male: Exploring Masculinities in the Hollywood Cinema*, ed. Steven Cohan and Ina Rae Hark. London and New York: Routledge, 1993, 118–33.

Flitterman-Lewis, Sandy. 'Psychoanalysis, Film, and Television', in *Channels of Discourse: Television and Contemporary Criticism*, ed. Robert C. Allen. London: Methuen & Co. Ltd, 1987, 172–210.

Freud, Sigmund. *A General Selection from the Works of Sigmunt Freud*, ed. John Rickman. New York: Liveright Publishing Corporation, 1957.

Friedberg, Anne. *Window Shopping: Cinema and the Postmodern*. Berkeley, CA and Oxford: University of California Press, 1993.

Gallop, Jane. *Reading Lacan*. Ithaca, NY and London: Cornell University Press, 1985.

Grosz, Elizabeth. *Space, Time, and Perversion*. London and New York: Routledge, 1995.

Irigaray, Luce. *The Irigaray Reader*, ed. Margaret Whitford. Oxford and Cambridge, MA: Basil Blackwell, 1991.
Lesnik-Oberstein, Karin. 'Childhood and Textuality: Culture, History, Literature'. *Children in Culture: Approaches to Childhood*. ed. Karin Lesnik-Oberstein. New York: Palgrave Macmillan, 1998, 1–28.
Metz, Christian. "The Imaginary Signifier". *Screen* 16, 2 (Summer 1975): 14–76, <https://doi.org/10.1093/screen/16.2.14>, accessed 1 June 2022.
Mulvey, Laura. *Visual and Other Pleasures*. London: Macmillan, 1989.
Penley, Constance. *The Future of an Illusion: Film, Feminism, and Psychoanalysis*. London and New York: Routledge, 1989.
Roof, Judith. 'A Verdict on the Paternal Function: Law, the Paternal Metaphor, and Paternity Law', in *Lacan, Politics, Aesthetics*, ed. Willy Apollon and Richard Feldstein. New York: State University of New York Press, 1996, 101–26.
Rose, Jacqueline. *Sexuality in the Field of Vision*. London and New York: Verso, 1986.
Summers, Frank. 'Self Psychology and Its Place among Contemporary Psychoanalytic Theories', in *The Annual of Psychoanalysis*, Volume XXIV, ed. Jerome A Winer. Chicago: Chicago Institute for Psychoanalysis, 1996, 157–71.
Winnicott, D. W. *The Child and the Family: First Relationships*, ed. Janet Hardenberg, second publication. London: Tavistock Publications Ltd, 1962a.
Winnicott, D. W. *The Child and the Outside World: Studies in Developing Relationships*, ed. Janet Hardenberg, second publication. London: Tavistock Publications Ltd, 1962b.
Winnicott, D. W. *The Child and the Outside World: Studies in Developing Relationships*, ed. Janet Hardenberg, second publication. London: Tavistock Publications Ltd, 1962c.
Winnicott, D. W. *Playing and Reality*. London and New York: Routledge – Institute of Psychoanalysis, 1999.
Winnicott, D. W. *Donald Winnicott Today*, ed. Jan Abram. The New Library of Psychoanalysis (general editor Alessandra Lemma). London and New York: Routledge – Institute of Psychoanalysis, 2013.

CHAPTER 5

Erased Ghost: The Deriddean Spectrality of Angelidi's Signs in *Idées Fixes / Dies Irae*

Ioannis Mazarakis

Antoinetta Angelidi's cinema is not easily classified into certain film genres or modes of filmmaking. Although most of her films do not follow the paradigm of classical narrative, labels as 'experimental' or 'lyric film' nevertheless do not adequately describe her work. Consequently, writing about Angelidi's cinema is not an easy task; being unable to fit into pre-designed schemes of narrative and filmic comprehension, her films demand a new vocabulary capable of describing, analysing and portraying their deconstructive function. Especially in her debut film, *Idées Fixes / Dies Irae* (1977), the absence of linear narrative, plot, main characters and even the slightest suspicion of a story development challenges the spectator's perception of what a film is supposed to be and, at the same time, produces a constant feeling of *knowing* without *understanding*; of watching familiar visual (and audio) elements being transformed into weird, unknown riddles, ready to be solved.

In many of her essays and interviews, Angelidi refers to the process of *ostranenie* ('defamiliarisation') as an artistic technique which plays a central role in the filmmaking process. Based mostly upon Freudian theory and Russian formalism, the process is described by Angelidi as the transformation of the familiar into the uncanny as the base of an alternative poetics of cinema, where films are no longer simple audiovisual representations of linear stories but function as artistic articulations between the imaginary and the symbolic order. However, although the Freudian 'uncanny' and the formalist concept of 'defamiliarisation' are valuable guides for the exploration of Angelidi's filmic universe, a closer look at the mechanism of the semiotic transformation realised through the defamiliarisation technique would highlight its central role in the meaning production process of Angelidi's films.

In this chapter I will strongly focus on the Derridean concept of *writing-under-erasure*, according to which we should be able to gain a valuable insight into the usage and interaction of the semiotic elements in Angelidi's films. According to Jacques Derrida in *Of Grammatology* (1967), *writing-under-erasure* is a method where a term is crossed out (~~like that~~) and its meaning is at the same time recalled and presented as an absence. Similarly, Angelidi's filmic signs acquire this double role of presence and absence, arriving at the Freudian uncanny through defamiliarising mechanisms. This 'spectrality' of Angelidi's signs, their condition of being at the same time present and absent, turns them impenetrable and renders them reflectors of thought – 'crystallizations of thought as images, [. . .] thoughts that have been turned back, rendered spectral'.[1]

This chapter analyses Angelidi's first film, *Idées Fixes / Dies Irae* (1977), through the prism of Derrida's concept of *writing-under-erausre* in order to present an alternative description of the defamiliarisation technique, which is at the core of her filmic signification.

FREUDIAN PSYCHOANALYSIS AND RUSSIAN FORMALISM

In her essay «Το παιχνίδι με το ανοίκειο – Μια ποιητική του κινηματογράφου» (i.e., 'Play with the Uncanny – A Poetics of Cinema', 2005),[2] Angelidi detects the similarities between the Freudian uncanny and the defamiliarisation artistic technique, as presented by the Russian formalists, in order to describe the basic functions of art, and especially of cinema. Although the two terms have a totally different background, with the first being developed in the academic field of psychoanalysis and the second being part of an aesthetic theory, they both seem to be related to the phenomenon of art and the way it is produced, received and interpreted.

In his well-known essay 'The Uncanny' (1919), Sigmund Freud begins his analysis of the *unheimlich* ('uncanny') by taking a closer look at the etymology of the word and its antonym *heimlich*, in German and in other languages. At the end of the first part of the essay, Freud concludes:

> (A)mong its different shades of meaning the word heimlich exhibits one which is identical with its opposite, unheimlich. What is heimlich thus comes to be unheimlich. (Cf. the quotation from Gutzkow: 'We call it unheimlich; you call it heimlich.') In general we are reminded that the word heimlich is not unambiguous, but belongs to two sets of ideas, which without being contradictory are yet very different: on the one hand, it means that which is familiar and congenial, and on the other, that which is concealed and kept out of sight. [. . .] Thus heimlich is a word the meaning of which develops towards an ambivalence, until it finally coincides with its opposite, unheimlich. Unheimlich is in some way or other a sub-species of heimlich.[3]

In the subsequent pages, Freud analyses the concept of the 'uncanny' by making references to several literatary examples, in order to depict, through them, some important phases of the development of the human psyche, especially through the process of repulsion: the fear of being robbed of one's eyes in E. T. A. Hoffmann's *The Sandman* (1817), the theme of the 'double' in the work of Otto Rank, the literary instances in which we are confronted with random repetitions of the same thing (and which are linked with the repetition compulsion phenomenon), and the omnipotence of thought in stories such as Schiller's *The Ring of Polycrates*. In most of those cases, the uncanny feeling is associated either with the repulsion and the recurrence of personal, childhood complexes or with historically repressed beliefs or primitive feelings which 'recur in the shape of an uncanny effect'.[4]

However, in the final part of his essay, Freud notes:

> It may be true that the uncanny is nothing else than a hidden, familiar thing that has undergone repression and then emerged from it, and that everything that is uncanny fulfils this condition. But these factors do not solve the problem of the uncanny. For our proposition is clearly not convertible. Not everything that fulfils this condition – not everything that is connected with repressed desires and archaic forms of thought belonging to the past of the individual and of the race – is therefore uncanny. [. . .] It is evident that we must be prepared to admit that there are other elements besides those set down here determining the production of uncanny feelings. We might say that these preliminary results have satisfied psychoanalytic interest in the problem of the uncanny, and that what remains probably calls for an aesthetic valuation.[5]

In other words, Freud realises that the psychoanalytic aspect of the uncanny feeling, although important for a deeper understanding of the human psyche, does not encompass the totality of the Uncanny. Beyond its role as a signifier of a personal repulsion, the Uncanny stands for every familiar element which is converted into an unfamiliar one.

In her attempt to expand the Freudian uncanny into the aesthetic field and to delineate its role in the creation of an artwork, Angelidi counterposes Freud's term with Victor Shklovsky's concept of defamiliarisation, the process of making something familiar look strange through the creation of art. In line with Russian formalism's attempt to discover a scientific grounding of the art experience, Shklovsky analyses the poetic function of language and its capacity to refresh our mental operations by disrupting the automatism of perception and re-introducing the world to us:

Habitualisation devours work, clothes, furniture, one's wife, and the fear of war. If the whole complex lives of many people go on unconsciously, then such lives are as if they had never been. And art exists that one may recover the sensation of life; it exists to make one feel things, to make the stone stony. The purpose of art is to impart the sensation of things as they are perceived and not as they are known. The technique of art is to make objects 'unfamiliar', to make forms difficult, to increase the difficulty and length of perception because the process of perception is an aesthetic end in itself and must be prolonged.[6]

The process of making strange or difficult something familiar which has been rendered invisible through our ordinary perception of the world is presented as the central difference between everyday language, which is designed in order to transfer a message from an addressor to an addressee in the most accurate way, and poetic language, which is destined to disrupt the over-automatisation of human perception and to revitalise the ordinary by portraying it in a new, more ambiguous and strange way. Taking also into consideration the strong focus of Russian formalists on the constructed nature of the artwork and the possibility to understand it as a system of signs, *ostranenie* becomes the basic guideline to recognise and decode the status of those signs and the interactions between them.

The concept of defamiliarisation had a great impact upon the art theory of the twentieth century, which gradually moved from a conception of art as a mechanism of representing physical phenomena towards art as an apparatus of re-inventing the world. The Russian formalist poetics, combined with Ferdinand de Saussure's linguistics. lead us to Christian Metz and his *Grande Syntagmatique du Film Narratif* (1966) ('The large syntagmatic category of narrative film'), while in Bertolt Brecht's work, *ostranenie* was transformed into *Verfremdungseffekt* ('estrangement effect') – a type of aesthetic estrangement which blocks the spectator's involvement with the characters and the actions of the narrative, and confers upon the latter an elevated, intellectual stimulus. David Bordwell's and Kristin Thompson's neoformalist approach to cinema and its historical poetics was also heavily influenced by the Russian formalists and especially by the famous film theory anthology *Poetika Kino* (1927), edited by Boris Eikhenbaum. In the third part of her essay, Angelidi tracks the traces of Freud's *unheimlich* and Shklovsky's *ostranenie* in Bordwell's and Thompson's film theory, where the uncanny becomes once again a central concept of the analysis of film and its perception by the audience. Their strong focus on cinematic form, part of which is also the meaning of the film itself, leads them to a specific methodological approach to film where the basic goal is not to interpret the 'hidden' meaning of the filmic text but to accurately describe and represent the unique mechanism through which it is constructed:

from the movement of the camera to costumes and the lighting setup, film depicts reality and, at the same time, defamiliarises it.

However, this dedication to the cinematic form led Bordwell to reject the hermeneutic approaches to cinema, such as the post-structuralist trend in film theory and Lacanian psychoanalysis. In *Post-Theory: Reconstructing Film Studies* (1996), Bordwell, along with Noël Carroll, presents all such theoretical approaches as 'Grand Theories'; sets of pre-determined theoretical schemes which describe films as instances of their proposed worldview. Several aspects of art and its impact on human perception, such as the status of the viewer-subject, the process of identification, the socially constructed practices and institutions or the linguistic nature of meaning, according to Bordwell and Carroll, are detected in filmic texts through specific interpretive prisms and analysed in such ways that they inevitably lead to the confirmation of their pre-established, theoretical framework.

Although there are many similarities between the Freudian conception of the uncanny and the (neo)formalist concept of defamiliarisation, there seems to be a theoretical incompatibility concerning the way in which they can be used alongside each other in order to describe the construction of an artwork and the process of its reception by the spectator. Its strict focus upon the cinematic form and the rejection of interpretive approaches in film theory renders Bordwell's neoformalism severely incompatible with the psychoanalytic film approach and any attempt to unify them in an alternative poetics of cinema will meet at least some considerable theoretical obstacles.

Despite the theoretical discontinuity between the psychoanalytical and the neoformalist approaches to film, the value of the concepts of the uncanny and the process of defamiliarisation in the understanding of the structural mechanisms of films should not be underestimated. Instead of taking a strong stance in the debate between the conflicting approaches, in this chapter I will attempt to analyse this feeling/mechanism, without getting engaged in an interpretative approach. In the following sections, I will present an alternative approach to the defamiliarisation technique based on Derrida's concept of *writing-under-erasure*, which I will later use to describe the way in which meaning is produced in Angelidi's debut feature film.

DERRIDA'S CONCEPT OF *WRITING-UNDER-ERASURE*

Although Derrida's theoretical starting point is Husserl's phenomenology, the link between his work and structuralism is a really important one: the notions of *différance*, *écriture* and the conception of language as a never-ending chain of signifiers are, in some way, the products of his critique of Saussurean linguistics and structuralism.

Saussure is faithful to the tradition that has always associated writing with the fatal violence of the political institution. It is clearly a matter, as with Rousseau, for example, of a break with nature, of a usurpation that was coupled with the theoretical blindness to the natural essence of language, at any rate to the natural bond between the 'instituted signs' of the voice and 'the first language of man'.[7]

For Derrida, the Saussurean distinction between the signifier and the signified is a dichotomy which bears important resemblances to other traditional dichotomies in Western thought, such as matter and spirit or idea and object. According to Derrida, 'the distinction between signifier and signified can only be rigorously maintained if one term within the realm of signification is believed to be final, incapable of referring beyond itself to any other term',[8] – that is, if they are forming a *binary opposition*. And all those binary oppositions, for Derrida, are indications of strong metaphysical tendencies in our thought which lead to contradictions and prevent us from realising that the terms of such oppositions are complementing each other.

By contrasting the metaphysical conception of those binary oppositions, Derrida describes signification as a 'scandalous supplementarity', where meaning is never fully present but is produced by the acentric play between the signifiers. He borrows the notion of *supplement* from Freud (*nachträglich*),[9] who uses it to describe 'a mode of belated understanding or retroactive attribution of sexual or traumatic meaning to earlier events [. . .]',[10] and goes further to suggest that psychic life is produced by 'a logic that relates missing meaning to a surplus of meaning, a "not enough" to a "too much", and acknowledges a "too late" at the heart of the feeling and meaning of now'.[11] Derrida detects this type of supplementarity in Strauss's description of 'floating signifiers': words like 'mana', which simultaneously denotes the life force, the spiritual power and the act of healing in the culture of the Melanesians and Polynesians, and can be at the same time a noun and a verb, and can refer to forces and actions, qualities and states.

> But is it not precisely because it is none of these things that *mana* is a simple form, or more exactly, a symbol in the pure taste, and therefore capable of becoming charged with any sort of symbolic content whatever? In the system of symbols constituted by all cosmologies, mana would simply be a zero symbolic form, that is to say, a sign marking the necessity of a symbolic content supplementary to that which the signified is already loaded, but which can take on any value required, provided only that this value still remains part of the available reserve and is not, as phonologists put it, a group-term.[12]

This 'overabundance of the signifier' in Claude Lévi-Strauss, which contradicts the Saussurean symmetry between the signifier and the signified, this 'surplus of signification' is the basic presupposition of the symbolic thought, which constantly rearranges those excessive or lacking units of meaning in order to produce meaning. 'Signification plays against the organisation of signifiers in relation to signifieds that thought is – and that same play provokes thought to try to bind signifiers into conceptual systems and maintain itself.'[13] However, those signifieds are never absolutely present but at any time they can be transformed into signifiers and start a new play of signification. Yet if there is no symmetry between signifier and signified, if sign is not a complete unit of meaning but marks a lack of it, if every signified is a potential signifier, then what is the reason for us to keep using those Saussurean terms after their, almost complete, conceptual subversion?

As we have already seen, Derrida strongly criticises the Saussurean distinction between the signifier and the signified as a metaphysical, binary opposition. However, every attempt to express such concepts in a new, non-metaphysical way is destined to fail. For this reason, Derrida uses all those concepts borrowed from the Western philosophical (and metaphysical) tradition *under erasure*: a method, adopted by Heidegger, where terms are crossed out as 'a means of clearing away the centuries of metaphysical connotations that had acquired to them and returning to their original [. . .] meanings'.[14] As Derrida himself notes with regard to the similarly metaphysically charged concept of experience:

> Like all the notions I am using here, it belongs to the history of metaphysics and we can only use it under erasure [sous rature]. 'Experience' has always designated the relationship with a presence [. . .]. At any rate, we must, according to this sort of contortion and contention which the discourse is obliged to undergo, exhaust the resources of the concept of experience (or sign – again, my comment) before attaining and in order to attain, by deconstruction, its ultimate foundation.[15]

In the case of Derrida's version of *sous rature*, the crossed-out term is not destined to return to its pure semiotic origins (as in Heidegger) but to reveal the status of its meaning, which is simultaneously present and absent: a temporary stage between the eternal conversion of the sign into a signifier, the signifier into a sign, and so forth. Meaning is never stabilised and revealed in its totality but always remains unfinished and incomplete, a middle point between 'not enough' and 'too much'. This eternal incompleteness of meaning, this 'always already absent present' (1970), becomes the theoretical base of Derrida's alternative to all the previous philosophical ontologies which are rooted in the field of the *metaphysics of presence*[16] – a new glance to a world, a reality and a history which is not inhabited by complete units of meaning and things in-themselves but by ghosts and spectres: What is a ghost? What is the effectivity or the presence of a spectre, that is, of what seems to remain as ineffective, virtual, insubstantial as a simulacrum? Is there *there*, between the thing itself and its simulacrum, an opposition that holds up? Repetition and first time, but also repetition and last time, since the singularity of any first time makes of it also a last time. Each time it is the event itself, a first time is a last time. Altogether other. Staging for the end of history. Let us call it a hauntology.[17]

Every time a term is crossed out, every time something familiar is recalled *under erasure*, a spectre of it is born and stands out as a singular and unique existence, a repetition which is never the same as an older one and will never be the same as a future one – a ghost whose *uncanny* temporality makes it return from the past and simultaneously, be born for the first time.

In his attempt to detect a link between Derrida's hauntology and the mechanism of self-reflection in experimental cinema, Akira Mizuta Lippit recalls the concept of the Derridean spectre and explores the relation between visibility and invisibility as positive forms of the image which, when superimposed over one another, form a unique *seeing blindness* – a phenomenon which is bound to both reflection and representation – in every attempt of depicting familiar thoughts that return and are converted into unfamiliar reflections, 'crystallizations of thought as images, but also thoughts that have been turned back, rendered spectral'.[18] Cinema, as well as photography, is a medium that reproduces such reflections and functions as a mechanical double of this *seeing blindness* by reproducing visible images of familiar things and rendering them invisibly unfamiliar through the *sous rature* technique.

The similarities between the Derridean conception of *writing-under-erasure* and *spectrality* with the Freudian uncanny and the formalist defamiliarisation are obvious: in all those cases, we are confronted with familiar elements which are turned into unfamiliar through a specific process and acquire a unique existential status, either artistic, in the case of formalism, or not. However, Derrida gets beyond the observation of the human psyche or the constructive base of the artwork and, through his own version of the 'uncanny', synthesises an ontology of meaning itself. In the following sections, I will attempt to trace the *writing-under-erasure* technique in Angelidi's debut film, recognise and present its filmic *spectres* and delineate the meaning production process of this filmic text. However, it is important to note at this point that the Derridean concepts will be used mostly as an alternative scheme of representing the filmic uncanny; their philosophical and semiological content is of course much wider and their use in a film analysis does not exhaust their theoretical potentials.

IDÉES FIXES / DIES IRAE: 'VARIATIONS ON THE SAME SUBJECT' (1977)

Angelidi's film begins with a static, wide shot of a graveyard. The image is accompanied by a continuous, monotonous sound produced by a wind instrument, probably a saxophone. The duration of the shot is about 8 minutes and the only movement inside the frame is the slow walk of two dark figures who seem to walk away from the cemetery. The whole frame functions as a transparent, painting canvas and we can still see the upper and the lower part of its tripod, as in René Magritte's painting *The Promenades of Euclid* (1955) (Figure 5.1).

In this first shot, both the Derridean concepts of *sous rature* and *spectrality* are at work. Magritte's painting is recalled *under erasure* – its main theme (the twin forms of the cupolas) is replaced by the static cemetery and the painting's central theme, illusion versus reality, is recalled and re-written in the new, audiovisual medium. The familiar moment of Surrealist art history is rendered unfamiliar, erased by its previous semiotic content and re-filled with a new one.

The scenery of the cemetery is a perfect representation of the simultaneous presence and absence, a topographic signifier which marks the absence of life through the presence of the cemetery's site – the absence of meaning through the use of a filmic sign. And this attempt to represent the absent, to create an image of what is missing, will be a central theme of the whole film. And Magritte's painting functions as a *supplement* of this semiotic absence, which nourishes the shot's *not enough* with a semiotic *too much*. And through Angelidi's attempt to represent this absence, image accents both of its positive forms – the visible and the invisible – and renders its viewing as a process of a *seeing blindness*. And the same holds for the sound which accompanies the shot: after the first two or three minutes, the continuous and monotonous sonic background is converted into an audible silence, a sound which is there but which, due to the total ellipse of any rhythmic melody, seems to function as an audio representation of the absence – a sound which is not a sound.

This static shot also blurs the boundaries between cinema, photography and painting. The three media and their shared capability of visual representation are *erased* and cinema (or, most accurately, its common conception) is almost eliminated and becomes an empty, 'invisible' canvas in order for Angelidi to re-invent it in the following shots. The faint movement of the two black figures in the upper part of this static frame seems also to function as a spectre of cinematography at the core of an immobile picture – a visual supplement of immobility. And although all those antithetical pairs seem to recall binary oppositions (life/death, presence/absence, visible/invisible, movement/immobility), their representation becomes possible only through the supplementary synergy of their two poles.

After the cemetery shot, we are once again confronted with another static shot, this time of a corridor, with three still human figures in the middle of it, and a fourth slowly walking across the long path. The duration of the shot is almost 7 minutes and, this time, the accompanying sound is the locational atmosphere of an urban road.

While the dialectics between immobility and movement, mentioned above, remains the same, a new antithetical pair emerges in this shot, which adds one of the basic semiotic layers of the whole film. The gender of the four human figures is not easily established from this wide shot: the three still figures seem to wear black suits but they also seem to have long hair. The moving figure is bold and wears a long black robe. Gender in this shot (and in the whole movie) seems also to be written *under erasure:* recognisable gendered traits (hair and clothing) are recalled through *sous rature* and lose their descriptive ability by being antithetically counterposed.

The movement of the bold figure, centred in the frame and constituting the only motion element of this still frame, makes the viewer wonder about its direction: does this figure go towards an unknown destination or is it moving away from somewhere? Is she or he moving into the corridor or moving out of it? This simultaneous presentation of in and out spatiality structures, once again, an antithetical part which is deconstructed through its spectrality.

The bold figure is finally out of the frame and the shot ends. In the next shot, we find the three still figures now placed in an interior space, probably a house, and their ambiguous gender is revealed: they seem like men, dressed in black suits, while their polished, long hair signals the incomplete presence of femininity. The big bold figure is also in this house, now wearing a long white robe, and is revealed to be a hairless woman. The contradiction of pure black-

Figure 5.1 Still, Angelidi, *Idées Fixes / Dies Irae* (1977).

and-white elements, mostly in the clothing of the characters, marks another antithetical pair which is semi-tonally incorporated in the grey tones of the black-and-white film.

The semiotic play between black and white is developed further in the subsequent shots, where we are confronted with a frame which is vertically divided into two parts (Figure 5.2). The left side of the frame is completely black, while the right side is totally white. The bold woman, placed in the white side of the frame and still wearing her white robe, sits on a chair and holds a black fowl in her hands. She seems to play with it and the shot is accompanied by a strange, distorted nursery rhyme which is suddenly disrupted by the woman's intense laughter. She stands up, moves towards the black side of the frame before soon after coming back holding the dead body of the fowl, which she begins to pluck. Finally, she moves towards the camera, vanishes from the frame and a word appears in the left side of the white part of the frame

Once again, Derrida's concepts all work together at this point of the film. The *writing-under-erasure* of the nursery rhyme recalls a familiar sound of childhood and crosses it out, in order to convert it into an uncanny, strange and almost horrifying soundtrack of the fowl's coming death. And this simultaneous representation of a tender and playful atmosphere with a dangerous and horrifying one supplements the bold woman's interaction with the fowl, starting with a tender hug and ending up in the plucking of its corpse.

This play between the opposites is intensified by the graphical construction of the frame. The supplemental co-existence of visibility and invisibility inside the image is depicted through the vertical division of the frame, which allows the invisible to be represented (but not viewed) alongside the visible. Invisibility always penetrates the visible, in the same way that black colour enters the white side of the frame (fowl's feathers). Invisibility, or blackness, or blindness, always renders the visible incomplete and in need of a supplement – it is a necessary ELLIPSE which allows the constant recall and re-writing of the signifiers. And for the first time, a printed word appears on the screen, as a linguistic supplement of the visual – a technique which will also play a central role throughout the whole film.

In the next scene, more printed words appear on the screen: MIMESIS and FEMME NUE. The bold woman sits in front of a giant advertising poster (probably of a detergent) and two women dressed in black stand either side of her. The two little girls depicted on the poster, although printed replicas, seem to participate in this filmic portrait as actual members of it. The advertisement catchphrase '. . . *maman sans se fatiguer c'est simple comme* . . .' ('. . . mother without getting tired, it is as easy as . . .') is not fully exposed. The shot is accompanied by a distorted nursery rhyme.

The familiar advertisement is erased and its depictions of femininity through the innocent little girls laughing in the picture and the housewife-mother in

Figure 5.2 Still, Angelidi, *Idées Fixes / Dies Irae* (1977).

the catchphrase are recalled in order to be counterposed with the uncanny, neutralised women figures in front of the poster. There is a *mimesis* here, a mimesis of a mimesis – a reproduction of an advertisement which is a photographic reproduction of two girls. But all the reproductions, all the repetitions, are unique singularities, ghosts which do not 'always return only later [. . .] (but) are always there in the living, and haunt the present in advance. They are [. . .] the condition of possibility of all work.'[19] And the counterposition of the advertising replica with the film's estranged depictions of the female lead to the *femme nue:* the image of woman *under erasure*, stripped of its cultural context and reinvented as a blank canvas, ready to be re-written.

The *writing-under-erasure* technique is depicted in exemplary fashion in the next scene of the film, where two men, wearing female underwear, are posing in front of another advertising poster and soliloquise a prose, half in Greek and half in French, based on free association. Among other lines, one of the men says in Greek: 'The political position, as well as femininity, are merchandises.' Diagonal black lines *cross out* the whole frame while the words *famille* ('family') and *état* ('state') are screened upon their almost naked bodies. Finally, the camera zooms out and we are confronted with a studio set of cameras, lights and microphones. The viewer realises that she was watching the recording of a strange tv spot while the catchphrase of the poster advertisement is also revealed: *Êtes-vous a gauche ou a droite?* ('Are you on the left or the right?') In the next shot, a French man, dressed in men's clothing, stands once again in front of the advertising poster. This time, the diagonal lines are crossing out the poster and not the filmic frame (Figure 5.3). The man says in Greek: 'The political position, as well as femininity, are *not* merchandises.'

The popular political advertisement is literally *crossed out* and recalled *under erasure*. The polarised, political dilemma between the left-wing and the right-wing political parties is visually deconstructed (once again through the graphical construction of the frame), while most of the lines uttered by the male models acquire a simultaneously realistic and ironic aspect: femininity, as well as political positions, become saleable objects used by marketing and advertising in the capitalist era. However, in the final shot of the film, the French man (who utters a Greek phrase) stands in front of the erased advertisement and states clearly his opinion – an opinion which is not susceptible to the *under erasure* technique and may be echoing the director's personal set of beliefs.

The superimposition of the advertisement video inside the film creates, once again, a filmic field of spectrality – a repetition filmed by the cinematic camera, a reproduced reproduction which is, at the same time, a second-order simulacrum and a unique singularity. The cinematic mechanism is also recalled *under erasure* – the camera creates an image of an image, re-invents its creative capabilities while, at the same time, reveals the construction behind the creation of every image.

The cinematic play with the printed words reappears in the next scene in the form of the static wide shot of the neon sign LA DEFENSE inside the Paris Metro. The spectator's gaze follows the camera's pause of movement in front of the station's sign. The shot's duration is about 7 minutes, while the audio background is the locational atmosphere of the underground station.

The double message of the sign, although not self-contrasting, functions as a reminder of the instability of linguistic signs. This is the station of La Défense, but the sign defends itself from a singular interpretation and functions as a fence against any semiotic totalitarisation. The familiar neon sign is recalled *under erasure* and, as the spectator focuses upon its filmic replica, it is transformed into Angelidi's aesthetic warning: this film is defending itself and its meaning. It is not a common piece of merchandise. As Christos Vakalopoulos notes about this shot:

> The shot in the tunnel which violently falls upon this sign, the DEFENSE, the defence of us all in the cinema, the defence of cinema itself, the defence of this image. How will the phallic wandering in the tunnel end up? Here is something closed, unknown. DEFENSE, who bore to watch this shot and this game? [. . .] the autonomy of the signifier is unbearable, until you surrender to your confrontation with it.[20]

The filmic play with the printed words and the signs continues in the next shot where two random commercial signs are framed in order to synthesise a single phrase: 'Jouets' 'Organiques' (i.e., organic toys). Their counterposition in the same frame marks their double *erasure* and their transformation into a linguistic sign of one of the film's main themes: the objectification of the female body and its transformation into merchandise.

This double encoding of the female body, as an organic entity and as a saleable and usable object is also revisited a few moments later, in the close-up of a vulva, upon which are screened the words: *usage externe* ('external use'). At

DERRIDEAN SPECTRALITY IN *IDÉES FIXES / DIES IRAE*   119

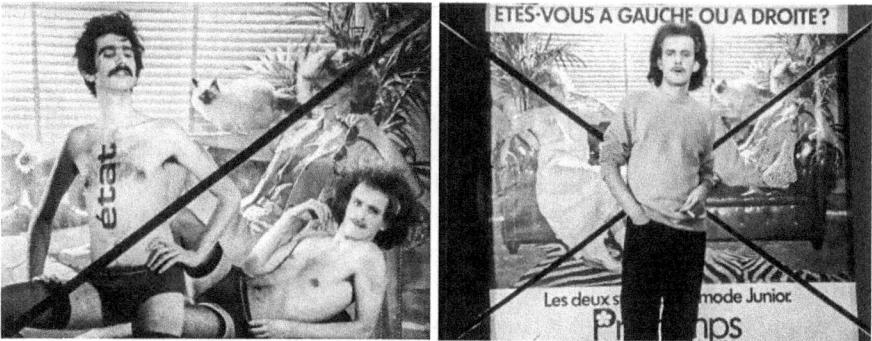

Figure 5.3 Still, Angelidi, *Idées Fixes / Dies Irae* (1977).

the same time, a female voice sings the lyrics 'I am fine, I am fine, really fine, I wish the same for you'. The screened words seem to function also as labels of the vulva, informing us about its use and, at the same time, parodying our conception of the female body. The symbol of femininity is *erased* through its portrayal as an object which can be used externally. The lyrics of Mikis Theodorakis's song, 'The Letter', which is based upon the letter of a political prisoner, are also recalled *under erasure* – the familiar song is *erase*d and re-written, acquiring the autonomy described by Derrida as the singularity of the repetition. The uncanny song, whose utterance opens up a dialogue with the screened image, functions as double, semi-ironic statement of the contemporary female, who is fine, despite her external use but also pretends to be fine, due to the fact that she has been converted into an external use object – a prisoner in her own body, due to gender stereotyping and patriarchy.

The *writing-under-erasure* of linguistic signs reaches its maximum in the next scene, where women wander inside a room while Angelidi herself soliloquises words from a Greek dictionary, all of them starting with the letter A. The enunciation of the words is rhythmical, with an emphasis on their first letter, while the sound of a drum highlights the sound of the first two syllables of each word.

All those worlds are recalled *under erasure* and appose each other not as linguistic signs but as sounds which synthesise an uncanny melody. The absence of the linguistic meaning at the core of spoken words becomes audible, while their meaning is totally *erased* and replaced by its aesthetic function. Words become the spectres of their selves while the strange melody, produced by their utterance, transforms them into semi-empty forms, ready to be also *externally used*. Gradually, the frame is emptied by the presence of the women, and we are confronted with a white screen – a present absence of filmic content, a seeing blindness which penetrates the spectators' perception and once again, *erases* cinematic experience itself.

The close-up of a female mouth follows, where the tongue licks the perimeter of the lips in an extremely slow tempo. The human organ and the moving tongue are portrayed as estranged and as we focus on this slow movement, we almost forget we are watching a human mouth. The erasure of the human body, once again playful and terrifying, is graphically linked with the close-up of the vulva and seems to echo a similar spectrality: an organ which loses its primary functions (to speak, to eat, etc.) and becomes an aesthetic object in front of a camera – a semi-empty form ready to be *used externally* by the director in order to fulfil her aesthetic goals. Finally, the mouth opens, and a pair of hands put a razor blade on its lips: playing (with the signifiers) is paired, once again, with an unknown danger, as in the scene with the bold lady and the fowl.

In the next close-up, Angelidi reads another text, again based on free association, in front of the camera. The text, spoken half in Greek and half in French, highlights most of the film's themes without analysing them in a strict and logical way. Mostly presented as splinters of speech, her lines succeed one another at high speed, and the meaning is once again in a state of simultaneous presence and absence. At some point, Angelidi begins to repeat in Greek the phrase 'Their men died relatively young', with slight syntactic differentiations (their men relatively young died, died relatively young their men, etc.). In front of her face appears written a complete list of all the possible syntactic rephrases of the line in French. In this playful experiment with language, Angelidi once again tests the capability of the signifiers to empty themselves and be instantly re-filled through slight differentiations in their organisation. The phrase is crossed out, erased and instantly re-written with the same words, without, however, retaining its previous meaning. And through this audio experiment, the *sous rature* technique is once again presented through the absence of meaning's stability.

Angelidi's monologue is followed by a static shot of Angelidi inside a bath, wearing a white turban. Another printed word is screened upon the filmic image: HORIZON (Figure 5.4). The shot is a clear reference to Jacques-Louis David's painting *The Death of Marat* (1793), which is recalled again *under erasure* – the director represents one more classical and familiar representation and re-writes its content by replacing its central character with herself. In one of her interviews, where she was commenting on the political aspect of her debut film, Angelidi notes:

> In one point of the film there is a representation of David's painting *The Death of Marat*, where I myself re-enact Marat inside the bath. First, we have to note that the painting itself describes the dead-end of a revolutionary historical persona: this dead-end is David's painting itself, the fact that David created that painting and not that he represents the dead Marat. My choice to represent the representation of a revolution inverts the logic of this representation. But, by placing also myself inside the

painting, I also become an object of such reversions and self-criticisms. When the person who writes acquires a place inside its film, this person reverses and parodies itself. And this is a political action.[21]

At this point, the *writing-under-erasure* has a double goal: to empty the popular painting from its previous meaning, re-invent its content and re-write it through the replacement of Marat with the image of the film's creator, who also appears *under erasure* – a self-critique of the director which is incorporated into her work. Once again, spectrality is at work: the woman inside the bath is Angelidi's spectre, a present absence formed under the eye of an external creator who tries to get inside her work and subvert both David's painting and her.

In the final scene of the film, there is a middle shot of a living room, with a window behind the sofa and a chessboard upon the coffee table. The printed word ELLIPSE appears vertically on the screen and soon, a team of young soldiers appear behind the window and stand still in front of the camera, while the popular Greek song 'Olaria Olara' (1972) plays in the background. Once again, the camera reproduces a representation: chess, a board game which represents a war battle, is situated in the centre of the frame while actual, living soldiers approach the scene and are counterposed with the game's imaginary setting. However, both the simulacra (chess pawns) and the actual soldiers are part of Angelidi's filmic representation and all of them are engaged in a dialectic between reality, illusion and replica. Finally, another printed word appears on

Figure 5.4 Still, Angelidi, *Idées Fixes / Dies Irae* (1977).

the screen and we hear a female voice read it aloud: CUISINE. The next shot, which is also the final shot of the film, is a static shot of the interior of a kitchen – a gendered space which will become the starting point of a new, both actual and spectral, revolution.

CONCLUSION

The main goal of this chapter was to propose an alternative method of reading and understanding Angelidi's filmic texts, beyond the theoretical tools provided to us by psychoanalysis or (neo)formalism. It is important to note that the Derridean concepts of *writing-under-erasure* and *spectrality* were not used in order to construct a strict and stable interpretative method, which would lead the spectator of Angelidi's film to the decoding of their 'secret symbols' and to the revelation of their 'true meaning'. On the contrary, the goal of the application of the Derridean concepts (as theoretical schemes) was the revealing of the unstable nature of meaning itself and the way in which it is constantly transformed, erased and re-created. This semiotic instability, along with the dialectic between the spectral and the actual, is also one of the main aesthetic tools used by Angelidi in the construction of her debut feature film and its central theme, the *variations* of which are visualised through the lenses of all her unconscious *fixed ideas*.

NOTES

1. Akira Mizuta Lippit, *Ex-Cinema: From a Theory of Experimental Film and Video* (London: University of California Press, 2012), 90.
2. Antoinetta Angelidi, 'The Game with the Uncanny – Poetics for the Cinema', in Angelidi, *Writings about Cinema: Interdisciplinary Approaches* (Athens: Nefeli, 2005).
3. Sigmund Freud, *The Uncanny*, trans. Alix Strachey (Boston, MA: MIT, 2001), 4, <https://web.mit.edu/allanmc/www/freud1.pdf>, accessed 1 June 2022.
4. Freud, *The Uncanny*, 14.
5. Ibid., 15–16.
6. Viktor Shklovsky, 'Art as Technique', in *Literary Theory: An Introduction*, ed. Julie Rivkin and Michael Ryan (Oxford: Wiley Blackwell, 2017), 9.
7. Jacques Derrida, *Of Grammatology*, trans. C. G. Spivak (Baltimore: The Johns Hopkins Unveristy Press, 1997), 36.
8. Kaja Silverman, *The Subject of Semiotics* (USA: Oxford University Press, 1983), 33–4.
9. 'Everything begins with reproduction Always already: repositor- ies of a meaning which was never present, whose signified presence is always reconstituted by deferral, nachträglich, belatedly, supplementarily: for the nachträglich also means supplementary.' Jacques Derrida, *Of Grammatology*, trans. A. Bass (New York: Routledge, 2001), 266.
10. Teresa de Lauretis, *Freud's Drive: Psychoanalysis, Literature and Film* (Basingstoke: Palgrave Macmillan, 2008), 118.
11. Sarah Wood, *Derrida' s 'Writing and Difference': A Reader' s Guide* (New York: Continuum, 2009), 148.

12. Claude Lévi-Strauss, *Introduction to the Work of Marcel Mauss*, trans. F. Baker (London: Routledge & Kegan Paul, 1987), 64.
13. Wood, *Derrida's 'Writing and Difference'*, 152.
14. Arthur Bradley, *Derrida's Of Grammatology: An Edinburgh Philosophical Guide* (Edinburgh: Edinburgh University Press, 2008), 151.
15. Jacques Derrida, *Of Grammatology*, trans. C. G. Spivak, 60.
16. The main focus of the Western philosophical tradition on the completeness of meaning, which is always present and can be easily and immediately be accessed and processed.
17. Jacques Derrida, *Specters of Marx*, trans. Peggy Kamuf (New York: Routledge, 1994), 10.
18. Lippit, *Ex-Cinema: From a Theory of Experimental Film and Video*, 90.
19. Ibid., 87.
20. Christos Vakalopoulos, 'Chronicle 1978', in *Time-Letters-Arts* (Athens: Gallery Ora, 1978), my translation.
21. Antoinetta Angelidi, 'Discussion with A. Angelidi and Fr. Liapa with Chr. Vakalopoulos and M. Dimopoulos', in *Contemporary Cinema* 17/18 (1978).

BIBLIOGRAPHY

Angelidi, Antoinetta. «Το παιχνίδι με το ανοικείο – Μια Ποιητική του Κινηματογράφου», in *Γραφές για τον Κινηματογράφο, Διεπιστημονικές προσεγγίσεις*, ed. Chrysanthi Sotiropoulou. Athens: Nefeli, 2005, 11–35.
Angelidi, Antoinetta. «Συζήτηση με την Α. Αγγελίδη και τη Φρ. Λιάππα με τους Χρ. Βακαλόπουλο και Μ. Δημόπουλο». Interview by Christos Vakalopoulos and Michalis Dimopoulos, in *Σύγχρονος Κινηματογράφος*, Athens, no. 17/18, 1978.
Bordwell, David, and Kristin Thompson. *Film Art: An Introduction*. Boston: McGraw-Hill, 2001.
Bradley, Arthur. *Derrida's Of Grammatology: An Edinburgh Philosophical Guide*. Edinburgh: Edinburgh University Press, 2008.
Carroll, Noel and David Bordwell (eds). *Post-Theory: Reconstructing Film Studies*. Madison: University of Wisconsin Press, 1996.
Derrida, Jacques. *Specters of Marx*, trans. Peggy Kamuf. New York: Routledge, 1994.
Derrida, Jacques. *Of Grammatology*, trans. C. G. Spivak. Baltimore: The Johns Hopkins Unveristy Press, 1997.
Freud, Sigmund. *The Uncanny*, trans. Alix Strachey. Boston, MA: MIT Press, 2001.
Lauretis, Teresa de. *Freud's Drive: Psychoanalysis, Literature and Film*. Basingstoke: Palgrave Macmillan, 2008.
Lévi-Strauss, Claude. *The Raw and the Cooked*, trans. J. and D. Weightman. London: Cape, 1969.
Lippit, Akira Mizuta. *Ex-Cinema: From a Theory of Experimental Film and Video*. London: University of California Press, 2012.
Shklovsky, Viktor. 'Art as Technique', in *Literary Theory: An Anthology*, ed. Julie Rivkin and Michael Ryan. Oxford: Wiley Blackwell, 2017, 8–15.
Silverman, Kaja. *The Subject of Semiotics*. USA: Oxford University Press, 1983.
Vakalopoulos, Christos. 'Chronicle 1978', in *Time-Letters-Arts*. Athens: Gallery Ora, 1978.
Wood, Sarah. *Derrida's 'Writing and Difference': A Reader's Guide*. New York: Continuum, 2009.

CHAPTER 6

The Cinematic Sublime in Antoinetta Angelidi's *Thief or Reality*

Evdokia Stefanopoulou

'What in me is dark, illumine.'

John Milton, *Paradise Lost* (1667)

Antoinetta Angelidi's cinema has been characterised as non-narrative, poetic, or visual. Indeed, her unique visual style and imagery often eludes classification, thus exemplifying a central aspect of the experimental film. Experimental or avant-garde cinema is a kind of non-conformist type of filmmaking that 'challenge[s] normal notions of what a movie can show and how it can show it', constantly subverting and reconfiguring the cinematic language.[1] Avant-garde cinema has also been associated with a politically enabling artistic practice that unsettles conventions and questions taken-for-granted values and structures. Angelidi's cinema exemplifies such definitions of the avant-garde or experimental, since her films constantly re-invent the cinematic language by using signifiers and codes in unexpected ways that challenge traditional ideas, and are usually inspired by the poetic strangeness of dreams. The director describes her film poetics as a

> particular approach to heterogeneity and codes, a play between defamiliarization and the uncanny, and the incorporation of lived experiences and fragments of re-interpreted artworks. Meaning-formation in dreams is a good model on which to conceptualize and understand synthetically all these elements.[2]

As evident from the above statement, the dream-mechanism, defamiliarisation and the uncanny are central aspects of Angelidi's radical poetics. However, as the director stresses, the concept of the uncanny does not refer to themes, as in the case of horror films, but rather to a structure: 'the entire film partakes of a structure of strangeness, thus producing the defamiliarizing effect of revealing the world in a novel way'.³ Despite the unquestionable centrality of the uncanny in Angelidi's work, I would like to suggest another related concept that can describe her cinema: the sublime.

The sublime and the uncanny are associated, since the latter has been described as 'the aesthetic outgrowth of the Burkean sublime, a domesticated version of absolute terror'.⁴ The sublime is 'a response to a shock of imaginative expansion, a complex recoil and recuperation of self-consciousness coping with phenomena suddenly perceived to be too great to be comprehended'.⁵ Similar to the uncanny, the sublime in Angelidi's cinema does not refer to themes, as for example in the case of fantastic films where the sublime is associated with the representation of spectacular vistas or extraordinary phenomena. Rather the sublime refers to the production of certain rhetorical and poetic effects that shape the director's unique cinematic language. The aim of this chapter is to describe how Angelidi's *Thief or Reality* (2001) expresses the sublime in cinematic form. Firstly, I present briefly two major theorisations of the sublime, while also expanding upon notions of sublimity in art and more specifically in cinema. In the second part, I discuss how Angelidi's *Thief or Reality* exemplifies some of the characteristics and concepts associated with the sublime in art, as presented in the first section. Finally, the chapter concludes that the sublime as the aesthetic expression of the dual structure of transcendence, enables the expansion and transformation of cinematic vision.

BURKE, KANT AND THE CINEMATIC SUBLIME

The concept of the sublime has its origins in a Greek treatise entitled *Περί Ύψους (On the Sublime)*, which is attributed to Longinus and dated to the first century. The manuscript was discovered in 1554, but gained critical attention only after its French translation by Nicolas Boileau in 1674. Boileau's preface of the translated manuscript was highly influential and introduced the concept of Ύψος – translated as sublime – to the European literary criticism of the late seventeenth and early eighteenth centuries. The sublime gradually became one of the most significant concepts in the field of aesthetics, philosophy and modern thought in general.⁶ The concept was established and solidified with Edmund Burke's *A Philosophical Enquiry into the Origin of Our Ideas of the Sublime and the Beautiful* (1757) and even more with Immanuel Kant's *Critique of the Power of Judgment* (1790). Notwithstanding that there have been numerous publications discussing the notion of sublimity (included in the work of John Dennis, Friedrich Schiller, Arthur Schopenhauer, Samuel Taylor Coleridge, G. W. F. Hegel, Jacques Derrida, Jacques Rancière, Jean-François

Lyotard, etc.), no treatise has been more influential than Burke's or Kant's exploration of the sublime. Therefore, this chapter focuses on these seminal theories of the sublime, which are used as a theoretical background in order to explore the cinematic sublime in Angelidi's work.

In his book *A Philosophical Enquiry into the Origin of Our Ideas of the Sublime and Beautiful*, first published in 1757, Edmund Burke conceives the sublime as an aesthetic simulation of risk perceived from a position of aesthetic distance, where the primary feeling is that of astonishment – a 'state of the soul, in which all its motions are suspended, with some degree of horror.'[7] The sublime elicits the contradictory sensation of 'delightful terror', a complex pleasure that both attracts and repels the subject. Unlike the beautiful, which is light, smooth and polished, the sublime must be necessarily obscure, because 'when we know the full extent of any danger . . . a great deal of the apprehension vanishes',[8] and therefore acquaintance alleviates even the most striking phenomena. Burke describes the sublime in terms of negations, or general privations, such as vacuity, darkness, solitude and silence. Other sources of the sublime include greatness of dimension, especially depth, where an immediate fear of the abyss is generated; infinity, which overwhelms the mind when trying to perceive it as a whole; magnificence; darkness or excessive light, as well as the sharp transitions between them; loudness, and great, confused, sudden or intermitting sounds. Sublimity is also induced by what Burke calls the 'artificial infinite', a vast construction characterised by succession and uniformity of parts, which give the impression of endlessness on bounded objects. Another artificial source of the sublime is difficulty, that is, 'when any work seems to have required immense force and labour to effect it, the idea is grand'.[9] As evident from the above descriptions, Burke draws examples from both the natural and the artificial world (art, culture), thus associating and converging the sublime in nature and in art. The artistic sublime engenders a similar experience and functions as an aesthetic simulation of a physical encounter with the sublime in nature. Burke thus acknowledges the possibility that human constructions and work of arts can elicit sublime wonder in the viewer.

Immanuel Kant in his *Critique of the Power of Judgment* (third critique), first published in 1790, stresses that the sublime – similarly to the beautiful – comprises judgements based on feelings, that is, not an evaluation that refers to objects themselves, but rather to the mind. Similar to Burke, the sublime is described as a complex feeling that merges pleasure with dread, and is distinguished from the beautiful not as mere opposition but as a 'counterweight'.[10] In contradiction to the beautiful, the sublime is characterised by three main traits: formlessness, limitlessness and the idea of totality. As Kant asserts, the sublime 'is to be found in a formless object insofar as limitlessness is represented in it, or at its instance, and yet it is also thought as a totality'.[11] Kant discerns two kinds of sublime: the mathematical and the dynamical, the one relating to ideas of grandeur (magnitude) and the other to power (terror).[12] The mathematical sublime is generated from the effort to aesthetically perceive magnitude, such as the infinity of the universe. In opposition, the dynamic sublime is an aesthetic response to nature as threatening power. Both categories of sublime evoke the Kantian idea of humans' ability to transcend limitations through reason's 'supersensible' vocation, that is, 'a faculty of the mind that surpasses every measure of the senses' in its attempt to approach unfathomable phenomena.[13] This is also the basis of the notion of immanent transcendence, a transcendence originating from within but also going beyond common human experience. However, the only way to grasp this extraordinary experience is through displaced representation, that is, by using the tools of science or art. Thus, although Kant privileges the perspective of nature in his discussion of the sublime, it is artistic representation that provides the model for 'the noncognitive experience of nature'.[14] According to Doran, despite the fact that Kant did not theorise the sublime in art in any sustained manner, some general remarks can be drawn mainly from scattered observations throughout the third critique in combination with Kant's *Anthropology from a Pragmatic Point of View*.[15] For example, Kant argued that while artistic representation must be beautiful, it can at the same time be sublime. The author favoured poetry as the medium most suited to express the sublime, often invoking Milton's *Paradise Lost* (1667) as the sublime artwork par excellence.[16] When it comes to visual art, Kant contended that due to its resemblance to what it represents, the sublime can be achieved with the use of indirect presentation. This suggests that sublimity in visual art may indeed have to be non-mimetic or para-mimetic.[17] Thus, from a Kantian perspective, the presence of sublimity in artistic representation is associated with indirect presentation and poetic figurations.

From the above brief presentation of the two major theorisations of the sublime we can trace certain oppositions and similarities. For Kant, who introduces the notion of the 'super-sensible', the sublime can be explained or negotiated rationally and therefore 'tends toward the noetic (the mental, the intellectual, the rational)'.[18] In contrast, for Burke the mental and rational explication of the sublime remains unattainable and subsequently the sublime is 'orientated toward the pathetic (terror, the irrational, the sensational)'.[19] However, both authors describe the sublime as generative of a complex pleasure that combines both attraction and repulsion and reflects its dual 'transcendence-structure'.[20] The sublime induces on the one hand the painful feeling of being overpowered, a feeling of inferiority or submission, and on the other hand it elicits the pleasure of ecstasy, that is, going outside or beyond oneself. This paradoxical experience of being at once overwhelmed and exalted by the encounter with the sublime recalls and to some extent reconfigures aesthetically the religious or mystical experience of transcendence.

The sublime's dual structure involves not only the natural world but also art. Burke alternated between examples of the sublime in nature and in art and included the notion of an aesthetic or artificial sublime. Kant mainly focused on the sublime in nature; however, as discussed, some general remarks about sublimity in art can be found throughout his work. Burke regarded the sublime in art as a simulated experience of a physical encounter with magnificent natural phenomena, while Kant similarly contended that artistic representation is a way to approach the sublime experience in nature. Although the authors did not provide a systematic analysis of the artistic sublime, Burke's privations (vacuity, darkness, solitude and silence) and Kant's ideas of formlessness, limitlessness and totality are concepts that can be extended, adapted and accommodated in artistic representation. What is more, Kant also set another parameter for the artistic sublime, especially in the visual arts: a degree of abstraction, or indirect presentation. Yet, when it comes to cinema – a medium well beyond Burke's and Kant's timeline – how is the sublime articulated? In what follows, I will not be delving into the literature of the sublime in cinema, since this would far exceed the scope of the chapter; rather, I focus on two particular theorisations, which are deemed most relevant to our topic.

One of the first discussions about the sublime in cinema is found in Gilles Deleuze's *Cinema 1: The Movement-Image* (1986). Deleuze associates the two types of Kantian sublime – the mathematical and the dynamic – with two cinematic movements, French impressionism and German expressionism, respectively. The two movements, each with its distinct characteristics, mark a break with the tradition of organic unity exemplified in classic American cinema, and in this disruption of unity the sublime emerges. French impressionism – as exemplified in the films of Abel Gance – displays an interest in 'the quantity of movement and in the metrical relations which allow us to define it', and is distinguished by 'a vast mechanical composition of movement-images'.[21] In the films of impressionism, one goes beyond the organic composition of bodies and the dialectical synthesis of their movements in order to abstract a single form, to extract 'a geometrical configuration of parts which combine, superimpose or transform movements in homogeneous space'.[22] Editing techniques gradually transform objects and elements into pure movement, thus abstracting the set of movements as a whole. It is exactly this gradual abstraction into a totality and simultaneity that Deleuze associates with the mathematical sublime, since the absolute maximum of movement is in itself 'identical to the incommensurable or the measureless, the gigantic, the immense'.[23] On the other hand, German expressionism is considered representative of the dynamic sublime. Here, impressionism's totality of movement is translated as the intensity of light and its stark opposition with darkness. This sharp opposition between light and darkness defines and organises not only the image but also the fictional worlds of expressionism, where the hero/heroine falls from lightness to dark. Contrary to the French school, German expressionism 'does not invoke the clear mechanics of the quantity of movement',[24] but a violent zigzagging between objects which are rendered bottomless or formless, merging into an intense totality. It is this powerful intensity which brings about a delightful terror that invokes Kant's dynamic sublime. Both impressionism and expressionism as antipodes of a realistic aesthetic tradition disrupt the organic unity of the image, thus invoking the mathematical and the dynamic sublime – the first by going beyond organic composition, the second by breaking it.

Other discussions related to the cinematic sublime tend towards the delineation of a specific film style. Film theorists, such as Paul Schrader (1972), Joseph Kickasola (2004), Richard Leonard (2009), and Vivian Sobchack (2015), among others, were interested in forms of sublimity in cinema which were described in terms of a transcendental film style. These film theorists suggested, in different ways, that films, whether narrative, non-narrative or experimental, and regardless of subject matter and form, can use different methods to inscribe the sublime in cinematic form. Specifically, Schrader's (1972) *Transcendental Style in Film: Ozu, Bresson, Dreyer* is quite instrumental in delineating specific stylistic techniques related to an aesthetic expression of transcendence. Schrader argues that the films of Robert Bresson, Yasujirō Ozu and Carl Theodor Dreyer, despite originating in different cultures and time periods, exemplify a style that can be called transcendental. Schrader defines the transcendental film style as a specific film form which aims to express the transcendent (i.e., the religious, the metaphysical). Although Schrader does not refer to the sublime per se or the Kantian transcendence,[25] I argue that his formulation of the transcendental style is illuminating and can delineate the cinematic sublime. Therefore, I am making a selective use of Schrader's argument by referring solely to his description of a specific style, relevant to the cinematic sublime. This style seeks to 'maximize the mystery of existence' and 'it eschews all conventional interpretations of reality'[26] by a subtle interplay between abundant and sparse means. Abundant means include cinematic tools and techniques that foster mimesis, sensation, realistic portraiture and empathy. In contrast, sparse means are 'cold, formalistic, hieratic. They are characterized by abstraction, stylized portraiture, two-dimensionality . . . [and] encourage . . . appreciation.'[27] It is exactly this ascetic movement, this gradual progression from abundant to sparse means, which exemplifies the sublime in cinema.

From Burke and Kant to Deleuze and Schrader, the sublime in art is closely associated with vacuity, indirect representation, abstraction and sparseness that 'forc[es] us to think an absolute of the movement of bodies, an infinity of the movement of light, a backgroundless of the movement of souls',[28] and foregrounds that which goes 'beyond normal sense experience'[29] and a familiar conception of reality. The cinematic sublime, through abstraction and suggestion, reflects the dual structure of transcendence – a complex recoil and recuperation of the mind towards images and sounds that disrupt the organic and familiar unity of mimesis, thus stretching the imagination to its limits. In what follows, I contend that Angelidi's *Thief or Reality* articulates the cinematic sublime in a unique way, combining certain of the aforementioned techniques and elements and transcending the established boundaries of cinematic vision.

A SUBLIME CINEMATIC VISION: *THIEF OR REALITY*

In *Thief or Reality*, three characters experience their own version of reality, producing different perspectives on life which are interwoven by the Thief – the invasion of reality, that is, time, finitude and mortality. The film presents three different versions of one Good Friday, a day of mourning in Holy Week, as experienced by three siblings: The Sculptress who has visions of the Last Judgement, the Scientist who mourns for her dead son, and the Actor who rehearses *Antigone*. These overlapping realities are organised in three segments, the Net, the Dice, and the Will, each one representing a different worldview (fate, chance and free will). This elliptical narrative is perfectly conveyed by an equally sparse and abstract style, articulating a unique cinematic sublime.

The film begins with an image of candles being blown out and the ensuing darkness – a source of sublimity – sets the main aesthetic tone that informs the entire cinematic text. The first part of the film, entitled the Net, is silent and begins with the dream/vision of the Sculptress. The frame is symmetrical, its synthesis organised around the centre of the image. The camera is static and the light is harsh, creating a desaturated and flat space devoid from the illusion of perspective. Blackness enfolds this brief, muted and de-colourised part, composing a *mise-en-scène* that alludes to silent cinema and especially Dreyer's *Vampyr* (1932).[30]

According to Schrader, Dreyer's works are informed by a perpetual disparity between different techniques, between abundant and sparse means, rendering his style similar to that of Gothic architecture.[31] Like a Gothic cathedral, Dreyer's films are characterised by unresolved incongruity, by tensions and contradictions between heterogenous elements – corporeality and spirituality, human passion and divine ecstasy, naturalistic empathy and stylistic abstraction. The sublime in Dreyer's films emerges from an abstraction composed from an intense dialogue between diverse forms. The sublime in *Thief or Reality* is also informed by such heterogeneity and monumentality. As Karalis claims, '[Angelidi's] distinct scenes could have been large panels or murals on the walls of cathedrals and prehistoric caves.'[32] The film's heterogenous sources of sublimity are further enhanced with allusions to and re-interpretations of other artworks.

Inspired by expressionistic films (e.g., the aforementioned *Vampyr* and *Faust* (1926)), the first part of the film goes beyond and reconfigures these references by creating an abstract space of geometric patterns. The dark world of the Sculptress's dream not only evokes the distorted spaces of expressionism, but also rearranges them in new symmetrical and frontal compositions. The film also hints at Byzantine iconography, which is characterised by 'frontality, non-expressive faces, hieratic postures, symmetric compositions, and two-dimensionality'.[33] I would argue that the first part of the film combines the aesthetics of both Gothic architecture (expressionism) and Byzantine icons in subversive and paradoxical ways, in a sort of 'heresy' that forms a unique cinematic sublime.

In the first scenes, we are gradually descending into the bleak dreamworld of the Sculptress, which oscillates between expressionistic intensity and Byzantine solemnity. The cinematic space does not resemble our common perception of reality; rather it emulates oneiric fragments surrounded by blackness. Similar to the cinematic worlds of expressionism, there is a constant and intense interaction between shadow and light. The first image is a ground plan of the Sculptress's home. A funeral memorial is placed at each of the four corners of the frame and their symmetrical arrangement surrounded by blackness forms an imaginary cross, whose centre coincides with that of the image. In the next scene, the Thief appears in the centre of this imaginary cross for a brief moment before darkness envelops the scene. An inverse close-up of the Sculptress's face is followed by a variation of the preceding ground plan, where now the tombs are replaced by living women's bodies, and a harsh light illuminates a hallway/vertical line of the imaginary cross. Throughout this segment, an alternation between darkness and light is constantly repeated, creating different geometric patterns, either symmetrical or asymmetrical. Bodies suspended over an abyss emerge and vanish into darkness, while patterns of light allude to both expressionistic and Byzantine artworks.

In certain images the expressionistic element is more prevalent and here the main source of sublimity is an intense contradiction between darkness and light, which Deleuze identifies with the Kantian dynamic sublime. For example, the scene in which the Sculptress holds up a diagonal wall, an allusion to Giotto's painting *La rêve du pape Innocent III* (1296),[34] creates an expressionistic intensity. Giotto was himself an artist influenced by both Gothic architecture and Byzantine iconography. As E. H. Gombrich puts it, 'his methods owe much to the Byzantine masters, and his aims and outlook to the great sculptors of the northern cathedrals'.[35] However, once again Angelidi does not simply replicate paintings but recomposes them, infusing them with other elements and references, and creating a new cinematic sublimity. The falling wall forms a diagonal line that traverses the frame, generating the impression of two converging bodies leaning against each other. The scene's side lighting creates sharp shades, while a secondary source of light gradually reveals in the background the Sculptress's family encased in a rectangular frame. These geometric patterns stage an intense interplay between darkness and light, generating a dynamic sublime image. Similar, the scene in which the Sculptress tries to repel the crows flying in the room – a reference to Max Klinger's expressionist artwork *Plague* (1903)[36] – also articulates a dynamic sublimity. This compelling scene reanimates and breathes new life into the dark and eerie expressionist worlds. The light enters the frame from left to right, from two windows covered by long white drapes, which are patterned with shadows cast on their floating surfaces. The Sculptress with hysterical movements tries to chase away the flying crows, and her excessive performance complements the light's intensity. The dynamic sublime emerges from the violent struggle of light, darkness and movement, connoting the Sculptress's dark revelation, as she identifies the Thief with the harbinger of (her) final Judgement.

These expressionistic images are interwoven with other influences, such as Byzantine and medieval illuminations, where 'the light seems to radiate out from the objects'.[37] Again, the original texts are reconfigured and expanded, since Angelidi employs the '[b]yzantine inverse perspective as seen from within a Renaissance and Baroque visual expressionism'.[38] For example, the women preparing the flowers for the epitaph resemble Byzantine icons, their inexpressive faces irradiating a luminosity from within. The scene is similar to the solemn splendour of Byzantine iconography, since 'no natural or realistic scene is enacted'.[39] These syntheses retain the hieratic frontal or symmetrical arrangements of Byzantine art, characteristic of the transcendental film style,[40] combined with the ritual movements of ancient theatre. However, they are not static imitations of old artistic expressions, but amalgamations of forms that produce new ideas. For example, the upside-down close-ups of the Sculptress reflect an inversed solemnity, a heretic icon of a Byzantine church. A similar erratic function is performed by the sacrilegious Communion of the two sisters and the Thief over the dead brother's body. The image is also mutually shaped by the soundtrack, which is replete with quotes from the Bible used in subversive ways, ominous sounds, and a deafening silence soliciting a feeling of dread and resembling a profane liturgy. The sparseness, the two-dimensionality and the solemnity of Byzantine iconography are traits entangled with unexpected and incompatible signifiers, creating a complex web of polysemous associations and sublime experiences.

Overall, in the first part the sublime is mainly invoked by the enveloping blackness and its intense contradiction with light that dissolves the illusion of the three-dimensional space, thus generating a sense of the abyss. As Burke maintains: '[w]hen the eye is not being able to perceive the bounds of many things, they seem to be infinite, and they produce the same effects as if they were really so.'[41] As the perspectival axes collapse and the boundaries are erased, the cinematic space becomes a 'bleak world [of] disorienting depthless, even horizonless, spatiality'.[42] However, as our ordinary perception of space is unsettled, the 'supersensible' vocation of the mind strives to rationally overcome this overwhelming attack on our imagination by creating a totality – the concept of the abyss or the infinite. Thus, the disruption of three-dimensionality engenders the disappearance of the humanist, Cartesian space and the parallel emergence of a new world, an unfathomable abyss of uncharted dimensions and equally concealed possibilities waiting to be explored. The formlessness of the space, and the lack of clear boundaries and limits, causes the resetting of the imagination and the production of new forms and perceptions. It is exactly this twofold movement, exemplified not only in the first part but throughout the film, which induces the double sense of attraction and repulsion, that is, the negative pleasure of the Kantian sublime.

In the second part, the Dice, the composition is asymmetrical and the movement of the camera continuous and smooth. The light is soft, highlighting the outlines and volumes of figures and objects. The dominant colour is blue, and in general cool hues underpin the image, reflecting the Scientist's cold viewpoint about the randomness that informs human existence.[43] However, the blue colour has also been associated with the spheres of the ethereal, the numinous and the otherworldly, especially in medieval illumination. As Eco points out,

> from the twelfth century onward blue became a prized colour: it suffices to think of the mystical value and the aesthetic splendour of the blue used in the stained-glass windows of cathedrals, which dominates the other colours and contributes to filtering the light in a 'celestial' manner.[44]

The blue colour thus connotes both the randomness of existence and the otherworldly, as expressed here in the 'afterlife' of memories. These themes underlie the second part, which unravels an imaginary encounter of the Scientist with her dead child, an encounter that engenders painful recollections and reflections. The segment begins with the Scientist and her lover sleeping. The sheets, the floor, the walls are coloured in a dark and sombre shade of blue, characteristic of the sublime.[45] In this blue atmosphere, the high-angle framing portrays the Scientist as if floating in a cold and opaque sea. In the next scene, the element of water is re-established with the symbolic sinking of the dead child's cloth in a liquid that resembles both water and amniotic fluid. Next, the Scientist is framed again from above, making violent and desperate movements and beginning her immersion into the obscure sea of memories/fantasies. Symbols of a dark turbulent sea of drowning bodies and surfacing memories transfuse the entire segment, connoting 'an abyss threatening to devour everything'[46] and articulating an idiosyncratic cinematic sublimity.

In a later scene, the Scientist clings to her son's burial mound, while reciting an elegiac soliloquy and immersing herself in the painful memory of love. The synthesis is stark, abstract and dream-like, surrounded by mist, while the background is covered in blackness. The austere composition is inspired by Max Klinger's *Yearnings – A Glove* (1881),[47] a black-and-white print, part of a series of 'elaborate visions of longing and loss, conveyed through dream-like distortions of scale and jarring juxtapositions'.[48] Like the expressionist artwork, the scene conveys abstractly the themes of loss and desire expressed through 'sparse' means,[49] via a denial of mimesis, of identification and empathy. It thus engenders appreciation and distance, which are the presuppositions of the aesthetic expression of transcendence, that is, the sublime. The vacuity of the image is accentuated by the hypnotic mobility of the camera that encircles the mourning Scientist. The blackness and the mist reinforce a sense of obscurity which causes grand impressions and thoughts. As Burke stresses, 'dark, confused, uncertain images have a greater power on the fancy to form the grander passions than those have [*sic*] which are more clear and determinate,' therefore 'a clear idea is . . . another name for a little idea'.[50] The scene's otherworldly atmosphere imbued with mystery and solemnity solicits such great feelings, and affects the imagination with ideas of infinity inscribed in the perpetual cycle of life and death, that is, with the grand ideas related to the sublime.

The Delirium sequence, the imaginary encounter of the Scientist with her dead son, marks the climax of this segment. The scene consists of a visceral and erotically charged choreography of mother and son immersed in the dark waters of a stone trough. The themes of water and drowning, already established at the beginning of the second part, are intensified and reach a climax here in this effective sequence. The first image is the inverse reflection of the child in the water. His hands appear in the frame, sinking a mirror – a connotation of the entrance to another world.[51] While the first words of the raving 'water libretto'[52] are articulated, the two naked bodies –mother and son – enter the frame and the rectangular tub from right and left respectively. The high-angle framing creates the impression of sinking, twisting bodies that are immersed in the liquid abyss of memories. Bodies, movements and words interpenetrate and intermingle, creating geometric patterns that alternate between fragile balance and violent delirium. This alternation and succession of patterns and rhyme merging into an abstract form recalls Deleuze's description of the mathematical sublime in cinema: bodies, movements, sounds and words gradually 'enter into very subtle relationships of reduplication, alternation, periodical return and chain reaction'[53] that induce the abstraction of a single form. The crescendo of the sequence coalesces the bodily movements into a single abstract form, transforming the organic composition into pure movement and totality, into the sublime.

The final part, the Will, revolves around the Actor rehearsing *Antigone*, and his decision to commit suicide. The synthesis of the frame is based on the principle of the golden section, while the camera performs elaborate movements.

The soft side lighting highlights the outlines of the objects, adding plasticity and the illusion of perspective in the image. These characteristics along with the warm and earthly colours render the final segment more 'grounded' in relation to the two previous parts, reflecting the equally 'earthly' attitude of the Actor towards life, which he regards as a series of choices in opposition to the determinism of Fate or the randomness of Luck that his sisters embrace. This part begins as a theatrical play where spectators still and watch the drama unravel. A high-angle view shows the Actor performing the monologue of Antigone after Creon has sentenced her to be buried alive in a cavern. In this monologue Antigone mourns her death but does not regret her choice to go against the laws of the king and bury her brother Polyneices. The acceptance of death as the outcome of his free will is inscribed not only in the monologue but also in the image. The floor is covered with soil where a phallic-shaped pile is symmetrically aligned with a hole in the ground, functioning as male and female symbols that engender the life/death cycle. The Actor spins around these two earthly bodies, his movement forming an imaginary symbol of infinity that unites male and female in the perpetual cycle of life. This choreography starts slowly and gradually escalates, while the equally intensified monologue infuses the scene with the gravitas of an ancient ritual. Earth, death, finitude and infinity – as the perpetual cycle of life/death – are all signifiers of the materiality and immanence of existence, and are all intertwined in the expression of the sublime.

The sequence in the bar interweaves some of these signifiers in the articulation of the sublime. A blind oracle stands behind the bar and gazes at the mirror. The signifiers of vision/knowledge apparent in this scene are further underscored by her conversation with a man about scientific/philosophical systems of belief. As the oracle turns to face her interlocutor the camera starts slowly to move rightward and gradually frames the mirror. We see, 'through a glass darkly', a distorted reflection of the Actor playing chess with the Thief/Reality/Death – an allusion to Bergman's *Seventh Seal* (1957). The reflection presents an anamorphic space where the curved floor, patterned with black-and-white squares, resembles a replication and enlargement of the chessboard extending to infinity and swallowing up the Actor and the Thief. This obscure image unsettles the fixed coordinates of the Cartesian space, thus presenting a warped reality that evokes a sense of sublimity. According to Anthony Vidler, warped space is a form of 'distorted' spatiality that 'rather than being understood as a passive container of object and bodies, [is] charged with all the dimensions of a relative, moving, dynamic entity'.[54] The warping of space involves a dynamic mobility that collapses fixed and clear boundaries, and disrupts the perspectival spaces of the Renaissance, thus paving the way for the sources of the sublime – formlessness, limitlessness and obscurity.

A similar warping of space takes place in the scene before the suicide where the Actor mourns about the emptiness of life. Similar to the previously discussed scene, the synthesis of the frame creates a distorted spatiality that confuses fixed coordinates and familiar perspectives and perceptions. We see the reflection of the Actor in a vertical, narrow mirror surrounded by the vagina-shaped folds of a sculptural black space. The Actor's reflection covers the lower part of the mirror as he lies face-down in the ground/earth. As the Actor occupies a small fragment of the image, he seems to be swallowed up and suppressed by this curved space pulsating with an imperceptible mobility and unfamiliar dimensions. This image evokes the overwhelming of the subject in their encounter with extraordinary experiences when facing the sublimity of the unknown.

In the final sequence the film comes full circle. After the Actor's suicide and the preparation for his funeral – a sequence that evokes Andrea Mantegna's *The Lamentation of Christ* (1480)[55] – the longing for life begins again. The darkness that falls when the candles are blown out in the first image is replaced in the final scene by a fierce fire that inflames the desire for life and transforms darkness to light. As the sisters watch the funeral pyre they laugh aloud at death, having embraced the life/death unity, the finitude and mortality as the preconditions of life, and remark 'the only certainty is that we die'.

TRANSCENDING THE LIMITS OF CINEMATIC ART

As already noted, the expression of the sublime has been associated with the dual structure of transcendence, of being at once overwhelmed and elevated by unfathomable experiences, by the encounter with the unknown, the incomprehensible, or the absolutely powerful. From this perspective, transcendence is understood as an expansion of our common and familiar perception of the world, even as it is located in the 'here' and 'now' of our sensual existence.[56] Sublime art provides 'a paradoxical experience of this outside of human sensibility, an outside that nevertheless remains the immanent and real condition of experience'.[57] This paradoxical experience is translated in cinematic terms as the sublime's ability to expand our imaginative capacity by transcending established rules and conventions of cinematic language. The cinematic sublime is expressive of the transcendence-structure, as our cinematic vision is overwhelmed and elevated, stretched and re-constituted through novel and unexpected forms that defy the boundaries of mimetic representations. Therefore, the aesthetics of the sublime facilitates our imaginative and mental expansiveness through artistic experimentation. As Lyotard asserts:

> The arts, whatever their materials, pressed forward by the aesthetics of the sublime in search of intense effects, can and must give up the imitation of models that are merely beautiful, and try out surprising, strange, shocking combinations.[58]

By pushing the boundaries of cinematic language and by 'allud[ing] to something which can't be shown, or presented',[59] the sublime bears 'expressive witness to the inexpressible'.[60] It creates an 'ontological dislocation',[61] freeing perception from the constraints of 'habitual or classical ways of looking'.[62] The transcendence-structure of the sublime thus generates an 'intensification of [the viewer's] conceptual and emotional capacity, an ambivalent enjoyment'.[63] *Thief or Reality* exemplifies all these aspects of the sublime as the dual transcendence-structure, re-envisioning cinematic art.

Thief's cinematic sublime moves us to an 'elsewhere' through its ability to generate new sensations/perceptions. In creating new worlds and broadening our ordinary perception of life/art, the film's cinematic sublime 'open[s] experience onto a transcendental realm of genesis, onto the realm of invention', or rather the re-invention of life/art, which is also a political praxis. As Stephen Zepke contends, 'the aesthetic features of sublime art not only actualise an ontogenetic and undetermined process of emergence, but also directly affect their historical and political conditions by pointing beyond them'.[64] The film's unique articulation of the sublime creates new ways of expression and feeling that pushes us outside the established limits of human consciousness, thus underscoring the 'political potentials of aesthetic invention'.[65] *Thief*'s sublime images juxtapose and reconfigure different codes, dreams and artworks through indirect presentation, obscurity and sparseness, thus providing 'an experience of the transcendental condition of the new, of the condition of emergence qua difference',[66] and enabling us to critically examine traditional concepts, codes and structures. The cinematic sublime in *Thief or Reality* exemplifies the paradoxical and transformative nature of Angelidi's cinematic art – a cinema that unsettles the fixed boundaries between mind/body, male/female, life/death, reality/fantasy, known/unknown, immanence/transcendence, creating sublime visions and disruptive possibilities.

NOTES

1. David Bordwell, Kristin Thomson and Jeff Smith, *Film Art: An Introduction* (New York: McGraw-Hill Education, 2017), 369.
2. Rea Walldén, 'Conversing with Dreams: An Encounter with Antoinetta Angelidi,' *Filmicon: Journal of Greek Film Studies* 4 (December 2017): 189.
3. Ibid., 190.
4. Anthony Vidler, *The Architectural Uncanny: Essays in the Modern Unhomely* (Cambridge, MA: MIT Press, 1992), 3.
5. Istvan Csicsery-Ronay Jr, *The Seven Beauties of Science Fiction* (Middletown, CT: Wesleyan University Press, 2008), 146.
6. Robert Doran, *The Theory of the Sublime: From Longinus to Kant* (Cambridge: Cambridge University Press, 2015), 8.
7. Edmund Burke, *A Philosophical Enquiry into the Origin of our Ideas of the Sublime and Beautiful*, ed. Adam Phillips (Oxford: Oxford University Press, 1990), 53.

8. Ibid., 54.
9. Ibid., 71.
10. Doran, *The Theory of the Sublime*, 219.
11. Immanuel Kant, *Critique of the Power of Judgment* (Cambridge: Cambridge University Press, 2000), 128.
12. Kant, *Critique*, 131.
13. Ibid., 134.
14. Doran, *The Theory of the Sublime*, 260.
15. Ibid., 276.
16. Ibid., 281.
17. Ibid., 279–82.
18. Ibid., 7.
19. Ibid., 7.
20. Ibid., 286.
21. Gilles Deleuze, *Cinema 1: The Movement-Image*, trans. Hugh Tomlinson and Barbara Habberjam (Minneapolis: University of Minnesota Press, 1986), 41.
22. Ibid., 41.
23. Ibid., 46.
24. Ibid., 50.
25. Schrader associates the transcendent with the metaphysical and religious, therefore it is different from Kant's secular (immanent) transcendence.
26. Paul Schrader, *Transcendental Style in Film: Ozu, Bresson, Dreyer* (New York: Da Capo Press, Inc., 1972), 10.
27. Ibid., 155.
28. Gilles Deleuze, *Cinema 2: The Time-Image*, trans. Hugh Tomlinson and Robert Galeta (Minneapolis: University of Minnesota Press, 1989), 238.
29. Schrader, *Transcendental Style*, 5.
30. Maria Katsounaki, «Συνέντευξη: Ο Πειραματισμός δεν είναι προνόμιο της Νεότητας» / 'Interview: Experimentation is not a Privilege of Youth', in *Antoinetta Angelidi*, ed. Stella Theodoraki (Athens: Aigokeros, 2005), 121.
31. Schrader, *Transcendental Style*, 138.
32. Vrasidas Karalis, *Realism in Greek Cinema: From the Post-War Period to the Present* (London: I. B. Tauris, 2017), 196.
33. Schrader, *Transcendental Style*, 99.
34. Eleni Mahaira, «Η Ζωγραφική Φύση στο Έργο του Κώστα Σφήκα και της Αντουανέττας Αγγελίδη» / 'The Painting Nature in the Work of Kostas Sfikas and Antoinetta Angelidi', in *Γραφές για τον Κινηματογράφο. Διεπιστημονικές Προσεγγίσεις/ Writings for Cinema: Interdisciplinary Approaches*, ed. Antoinetta Angelidi, Eleni Mahaira and Konstantinos Kyriakos (Athens: Nefeli, 2005), 184.
35. E. H. Gombrich, *The Story of Art*. Fourth Edition (London: Phaidon Publishers Inc., 1951), 144.
36. Mahaira, «Η Ζωγραφική Φύση» / 'The Painting Nature', 185.
37. Umberto Eco, *On Beauty: A History of a Western Idea*, trans. Alastair McEwen (London: Secker & Warburg, 2004), 100.
38. Karalis, *Realism in Greek Cinema*, 207.
39. Gombrich, *Story of Art*, 96.
40. Schrader, *Transcedental Style*, 53.
41. Burke, *A Philosophical Enquiry*, 67.
42. Karalis, *Realism in Greek Cinema*, 191.
43. Katsounaki, 'Συνέντευξη/ Interview', 121.

44. Eco, *On Beauty*, 123.
45. Burke, *A Philosophical Enquiry*, 75.
46. Kant, *Critique*, 153.
47. Mahaira, 'Η Ζωγραφική Φύση / The Painting Nature', 185.
48. Moma, 'Max Klinger', *Moma.org*, 16 April 2020, <https://www.moma.org/collection/works/128895>, accessed 1 June 2022.
49. Schrader, *Transcendental Style*, 154.
50. Burke, *A Philosophical Enquiry*, 58.
51. Rea Walldén, 'Το Μέσα είναι Έξω / The Inside is Outside', in *Antoinetta Angelidi*, ed. Stella Theodoraki (Athens: Aigokeros, 2005), 104.
52. Ibid., 102.
53. Deleuze, *Cinema 1*, 42.
54. Anthony Vidler. *Warped Space: Art, Architecture and Anxiety in Modern Culture* (Cambridge, MA: MIT Press, 2000), 2.
55. Mahaira, 'Η Ζωγραφική Φύση / The Painting Nature', 185.
56. Vivian Sobchack, 'Embodying Transcendence: On the Literal, the Material and the Cinematic Sublime,' *Material Religion* 4, 2 (2015): 197.
57. Stephen Zepke, *Sublime Art: Towards an Aesthetics of the Future* (Edinburgh: Edinburgh University Press, 2017), 16.
58. Jean-François, Lyotard, *The Inhuman* (Stanford: Stanford University Press, 1988), 100.
59. Lyotard, *The Inhuman*, 89.
60. Ibid., 93.
61. Ibid., 101.
62. Ibid., 102.
63. Ibid., 101.
64. Zepke, *Sublime Art*, 6.
65. Ibid., 4.
66. Ibid., 9.

BIBLIOGRAPHY

Bordwell, David, Kristin Thomson and Jeff Smith. *Film Art: An Introduction*. Eleventh Edition. New York: McGraw-Hill Education, 2017.

Burke, Edmund. *A Philosophical Enquiry into the Origin of our Ideas of the Sublime and Beautiful*, ed., intro. and notes by Adam Phillips. Oxford: Oxford University Press, 1990.

Csicsery-Ronay Jr, Istvan. *The Seven Beauties of Science Fiction*. Middletown, CT: Wesleyan University Press, 2008.

Deleuze, Gilles. *Cinema 1: The Movement-Image*, trans. Hugh Tomlinson and Barbara Habberjam. Minneapolis: University of Minnesota Press, 1986.

Deleuze, Gilles. *Cinema 2: The Time-Image*, trans. Hugh Tomlinson and Robert Galeta. Minneapolis: University of Minnesota Press, 1989.

Doran, Robert. *The Theory of the Sublime: From Longinus to Kant*. Cambridge: Cambridge University Press, 2015.

Eco, Umberto. *On Beauty: A History of a Western Idea*, trans. Alastair McEwen. London: Secker & Warburg, 2004.

Gombrich, E. H. *The Story of Art*. Fourth Edition. London: Phaidon Publishers Inc., 1951.

Kant, Immanuel. *Critique of the Power of Judgement*, ed. Paul Guyer; trans. Paul Guyer and Eric Matthews. Cambridge: Cambridge University Press, 2000.

Karalis, Vrasidas. *Realism in Greek Cinema: From the Post-War Period to the Present*. London: I. B. Tauris, 2017.

Katsounaki, Maria. «Συνέντευξη: Ο Πειραματισμός δεν είναι προνόμιο της Νεότητας» / 'Interview: Experimentation is not a Privilege of Youth', in *Antoinetta Angelidi*, ed. Stella Theodoraki. Athens: Aigokeros, 2005, 120–1.

Kickasola, Joseph G. *The Films of Krzysztof Kieślowski: The Liminal Image*. New York: Continuum, 2004.

Leonard, Richard. *The Mystical Gaze of the Cinema the Films of Peter Weir*. Carlton, Vic: Melbourne University Press, 2009.

Lyotard, Jean-François. *The Inhuman*. Stanford: Stanford University Press, 1988.

Mahaira, Eleni. «Η Ζωγραφική Φύση στο Έργο του Κώστα Σφήκα και της Αντουανέττας Αγγελίδη» / 'The Painting Nature in the Work of Kostas Sfikas and Antoinetta Angelidi'. In *Γραφές για τον Κινηματογράφο. Διεπιστημονικές Προσεγγίσεις / Writings for Cinema. Interdisciplinary Approaches*, ed. Antoinetta Angelidi, Eleni Mahaira and Konstantinos Kyriakos. Athens: Nefeli, 2005, 133–89.

MoMA. 'Max Klinger', *Moma.org*, <https://www.moma.org/collection/works/128895>, accessed 16 April 2020.

Schrader, Paul. *Transcendental Style in Film: Ozu, Bresson, Dreyer*. New York: Da Capo Press, Inc., 1972.

Sobchack, Vivian. 'Embodying Transcendence: On the Literal, the Material and the Cinematic Sublime'. *Material Religion* 4, 2 (2015): 195–203.

Vidler, Anthony. *The Architectural Uncanny: Essays in the Modern Unhomely*. Cambridge, MA: MIT Press, 1992.

Vidler, Anthony. *Warped Space: Art, Architecture and Anxiety in Modern Culture*. Cambridge, MA: MIT Press, 2000.

Walldén, Rea. 'Conversing with Dreams: An Encounter with Antoinetta Angelidi'. *FilmIcon: Journal of Greek Film Studies* 4 (December 2017): 184–94.

Walldén, Rea. «Το Μέσα είναι Έξω» / 'The Inside is Outside'. In *Antoinetta Angelidi*, ed. Stella Theodoraki. Athens: Aigokeros, 2005, 102–5.

Zepke, Stephen. *Sublime Art: Towards an Aesthetics of the Future*. Edinburgh: Edinburgh University Press, 2017.

PART 3

Means and Media

CHAPTER 7

From Orchestrated Noise to Elaborated Silence: The Audiovisuality of Antoinetta Angelidi's Films

Electra Venaki

In her four feature films, between 1977 and 2001, Antoinetta Angelidi's sonic practices, surpassing the common film sound production workflow of narrative Greek films during that period, explored subversive sound-based narratives and proposed new forms of audiovisuality.

Angelidi's daring decisions, even from her first mono feature film, propose an immersive audiovisual experience, where the audio-spectator consciously or unconsciously follows the seemingly parallel flows of two bifurcated worlds, that of the visual and that of the sound, to reach a perception of all the cinematic elements as a whole. Many parallel tracks – voices, sounds, music, moving images and written texts – are intertwined (horizontally and vertically in the editing timeline) in a tight and at the same time open structure. Angelidi's filming approach, along with that of her contemporaries in the avant-garde film world, disrupts the canonical hierarchy between a) visual, b) voice, c) music, and d) all other 'sounds', revealing, in that way, her films' audiovisuality.

Composed of four feature films, Angelidi's oeuvre, traversed the monophonic period, and the digital soundtrack era.

Angelidi directed her first feature film, *Idées Fixes / Dies Irae* (60 min, France-Greece, Black/White, 16mm/16mm,[1] mono), in Paris in 1977, edited in moviola, with magnetic sound and optical sound for the final print. Her second film, *Topos* (85 min, Greece, Colour, 35mm/35mm, mono) was produced in Greece in 1985, edited in moviola, with magnetic sound and optical sound for the final print. Her third film, *The Hours – A Square Film* (85 min, Greece, Colour, 35mm/35mm) was also produced in Greece, in 1995, edited in moviola, with final prints in Dolby SR. Her fourth film, *Thief or Reality – Three Versions* (83 min, Greece, Colour, 35mm/35mm, Dolby Digital), produced in Greece in 2001, is the only one edited on AVID, with final prints in Dolby Digital. The sound composition before the final mix in Dolby of the two last films was held by and finalised at Studio 19 in Athens, (headed by Kostas Bokos and Vasilis Kountouris) in a completely digital form before being printed in the 35mm optical prints.

Yet, little has been written about film sound practices, auditory perception and culture, in small cinemas, in the so-called 'low-production capacity countries' such as Greece. In other words, the geopolitical context that includes the modes of production, distribution exhibition and reception determined to a great extent Angelidi's choices in the construction of her soundtracks; therefore a brief industrial and cultural contextualisation seems fitting here to help provide to an overall understanding of the sound worlds in Angelidi's films.

Guided by Murray S. Schafer's well-known saying that 'individuals and societies of various historical eras [and various geographical ones, I add] listen differently',[2] the following hypothesis is presented: If individuals and societies listen differently, their artists create their soundscapes differently. That is to say, along with the filmmakers of her generation, Angelidi worked with given conditions offered by her environment: the Greek film production restrictions and practices paired with the influences of cultural, historical and technological factors. This chapter will focus on the sonic journey from her first mono film to the latest digital one, in order to showcase Angelidi's aesthetic choices based on sound technology, national sound practices and personal style.

THE CONTEXT OF ANGELIDI'S SOUNDSCAPES AND FILM WORLDS

Angelidi's sound worlds, the uniqueness of her audiovisuality, are closely interlinked via three key contextual factors: the artisanal mode of production in which she was operating; the emergence of avant-garde film feminist theory and practice; and the particular auditory cinema culture based on the common practice of subtitling foreign language films in Greece.

During this whole period, from 1977 to 2001, in an almost artisanal film production framework, Angelidi created her soundscapes meticulously, with a highly elaborated and sophisticated sound design including creation and alteration of sounds and voices, working with music, voice and sound compositions direct from the script, practices almost unknown to Greek film production of that period. Just as with mainstream narrative cinema worldwide, Greek films used sounds (effects, ambiences and music) mostly to enhance the reality and the '*affect*' of the moving images, and voices as the vehicle of the narration. The soundtrack (including all the above) was mainly anchored to the image field.

Those technological restrictions in the production as well as the screening experience resulted in the broadly accepted national assumption that soundtrack (mainly mono) does not solicit any field of aesthetic or narrative quest, but is a technicality, a self-explanatory and realistic necessity. The majority of Greek films were visually oriented, focused on the representational attributes of the sounds, bestowing upon the voice and the music a predominant role. The ultimate preoccupation was the clarity and the intelligibility of the voices that bore the narration, the dialogue, always shot in sync on location. The dominance of the voice, the 'vococentrism' of Michel Chion, and of music led to the neglect, to the marginalisation, of other sounds, and only some 'key sounds' and 'soundmarks', according to Schafer, were used to create the local characteristic soundscape along with ambient sounds captured on location.

In Greece, the first cinema equipped with Dolby Stereo appeared in 1986.[3] The first Dolby SR screens appeared in 1992 and the first Dolby Digital ones in 1994. It was during the late 1980s and early 1990s that Greek studios were able to perform a multichannel mix, and around 2000 the Dolby Digital mixes became possible. Location recording had already been digitised in 1992 and non-linear editing hardware entered the Greek film production market in 1996. It should be noted here that even during the first years of digital sound final mix in Greece, the propagation of sounds all around the surround loudspeakers was extremely limited, and only the music enjoyed this privilege, while some movements between left and right channels provided compensation to the film sound people for their eagerness to create 'sound immersion' by sound spatialisation. Digital multitrack sound was mostly appreciated for its new enlarged bandwidth qualities and multilayering possibilities.

Moreover, in film sound scholarship, based mostly on an analysis of Anglophone mainstream film paradigms, the soundtrack, even after the so-called 'second wave of film sound studies',[4] is often considered in relation to its visual source (whether it is 'in' or 'off'), its diegetic or non-diegetic functions, or limited to the study of the sonic elements of the filming event. On top of that, the 'unified approach' or 'intensified musicalization' of sound in recent cinema,[5] after the advent of digital sound, is restricted to the interesting ramifications of the blurring between music and sounds, thereby leaving the voice and the visual out of the equation.

Angelidi started to make films in the wake of avant-garde feminist cinema and theory. Texts and movies such as those of Laura Mulvey and Chantal Akerman, to name but a few, were part of the cultural landscape of that period, at least in Britain and in France. Angelidi was born in Athens, left for Paris as a political refugee during the junta, and returned after its fall. Her cinema is thus impregnated with this radical and highly interesting combination: a political, feminist, avant-garde, experimental and, later on, poetic cinema disrupting 'a woman's to-be-looked-at-ness, the way she is to be looked at into the spectacle itself'.[6] Furthermore, experimental cinema has explored soundscapes in an innovative and creative way, long before the advent of digital sound. Holly

Rogers and Jeremy Barham, in their seminal book *The Music and Sound of the Experimental Film*, summarise the history of avant-garde films as creating provocative, 'shocking audiovisual relationships'[7] and discuss how '[on] many occasions [. . .] *music and/or sound*[8] have been used in surprising, subversive and/or politically charged ways by those operating outside of the artistic and financial aesthetics that drive dominant commercial cinema'.[9] Some years earlier, Maureen Cheryn Turim pointed out that

> one principle of avant-garde sound track could be autonomy and disjunction, but [. . .] there are some avant-garde films that display a high degree of correspondence between sound and image. It is likely that in these cases the sound track determines the image track, but in a manner at once more abstract and more direct that 'narration'.[10]

Avant-garde or experimental films, however, did not really exist in Greece until the 1970s.[11] When they started to emerge, the audiovisuality of their approach was clearly different to that of mainstream narrative films. Notwithstanding their subversive visual and aural statements, these films were supported by national and European cultural institutions, such as the Greek Film Centre and MEDIA Programme, and participated along with narrative mainstream films in the Thessaloniki Film Festival, the main film festival in Greece.[12] In fact, Angelidi won the Best Soundtrack Award for the 'sound concept' in *Topos* (monophonic soundtrack, 1985) at the 26th Thessaloniki Film Festival; at that time, this award was meant to be bestowed for work in the field of sound recording. Angelidi was one of the first, if not the first, in Greece to work on her soundtracks (voices and sounds included) with a composer direct from the script. Even though she has been practising post-synchronisation and later sonification rather than field recording – which was and still is the canon in Greek film production – she has been collaborating closely with the whole sound and editing team from pre-production onwards: composer, actors, sound crew and editor.

Moreover, in Greece, subtitling of foreign films was – and still is – a common practice.

In subtitling cultures such as Greece the voice is not only considered as the bearer of meaningful speech but is unconsciously highly appreciated as a sound element of the cinematic soundscape for its materiality, for its tone, texture, or pitch, adding to the 'affect' of the scene.

As Tom Whittaker and Sarah Wright aptly summarise in the introduction to their edited volume on global practices regarding the voice in film:

> Original voice that provides meaningful articulation to one national audience can elsewhere be heard as sonority to another; their lack of semantic understanding of the language can instead lead them to be more highly attuned to its material poetics and unfamiliar rhythms.[13]

National cinemagoers are conditioned to appreciate more the verbal rhythm of the voice, its instrumentality, instead of the articulated, and they are aware of and accustomed to this effect when they become creators; they appreciate what Roland Barthes called 'the grain of the voice', 'the materiality of the body speaking its mother tongue'.[14]

The construction of Angelidi's soundtracks varied considerably over the aforementioned period, affected by the three main factors discussed above. She always appealed to the Greek audience's sonic cultural background. The films' materiality and the specific encounter between them and the audience, according to the film sonic culture of each period, are in evidence.

Cinema's 'social materiality'[15] is reflected in Angelidi's work and in her aesthetic decisions, a fact that should be taken into consideration when we talk about the use and style of sound in her films.

ANGELIDI'S SOUND WORLDS IN HER FILMIC UNIVERSE

Angelidi's work is renowned for its boldly structured visual compositions and visualized concepts. Vrasidas Karalis[16] among others underlines the geometrical structure of their filmic space; Greek critic Eleni Mahera[17] reveals the alteration of the perspective due to the frame composition and the camera shot, while Angelidi's colour palette, the light, and first and foremost the abundance of references to acclaimed and well-known paintings are almost always praised. Her strong connection to visual compositions probably emanates from her relation to painting: as she claimed: 'In the beginning was painting. It was through painting that I first felt this "thing-condensation" that nourishes our lives. I have been drawing ever since I remember myself, and I have come to know myself through painting.'

She continues:

> In 1972, after visiting the Documenta exhibition in Kassel, I had a life-changing dream. I saw an image that looked like a Magritte painting but included a slight, infinitesimal movement, internally, in the objects and the faces of people. This minimum movement shook me – yes, I am aware of the possible double meaning of this expression. What this minimum movement did was to introduce time into a painting. Time, the existence of time, haunted me, obsessed me, and has never left me since.[18]

In the same way Angelidi masters her visual space, she crafts her films' sound space, manipulating ingeniously the well-known strong relation of auditory phenomena to temporality.

The sound world in Angelidi's films is rather akin to the feeling we experience in a moving bus, where the soundscape covers or is limited to the interior of the bus, while the moving images – the image field is muted – follow their proper timefulness, outside the glass which separates the two nonetheless 'real' worlds: different moving images/different sound flow, different times.

The sounds do not derive from the pictorial synthesis, do not belong to the visual space; they do not interpret, or represent, or animate, or even enhance the image field, vocabulary very often used to describe the role of the soundtrack in a filmic event. This unique flow of Angelidi's sound world might guide us to perceive totally different meanings and/or sensations and to create totally different associations to the ones caused by the moving image alone. The quote from Rick Altman regarding sound film's fundamental lie of 'the implication that sound is produced by the image when in fact it remains independent of it',[19] paired with Chion's famous aphorism that 'there is no soundtrack', just 'sounds and images, both devot[ing] themselves to the constitution of [. . .] cinematic space-time',[20] finds in Angelidi's films its cumulative evidence.

All Angelidi's films were made for the big screen, for a movie theatre experience. This involves the black surroundings of the screen, different configurations of the one or more loudspeakers – according to the technical evolutions of the time – and an audience.

We cannot watch/listen to these films at home or on a mobile device, foremost because absolute silence (if any in the film) and absolute darkness (if any in the film) cannot be experienced correctly. In a Greek movie theatre, with the one and only loudspeaker in front of the screen until the 5.1 Digital Sound configurations, Angelidi demanded a very active listener-viewer and not a pathetic spectator. Nonetheless, Angelidi's sound (almost monophonic) construction predated the 'superfield' of Chion's terminology, where 'the space of the film, no longer confined to the screen, in a way became the entire auditorium, via the loudspeakers that broadcast crowd noises as well as everything else'.[21]

Indeed, even without surround loudspeakers, Angelidi's film sound is mainly outside the image, in front of the screen, in the space of the theatre, of each theatre with its particularities; a space created by the position of the microphone, by the lack of reverberation, by the lack of synchronisation; a space offered by the filmmaker to the audience; a space filled by the sound, or by the non-sound, a space where the body of the film 'talks'.

The often-dark parts of the frame's construction, created by well-constructed lighting, and the placement of the camera that disturbs the perspective and removes any exit, remove the borders, leaving the screen without any trace of the surroundings, and subvert any notion of 'continuity'. This works in tandem with the sounds' qualities and their position in the time flow that removes the same notion of the soundscape, becoming, in that way, timeless. Sometimes, in specific scenes and moments, the sound enters into the image field, participates in the action before exiting once again out of the screen, remaining in constant dialogue with the other elements of the filmic event.

Angelidi's sound concepts create their own worlds that co-exist and interact with the visuals, and together they create the films' audiovisuality. This is very much in harmony with Angelidi's own words, repeated in many interviews:

> My poetics involves working on and against the codes, the way dreams do, inverting and juxtaposing them. Moreover, it relies on a communication between the elements of heterogeneity; screeching noises transform into lights, body movements continue as screams, women's voices weep through inanimate objects.[22]

Angelidi's non-representational forms propose a different situatedness of narration linked with embodied experience more than with plot structure, thus suggesting a non-significative model of approach describing instead the films' affective potential and other possible connections between film and perceiver. Following Schafer's words, What the soundscape analyst must do first is to discover the significant features of the soundscape, those sounds which are important either because of their individuality, their numerousness or their domination,[23] we can easily discern what is Angelidi's important sound: the female voice.

THE FEMALE VOICE AS THE ULTIMATE SONIC DEVICE

Angelidi's soundscapes are haunted by the female voice.

Female voices are found in male bodies and deep female voices in bodies of young girls (*Topos*); a woman is the Thief and a man recites the part of Antigone (*Thief or Reality*).

Sounds are voices, music is voices, voices are sounds, voices are music; voices are noise. All melt into one another, without a reference point to realistic elements which articulate a specific and/or predictable type of narration. When the voices articulate meaningful speech, they swim around the bodies as if they don't belong to them, as if they are translating or rather complementing or even commenting on them, while their timbre and tonal qualities are generating a form of rhythm and/or music. By altering the timbre and the pitch, assembling sounds, music and voices, Angelidi gives birth to different auditory events; she creates musicality.[24]

Her voices-speeches are characterised by repetition, a peculiar repetition that works hand in hand with constant transformation. The perception of the filmic event through repetition is transformed by a kind of mantra, by a sensation of a ritual, where every single screening of the same film is perceived afresh in different times or eras and places by the same listener-viewer. Very often voices articulate fragments of spoken words, onomatopoeic words, or other types of linguistic prosody, which, through repetition, through their musicality, lose their evident meaning and are transformed into elements of initiation or of a dream. Words which 'hypnotize the mind, at which point they may give rise to new word-sounds. Such is the function of a mantra', as Murray R. Schafer points out.[25]

In her first film, the only one with sound recording on location, in Paris, the director herself, in a frontal close shot, recites words with the prefix 'a', which in Greek is used to form words expressing deprivation or negative and opposite forces in adjectives and their related verbs and nouns. And she continues in a mantra-like tone with the phrase, 'the men who died relatively young' (*I andres pou pethanan nei shetika*), in many different syntaxes, as voiced Greek words, while the image is covered by the same text, written in French, as the visual embodiment of language.[26] The same structure of the voice-speech can be found scattered throughout her four films, reaching its culmination in *Thief or Reality*, in many instances; a prominent example is the sequence in which the elder sister repeats, once again in many different syntaxes, the phrase 'My God give me the strength to distinguish . . .', while she sculpts the rock rhythmically with sound (49:45). By repetition and acceleration of the rhythm, her voice speaks a phrased orgasm leading to a liberating exhalation and then to silence – silence as spoken word and as movement of her hands that seal her lips.

Sometimes her female voices become noise, an irritating noise, which is the result of this meticulously modified repetition, alteration and multiple juxtapositions.

The image of the rooster on a sexually ambiguous body's lap (*Idées Fixes*, 00:19:00) is mixed in with a phrase from a high-pitched female voice, accelerated and multiplied to arrive at something close to the irritating song of the cicada, a common sound event during Greek summers.

Faithful to her pattern of repetition and transformation, Angelidi offers us different qualities of the female scream, with different connotations. In her first film, the scream is not quite clear; between a hysterical quasi-mocking scream and a female altered laugh. She juxtaposes many sounds with female voice-speech accelerated at high pitch, which leaves us with the sensation of hearing a scream which is not a scream, not a real female scream. Angelidi uses the ambiguousness of the female scream to disturb, to provoke our cultural auditory codes, to oppose her Greek, female filmmaker's gaze with the men's gaze towards female sexuality. Inasmuch, in the following shot, a tight close-up without sound (48:00–49:00) of a woman's mouth, the tongue licks the lips with movements that are the opposite of the 'erotic' connotation: this female scream, which is always ambiguous, between pleasure and fear, a sound that in male films oscillates almost always between sexuality and pain. Angelidi playfully uses aural stereotypes and twists them, distorts them, putting the perceiver in an uncanny situation, expressing at the same time subtle but clear political statements.[27]

In her other three films the scream is loud, pure, a raw female voice that disturbs the cinematic auditory canons.

As Philip Brophy explains at length:

> For when a woman's scream is audible, non-silent, locatable, unpossessed, unmanipulated, self-controlled, its raw texture colors it *as noise*. [. . .] Cinema has rarely allowed the noise of the female to corrupt the ruthlessly coded soundtrack and few films holistically import the female vocal machine into the cinematic apparatus.[28]

In all her films, we can say that the female scream is *a noise*. And when, sometimes, the scream is silenced, the breath, which is 'mirroring the frightening ambiguousness of the female scream', takes over. The 'breath on the soundtrack is both erotic and necrotic', as Angelidi ingeniously exposes in several sequences in *Thief or Reality*, one of which we discussed above.

Angelidi's films are very talkative too. The main voices are mostly female and they are talking all the time. As Sarah Kozloff argues, 'talkativeness has traditionally been allied with femininity, terse action with masculinity. Films that are "talky" come with the connotations "trivial" and "idle" and, ultimately, "female".'[29]

In *The Hours* (1995, Dolby SR, moviola), her most narrative film, the dominant voice is that of Spendo, the protagonist. Spendo's voice navigates through space and time: between embodied voices, voice-over and inner speech. The boundaries are blurred while the voice is suspended, levitated between the present and the past, between the space in front of the screen and its embodied moments on the screen. We (the protagonist included) watch the present or the present of the past of the moving images, while listening to the narration, in the present time, as a commentary on the unfolding of the Deleuzian 'image-mémoire'.[30] Spendo's voice constantly oscillates from the inner speech to the narration or dictation of monologues and parts of dialogues in sync with her body. These three different kinds of voices, according to (or depending on) the enunciation along with their position in relation to the microphone, enter and leave the image field, as each moment requires a different approach, as if the different voices talk to us or to the characters of the film when it is necessary to interfere, from diverse 'somewheres'. Spendo's disembodied voices embody the sense of time in this film. We are with Spendo, in her time and her space.

Both following and preceding well-known findings from recent scholarship in female voices, mostly in American films, by Kaja Silverman, Amy Lawrence, Sarah Kozloff, Britta Sjogren and Liz Greene, to name but a few,[31] Angelidi gave to Spendo-young girl and to Spendo-narrator and protagonist a smooth intimate articulation, without outbursts of emotion, while all the other voices, anchored in time and space to the image field, are mostly redundant. These other voices create a large acoustic profile, and thus, by dominating 'more acoustic space, they become more imperialistic':[32] This is true of Sophia's voice, the fierce housekeeper, or the voices of many of the men, especially the husband, while he is talking about feminism (42:00), or the voice of the uncle while he is talking about politics (46:00). Both male voices, that of the husband and that of the uncle, utter common gender stereotypes, banalities, with redundant voices, revealing in that way the absurdity of these scenes into their 'reality'.

Unlike her contemporaries, Angelidi chose to work with dubbing in her three Greek films. But, as she has mentioned in many interviews, she would like her films to have the feeling of 'metaglotism'. In Greek film industry jargon the word 'doublage' means the dubbing, the post-synchronisation and the automated dialogue replacement (ADR), while 'metaglotism' describes the dubbing in another language, for example in children's films. The female voices are treated mostly as metaglotism, while the male or 'realistic' voices are seen as a well-realised dubbing. That means that the dubbed voices seem to be in sync with the image, setting up depth on the screen, while the voices that follow the metaglotism practice seem to escort the pictorial flow, offering different auditory events that envelop the cinema hall and the audience.

An exquisite use can be found in *Topos* (1985, mono), where the male voices in the table scene (00:25) are placed in their space and time, in their realistic distance from the camera, in contrast with the voice of a young girl perceived as the voice of a mature woman, which is positioned just off-screen in the audience's position. In the Chionian context, 'The presence of the human voice structures the sonic space that contains it.'[33] This approach regarding the spatialisation of synched (dubbed in reality) male voices talking about the moon as an intruder, and the female voice, which interrupts them to ask to hear the story of the lost woman, disturbs the spatiality of the filming event, revealing at the same time the absurdity of this sole 'realistic' sequence of the film.

In *Thief or Reality* (2001, Dolby Digital), two clearly distinct voices, at the same level but with different pitch, with two different tonalities, offer a double dialogue or two monologues simultaneously, in parallel voice flows, mutually exclusive and/or complementing one another. The audience can choose: listen to one voice or the other, or listen to some words from each one, without grasping the meaning. Now it is commonplace to hear two voices in a film digital soundtrack, yet at the time such a handling of the soundtrack was impossible. Nevertheless, 'if the sound or voices are similar, only one can truly command our attention at one time, so with two going we usually flip back and forth, or perceive an overall pattern between the two without getting into details'.[34] Two voices, one of Antigone (the male voice) and the other of the Thief (the female voice), interact with and are superimposed upon one another as we are left to choose which to listen to (01:10:00), as if we are eavesdropping a discussion between our parents.[35] Similarly, on many occasions, double voices, even of the same person (34:00), repeat parts of the text, single words, with an accelerating tempo, pronounced with a different tonal mode, with different modulations, voicing different possibilities and open to different auditory experiences.

In the same vain in *Idées Fixes*, in a frontal close shot the director herself reads a text in Greek and French, without translation; in *Topos*, an acousmatic voice recites an excerpt from Dante's *Divine Comedy* without translation; in *The Hours* the music teacher recites an excerpt from Leonardo Da Vinci in Italian and after that in Greek; all these, just for the pleasure of listening to different languages, such that the pronunciation in her three later films is more emphatic, with rhythmically enounced accented vowels that give prominence to the musicality of the sound-speech.

In *Topos*, her second film (1985, mono), the human female voice is the exclusive, unique devise, the only instrument that unfolds the sound world of the film and demands particular praise and attention.

A woman, who gives birth and dies in the beginning of the film, is split into many facets, different aspects, different sights, different women; all fragments of the main body, in different or parallel times, embodied in her voice: one female voice, many women and, occasionally, men.

The actress, Annita Santorinaiou, closely miked, modulates a speaking voice and generates different fundamental frequencies or pitches to emit all the voices-speeches of the film through the manipulation of her larynx. The only two exceptions occur in the disembodied recitation of Dante's text in Italian, during the pre-credits and at the end of the film, which is voiced by Maya Liberopoulou, and in the men's table sequence mentioned above.

The 'voices of things' are also expressed vocally by a human female voice. For this film, Angelidi worked from the pre-production stage with the composer Georges Aperghis[36] and she uses his 'Récitations for Solo Voice, 1977–1978', performed by Martine Viard, for the creation of the entire sound and music tracks. In post-production, Angelidi collaborated closely for the registration of all vocal sounds with Martine Viard who improvised while watching the image track, remaining faithful to the written music and notes of Aperghis.

The voiced sounds of the wind, the cracks of a chair, of a table, a rolling wheel, a curtain, a breath, are quasi-synchronous with the image, with some moving elements in the shot. There are some points of synchronisation, that create 'synchresis' in Chionian terms,[37] but only a few shots later, sometimes even in the same shot, the corresponding sound changes and a new effort is solicited from the audience in order to create a new mental association. Both image and sound, in a strange symbiosis, create an uncanny 'synchresis', as Chion defines it:

> Certain experimental videos and films demonstrate that synchresis can even work out of thin air – that is, with images and sounds that strictly speaking have nothing to do with each other, forming monstrous yet inevitable and irresistible agglomerations in our perception.[38]

Indeed, the female voiced sound of the wind becomes the breath of the woman who gives birth and dies; the female voiced sound of the wheel becomes the sound of the cradle; the moving wheel belongs to the young daughter, its sound too. The same vocal sound illustrates, two shots later, the cradle of the tweens, the newborn. One can say that the sound of the wheel becomes a sound of the wind, when the first daughter loses her supremacy and offers her primary sound to the tweens. On the other hand, one can claim that the choices of the human voiced sounds are purely based on their instrumentality and musicality and have nothing to do with the need to seek meaning.

Sounds expose more their aesthetic value, lose completely their representational attributes, removing in that way the same notion of the soundscape, as happens with the image. There is no landscape or soundscape; there is no place out of the frame; there is no time or space, per se, with their accompanying linearity or perspective, but only fragments of timeless moments, so precious in the dream-mechanism. The voices as speech or musical sounds shape the non-topos, the a-topos – dystopia. Borrowing the interesting idea of a vocal *matrix* from Philip Brophy, Angelidi creates 'an expandable network of vocal lines which creates the space for vocal multiplicity, within which vocal ownership is a questionable investment'.[39]

ANTOINETTA ANGELIDI'S NON-SOUNDSCAPES

At a time when the soundscape of Greek films was limited to the "atmos", the ambiences of the scene usually in one or two mono tracks, recorded on location, with some additional sounds from very well-known sound libraries, Angelidi refused to follow the largely accepted practice of 'realistic' soundscapes and progressively removed all 'natural' sounds from her soundtracks. She refused to use ambient sound or sound effects that 'foster the intensified continuity style' of which Bordwell, Smith, Kerin and Donnelly, to name but a few, have already explored the representational attributes, because she didn't need them as such: the small-scale film sound production in Greece in the 1970s and 1980s, with its often poor results, would have perhaps altered and restricted her films' audiovisuality. She called attention, instead, to their aesthetic, emotional and oneiric functions by choosing single, pure sonic elements (such as the voice, for instance), with greater impact on the audience's perception than would have been produced by a 'realistic' ambient sound synthesis.

What is more, between her first film in 1977 and her fourth film in 2001, the environmental sound changed too. The easily located ambient sounds which could have been treated as sound marks of a city, of a specific place and time in the 1970s, were transformed into a more continuous heavy hum, a noise, with more electronic rather than mechanical sounds. This transformation, this evolution of the ambient sounds (technically as well as culturally) is reflected in many films' soundtracks and of course in Angelidi's films. In her first film she chose to create a continuous noisy – albeit orchestrated – irritating sound bath, while in her fourth film, with the advantage of digital sound, she preferred the musicalised silence and clear, naked voices.

She chooses her collaborators/composers with the main idea that every single sound participates in the creation of the musicalised forms and shapes the final musicality of the film.

The music of Angelidi's films mostly belongs to the electro-acoustic style and '*musique concrète*' (concrete music). As already mentioned, she collaborates, as many avant-garde filmmakers do, with acclaimed composers from the pre-production stage onwards. For her first film, *Idées Fixes*, she collaborated, in Paris, with the saxophonist Gilbert Artman, founder of Urban Sax.[40] The idea and the musical principle of this group is 'continuous sound'. Angelidi was also the editor of the film. In her first Greece-based film, *Topos* (monophonic sound), she worked from the outset with the composer Georges Aperghis,[41] as mentioned previously; with Dimitris Kamarotos,[42] for her film *The Hours*, the idea of a music score as a 'twisted lullaby' was discussed long before the shooting, while with Thodoros Abazis,[43] the collaboration for her fourth film, *Thief or Reality* (Dolby Digital), started from the pre-production stage.

Sometimes, Angelidi gives sounds their voices, their 'natural' (recorded) sounds, as in the 'water scenes' in her three later films, or the footsteps in her third film, or the industrial ambient-sync sound in her first film, but mostly she deprives her sound world of the so-called 'ambient' sound.

In her first film, the 'ambient' sound on the bridge, just after the sixteen saxophones, which were progressively added to the composition, playfully blurs the frontier between music and noise. At 00:16, in two almost static frontal shots, the sound reveals its non-static inner qualities and offers, in a way, a slight internal movement to the static image. The same happens in the (once again) 8-min static frontal shot in La Défense metro station, where some 'diegetic' music, along with disembodied footsteps and 'natural' ambient sounds, immerse the perceiver in the contemplation of the time flow.

In *The Hours* (1995, Dolby SR, moviola), Angelidi uses ambient sounds in some shots, where the limits of the frame are clear and offer the listener/viewer an almost realistic notion of space. Accordingly, in other shots, where the darkness removes the edge of the frame, of the screen, when the light creates a new rectangular frame in the frame, which removes even the same notion of the space, the human female voice or the absolute silence take up the torch. It's her only film in which we clearly and repeatedly hear footsteps. In Schafer's words:

> It is not in the heartbeat that the pulse of society is to be measured, but in the choreography of footsteps. The moderate movement of the Italian foot has given us the andante of music (andare, to walk). To know the momentum of a society, measure the footsteps of its citizens.[44]

The sound of the severe and even fearsome Miss Sophia, who walks with a limp (redundant single steps on a wood floor), and, on the other side, the sound of young Spendo when she plays hopscotch (immersed into its natural environmental sound), together form the musicality and the choreography of the whole filming event. In these two films we hear the sounds of some domestic activities, tiny sounds off-screen, close to the edge of the visual field, such as in the final sequence in her first film and in the domestic sequences in *The Hours*. Nevertheless, whenever Angelidi uses 'ambient-sync' sounds, they are tightly linked to sonic archetypes which offer the rhythms of life: water, fire, ground, breath, footsteps. And between them, there is either the voice or the silence.

SILENCE

'Silence is the horizon of sound', Ihde says, and 'the invisible is the horizon of sight'.[45] When the landscape is confined between the lighting zones of the frame, restricted and at the same time unlimited, without borders, the sound is silence.

In *Topos*, as was extensively presented previously, there is no ambient sound. There is silence. The 'dead' space acoustically in movie theatres was a taboo in mono cinema. It was the source of much frustration, and for that reason all technicians and directors usually added the room tone. *Topos* has *no* room tone. For the construction of its sound world the director took into consideration the available infrastructure, that is, the cinema theatres, their acoustics and the sound elements that would have interfered with the soundtrack. She dares, in a mono soundtrack, to leave entire shots in uncanny silence, where the sounds of the theatre hall and those of the audience (hums, cracks, etc.) have the place and the time to dialogue with what is happening on the screen. The audiences can focus on the environmental sounds that occur, or scrutinise what happens on the screen, waiting for a sign of sound. Alluding to John Cage's composition '4'33', where each interpretation changes the hums and the clacks of the audience, thereby changing the composition itself, each screening in the movie theatre changes the soundscape of the film itself. In Angelidi's films, the size of the theatres, the size of the audience, the quality of the amplifiers, the quantity and quality of the speakers, are in charge of this task and the result is always different, always random, and always uncanny.

In Angelidi's Dolby Digital era (*Thief or Reality*, 2001, AVID), when the hum of the optical sound has been 'corrected' and ambient musical sounds are propagated around the theatres using more visceral pathways, we (barely) hear eerie musical sounds in the surrounds similar to the black background of the frame, of the shot, while the listener/viewer strives to see, to hear, to depict something in the abyss that envelops the filming event. Angelidi took advantage of the new possibilities offered by digital sound, and, in this film, she combines voices in multiple layers with musical sounds, with silence.

As Abazis says in an interview in 2001, during the Thessaloniki International Film Festival,

> My collaboration with Antoinetta started long before the shooting of the film for its specific needs. We worked very closely with the sound people, because even a tiny sound, such as the opening of a curtain, or the flap of a bird's wings, along with the voices, the pure speech, should have been incorporated into the music form. We had many rehearsals with the actors before the shooting, and having in mind the extremely detailed storyboard, we started creating musical material from the actors' voices and from the mezzo-soprano Maria Georgakarakou. Nevertheless, when the edited image arrived we realised that we needed to remove some elements, to remove music.[46]

Silence here is different from that of the mono films. It is not aggressive. This digitally created and orchestrated silence with musicalised sounds and musical voices (again!) is abundant and ceases only when the voice-speech is present. Angelidi herself in an interview describes the first part of *Thief or Reality* as 'muted, as references to silent cinema',[47] and it's true, silent cinema always had musical accompaniment. There are no animating sounds, literally speaking; there is only musicalised emptiness which amplifies visuals' denaturalisation.

This elaborated silence of Angelidi's last film is perhaps related to the abundance of non-organised loud sounds (noise) in our acoustic environment, and the new possibilities offered by the digital sound for quitter-controlled soundtracks. Angelidi proposes another model of listening; perhaps, once again, the evolution of the soundscape across her four films and our understanding of it depend on the listening skills or, to use Schafer's passionate argument, on the 'sonological competence'[48] of the audio/viewer.

Angelidi conversed with silence throughout her four films. This emptiness of soundtrack isolates and reveals at the same time the richness of each sound created mainly by vocals, offering multiple and diverse auditory experiences. In the mono period, in *Topos*, when the sound wasn't there, the audience was invited to enter into the screen as the ultimate place for the filming event, so, moviegoers hunched over their seats to enter into the screen. It was pure and uncanny silence.

By contrast, in her digital film, the musicalised sound of silence goes out, towards the audience. What Angelidi was able to provoke in the perceiver during the mono period, with the uncanny silence, in the Dolby Digital era she achieved via the propagation of eerie sounds.

When the mourning Scientist is bent over the table, defeated by her pain (*Thief or Reality*, 20:00–21:00), knocking over and smashing some glasses, the sound is much longer than the distance we have in mind (as gestalt reaction) that separates the floor from the table. The duration of the crashing of the glasses suggests they have a greater distance to travel to the floor. This distance is translated by the perceiver as the necessity of the glasses' crash with what is beyond the image field. Unlike with the mono soundtrack in *Topos*, which almost forces one to bend forward into the screen, now the perceiver, almost frightened, steps back and waits for the sound to reach them. This unbearable torment slides down throughout the extended musicalised sounds of the glasses hitting the floor coming out of the screen, and is propagated all around the theatre until it reaches everyone's body. The place of the filming event is now, once again (albeit with the opposite use of sound), the entire theatre and not just the light screen in front of us.

From Luigi Russolo's futurist manifesto, *The Art of Noises*,[49] to Cage's performance of silence, '4'33', Angelidi navigates between orchestrated noise and elaborated silence in order to offer, in a highly sophisticated and meticulously constructed soundtrack of her notion of film sound, her sound worlds. The noise is here, but also the silence. She interrupts the flow of the visual moving parts in a harsh way as the listener-viewer registers the irritating voices-noise, and at the same time she provokes the listener-viewer in theatres with the silence of the screen and the noises of the audience (hums, cracks, etc.).

Angelidi chooses orchestrated noise – according to Russolo's argument[50] – in her first and third feature films and opts for silence in her second and fourth films. The pattern 'repetition and transformation' is followed once again (on a larger scale), detected via tiny sonic details.

All the examples discussed in this chapter, as part of the tripartite schema highlighted earlier, have attempted to identify the multiple factors influencing the final artistic choices, characterising and perpetually shaping the personal aesthetics of Angelidi's filming universe.

Angelidi's work challenges, especially during its specific era of production, the established sound approaches and taxonomies in terms of their diegetic functions or with regard to the location of their source, or even their categorisation and hierarchy in the filming event (voice, music, sound, effects, etc.), key issues for film studies research, especially about that period.

Visual and sonic practices developed and adopted by Angelidi throughout her four films require an almost somatically experienced participation, beyond consciousness or cognitive responses to the filming event. The awareness of this bodily sensation, the embodiment of these sophisticated soundtracks, leads to the immersion of the perceiver in Angelidi's film world. This chapter has contextualised the cultural and industrial specificities of a peripheral country such as Greece, specificities that film sound studies seem to neglect or even ignore, and stressed the particularities of soundtrack construction and its uniqueness in Angelidi's films.

AUTHOR'S ACKNOWLEDGEMENTS

I am indebted to Lydia Papadimitriou, Giorgos Papakonstantinou and Eliza Anna Delveroudi who made generous contributions of time, suggestions and ideas to this paper.

NOTES

1. The first is the production format and the second is the distribution format.
2. Murray R. Schafer, *The Soundscape: Our Sonic Environment and the Turning of the World*, Second Edition (Rochester, VT: Destiny Books, 1994), 151.
3. According to Dolby Laboratories' data, the first film with Dolby Stereo Optical 4-ch was released in 1976, the first Dolby SR Optical 4-ch in 1987 and the first Dolby Digital Optical 5.1-ch in 1992. In Joseph Hull, *Surround Sound: Past, Present and Future* (Dolby Laboratories Inc., 1999), 3, <http://docplayer.net/24307370-Surround-sound-past-present-and-future-a-history-of-multichannel-audio-from-mag-stripe-to-dolby-digital.html>, accessed 1 June 2022.
4. The second wave of film sound studies probably started with Claude Bailblé's articles in *Cahiers du cinema* ('Programmation de l'ecoute', 1978–1979) and was followed by the seminal issue 'Cinema/Sound', edited by Rick Altman, of the journal *Yale French Studies*, in 1980, and Michel Chion's *The Voice in Cinema* in 1982, with the advent of multichannel sound.
5. Kevin J. Donnelly, 'Extending Film Aesthetics: Audio beyond Visuals', in *The Oxford Handbook of New Audiovisual Aesthetics*, ed. John Richardson, Claudia Gorbman and Carol Vernallis (New York: Oxford University Press, 2013), 358; Holly Rogers and Jeremy Barham, *The Music and Sound of the Experimental Film* (New York: Oxford University Press, 2017), 1, among other works.
6. Laura Mulvey, 'Visual Pleasure and Narrative Cinema', *Screen* 16, 3 (Autumn 1975): 17.
7. Rogers and Barham, *Music and Sound of the Experimental Film*, 2.
8. Italics mine.
9. Rogers and Barham, *Music and Sound of the Experimental Film*, 4.
10. Maureen Cheryn Turim, *Abstraction in Avant-Garde Films* (Michigan: UMI Research Press, 1985, 1978), 35.
11. See Stella Theodoraki, 'L'anatreptikos dans le cinema Grec' [The Subversive in Greek Cinema], in *Le cinéma Grec*, ed. Michel Dimopoulos (Paris: Centre Georges Pompidou, 1995), 118–25. Further explored in Nikos Tsagkarakis, *I Elliniki Kinimatografiki Protoporia* (Greek Experimental Cinema), PhD dissertation, University of Crete, 2017, <https://elocus.lib.uoc.gr/dlib/1/3/a/metadata-dlib-1528975299-213682-26618.tkl>, accessed 10 January 2021.
12. Kostas Sfikas presented his film *Modelo*, without sound, at the Thessaloniki Film Festival and won the 1st Award (1974).
13. Tom Whittaker and Sara Wright (eds), *Locating the Voice in Film* (USA: Oxford University Press, 2019), 4.
14. Roland Barthes, *Image, Music, Text*, trans. Stephen Heath (London: Fontana Press, 1977), 182.

15. 'As a material product, cinema quickly reveals the location and nature of its sound track(s), the technology used to produce them, the apparatus necessary for reproduction, and the physical relationship between loudspeakers, spectators, and their physical surroundings'. Rick Altman, *Sound Theory, Sound Practice* (New York: Routledge, 1992), 6.
16. Vrasidas Karalis, *Realism in Greek Cinema* (London and New York: I. B. Tauris, 2016), 206–8.
17. Eleni Mahera, 'Painting the Matrix', in *Writings on Cinema*, ed. Antoinetta Angelidi, Eleni Mahera and Konstantinos Kyriacos (Athens: Nefeli, 2005), 176–7.
18. Rea Walldén, 'Conversing with Dreams: An Encounter with Antoinetta Angelidi', *Filmicon: Journal of Greek Film Studies* 4 (December 2017), 186.
19. Rick Altman, 'Introduction', *Yale French Studies* 60 (1980): 6.
20. Michel Chion, *Film, A Sound Art*, trans. Claudia Gorbman (New York: Columbia University Press, 2009), 228.
21. Michel Chion, *Audio-Vision*, trans. Claudia Gorbman (New York: Columbia University Press, 1994), 150–1.
22. Walldén, 'Conversing with Dreams', 189.
23. Schafer, *Soundscape*, 9.
24. Electra Venaki, 'Sound Spaces in the Four Films of Antoinetta Angelidi', in Stella Theodorakis (ed.), *Antoinetta Angelidi* (Athens: Aigokeros – Thessaloniki International Film Festival, 2005), 28–30, trans. Zoe Siapanta, <http://www.altcine.com/details.php?id=396>, accessed 5 January 2021.
25. Schafer, *Soundscape*, 160.
26. Don Ihde, *Listening and Voice: Phenomenologies of Sound* (New York: State University of New York Press, Albany, 2007), 197, 153.
27. For the feminist gaze of Angelidi's films see, Rea Walldén, 'The Spatio-Temporality of the Avant-Gardes: Feminist Avant-Garde U-Topoi in Greek Cinema from Transition to Crisis', in *Contemporary Greek Film Cultures from 1990 to the Present*, ed. T. Kazakopoulou and M. Fotiou (Bern: Peter Lang, 2017), 71–99.
28. Philip Brophy, 'I Scream in Silence: Cinema, Sex and the Sound of Women Dying', in *Cinesonic: The World of Sound in Film*, ed. Philip Brophy (Australia: Australian Film, Television & Radio School North Ryde, NSW, 1999), 67.
29. Sarah Kozloff, *Overhearing Film Dialogue* (Berkeley: University of California Press, 2000), 13.
30. I don't use the English translation as I believe there is a slight difference between 'image-mémoire' and recollection images.
31. In chronological order: Kaja Silverman *The Acoustic Mirror: The Female Voice in Psychoanalysis and Cinema* (Bloomington and Indianapolis: Indiana University Press, 1988); Amy Lawrence, *Echo and Narcissus: Women's Voices in Classical Hollywood Cinema* (Oxford: University of California Press, 1991); Sarah Kozloff, *Overhearing Film Dialogue*; Britta Sjogren, *Into the Vortex: Female Voice and Paradox in Film* (Urbana and Chicago: University of Illinois Press, 2006); Liz Green, 'Speaking, Singing, Screaming: Controlling the Female Voice in American Cinema', *The Soundtrack* 2, 1 (2009): 63–76, <doi:10.1386/st.2.1.63/1>. All these works have pointed out the silencing or softness of women's voices in American films, in contrast to the clear, loud male voices.
32. Shafer, *Soundscape*, 77.
33. Michel Chion, *The Voice in Cinema*, trans. Claudia Gorbman (New York: Columbia University Press, 1999), 5.
34. David Sonnenschein, *Sound Design: The Expressive Power of Music, Voice and Sound Effects in Cinema* (Studio City, CA: Michael Wiese Productions, 2001), 93.
35. From a private conversation with Angelidi, in which she alludes inevitably to Elisabeth Weis's paper, 'Eavesdropping: An Aural Analogue of Voyeurism?', in *Cinesonic*, ed. Philip Brophy, 79–107.

36. See <http://www.aperghis.com/>, accessed 10 January 2021.
37. Chion, *Audio-Vision*, 63: 'Synchresis (a word I have forged by combining synchronism and synthesis) is the spontaneous and irresistible weld produced between a particular auditory phenomenon and visual phenomenon when they occur at the same time. This join results independently of any rational logic.'
38. Chion, *Audio-Vision*, 63.
39. Brophy, 'I Scream in Silence', 64.
40. <https://urbansax.com/presentation/; https://en.wikipedia.org/wiki/Urban_Sax>, accessed 10 January 2022.
41. <http://www.aperghis.com/>, accessed 10 January 2022.
42. <http://dimitriskamarotos.com/bio/>, accessed 10 January 2022.
43. <http://composers.musicportal.gr/?lang=en&c=abazis>, accessed 10 January 2022.
44. Schafer, *Soundscape*, 164.
45. Ihde, *Listening and Voice: Phenomenologies of Sound*, 50, 51.
46. Theodoros Abatzis, 'Music of the Images', in *Antoinetta Angelidi*, ed. Stella Theodorakis, 113. The translation is mine.
47. Karalis, *Realism in Greek Cinema*, 211. In this extract, Angelidi refers to the pictorial synthesis as well.
48. Shafer, *Soundscape*, 153–5.
49. Luigi Russolo, *The Art of Noises* (futurist manifesto, 1913), trans. Robert Filliou (Ubu Classics, 2014).
50. Russolo, *The Art of Noises*, 11: 'We must replace the limited variety of timbres of orchestral instruments by theinfinite variety of timbres of noises obtained through special mechanisms.'

BIBLIOGRAPHY

Altman, Rick (ed.). 'Cinema/Sound'. Special issue of *Yale French Studies* 60, 1980, <doi:10.2307/2930000>.
Altman, Rick (ed.). *Sound Theory, Sound Practice*. New York: Routledge, 1992.
Angelidi, Antoinetta, Eleni Mahera and Konstantinos Kyriacos (eds). *Writings on Cinema*. Athens: Nefeli, 2005.
Barthes, Roland. *Image, Music, Text*, trans. Stephen Heath. London: Fontana Press, 1977, 182.
Birtwistle, Andy. *Cinesonica: Sounding Film and Video*. Manchester: Manchester University Press, 2010.
Bordwell, David. 'Intensified Continuity: Visual Style in Contemporary American Film'. *Film Quarterly* 55, 3 (2002): 16–28.
Bordwell, David. *The Way Hollywood Tells It*. Berkeley: University of California Press, 2006.
Brophy, Philip (ed.). *Cinesonic: The World of Sound in Film*. Australia: Australian Film, Television & Radio School North Ryde, NSW, 1999.
Buhler, James. *Theories of the Soundtrack*. Oxford: Oxford University Press, 2019.
Calotychos, Vaggelis. *The Balkan Prospect-Identity: Culture and Politics in Greece after 1989*. London: Palgrave Macmillan, 2013.
Cheryn Turim, Maureen. *Abstraction in Avant-Garde Films*. Michigan: UMI Research Press, [1978] 1985.
Chion, Michel. *La voix au cinéma*. Paris: Editions de l'Etoile, 1982.
Chion, Michel. *Le son au cinéma*. Paris: Editions de l'Etoile, 1985.
Chion, Michel. *Audio-vision*. Paris: Editions Nathan, 1990.

Chion, Michel. 'Quiet Revolution . . . And Rigid Stagnation', trans. Ben Brewster. *October* 58 (Autumn 1991): 69–80.
Chion, Michel. *Audio-Vision: Sound on Screen*, ed. and trans. Claudia Gorbman. New York: Columbia University Press, 1994.
Chion, Michel. *The Voice in Cinema*, trans. Claudia Gorbman. New York: Columbia University Press, 1999.
Chion, Michel. *Film, A Sound Art*, trans. Claudia Gorbman. New York: Columbia University Press, 2009.
Deleuze, Gilles. *Cinema 2: The Time-Image*, trans. Hugh Tomlinson and Robert Galeta. Minneapolis: University of Minnesota Press, 1985–1989.
Donnelly, Kevin J. 'Extending Film Aesthetics: Audio beyond Visuals', in *The Oxford Handbook of New Audiovisual Aesthetics*, ed. John Richardson, Claudia Gorbman and Carol Vernallis. New York: Oxford University Press, 2013, 357–71.
Flynn, Niall. 'An Intimate Encounter: Negotiating Subtitled Cinema'. *Open Library of Humanities* 2, 1 (2016): e1, 1–28.
Greene, Liz. 'Speaking, Singing, Screaming: Controlling the Female Voice in American Cinema'. *The Soundtrack* 2, 1 (2009): 63–76, <doi: 10.1386/st.2.1.63/1>
Greene, Liz, and Danijela Kulezic-Wilson (eds). *The Palgrave Handbook of Sound Design and Music in Screen Media*. London: Palgrave Macmillan, 2016.
Hull, Joseph. *Surround Sound: Past, Present and Future*. Dolby Laboratories Inc., 1999.
Ihde, Don. *Listening and Voice: Phenomenologies of Sound*. Albany: State University of New York Press, 2007.
Karalis, Vrasidas. *A History of Greek Cinema*. New York: The Continuum International Publishing Group, 2012.
Kerins, Mark. *Beyond Dolby (Stereo): Cinema in the Digital Sound Age*. Bloomington: Indiana University Press, 2011.
Kozloff, Sarah. *Overhearing Film Dialogue* (Berkeley: University of California Press, 2000).
Kytö, Meri, Nicolas Remy and Heikki Uimonen. *European Acoustic Heritage*. Tampere: Tampere University of Applied Sciences (TAMK), and Grenoble: CRESSON, 2012.
Lawrence, Amy. *Echo and Narcissus: Women's Voices in Classical Hollywood Cinema*. Oxford: University of California Press, 1991.
Mahera, Eleni. 'Painting the Matrix', in Antoinetta Angelidi, Eleni Mahera and Konstantinos Kyriacos (eds), *Writings on Cinema*. Athens: Nefeli, 2005, 176–7.
Mulvey, Laura. 'Visual Pleasure and Narrative Cinema', *Screen* 16, 3 (1975): 6–18, <https://doi.org/10.1093/screen/16.3.6>
Rogers, Holly and Jeremy Barham (eds). *The Music and Sound of the Experimental Film*. New York: Oxford University Press, 2017.
Russolo, Luigi. *The Art of Noise* (futurist manifesto, 1913), trans. Robert Filliou. Ubu Classics, 2014. Originally published as Luigi Russolo, Robert Filliou and Francesco Bailla Pratella, *The Art of Noise: Futurist Manifesto*. New York: Something Else Press, 1967.
Schafer, R. Murray. *The Soundscape: Our Sonic Environment and the Turning of the World*. Second Edition. Rochester, VT: Destiny Books, 1994.
Shingler, Martin. 'Fasten Your Seatbelts and Prick Up Your Ears: The Dramatic Human Voice in Film'. *Scope* 5 (June 2006). <https://www.nottingham.ac.uk/scope/documents/2006/june-2006/shingler.pdf>, accessed 13 November 2020.
Silverman, Kaja. *The Acoustic Mirror: The Female Voice in Psychoanalysis and Cinema* (Bloomington and Indianapolis: Indiana University Press, 1988),
Sjogren, Britta. *Into the Vortex: Female Voice and Paradox in Film*. Urbana and Chicago: University of Illinois Press, 2006.

Sobchack, Vivian. 'When the Ear Dreams: Dolby Digital and the Imagination of Sound'. *Film Quarterly* 58, 4 (Summer 2005): 2–15.
Sonnenschein, David. *Sound Design: The Expressive Power of Music, Voice and Sound Effects in Cinema*. Studio City, CA: Michael Wiese Productions, 2001.
Truax, Barry. *Acoustic Communication*. Second Edition. Westport, CT: Ablex Publishing, 2001.
Tsagkarakis, Nikos. *I Elliniki Kinimatografiki Protoporia* ('Greek Experimental Cinema'), PhD, University of Crete, 2017.
Walldén, Rea. 'Conversing with Dreams: An Encounter with Antoinetta Angelidi'. *FilmIcon: Journal of Greek Film Studies* 4 (December 2017): 186.
Walldén, Rea. 'The Spatio-Temporality of the Avant-Gardes: Feminist Avant-Garde U-Topoi in Greek Cinema from Transition to Crisis', in *Contemporary Greek Film Cultures from 1990 to the Present*, ed. T. Kazakopoulou and M. Fotiou. Bern: Peter Lang, 2017, 71–99.

CHAPTER 8

Dreyer, Magritte and Other Obsessions: Figural Invention in Antoinetta Angelidi's *Idées Fixes / Dies Irae – Variations on the Same Subject*

Kyriakos Dionysopoulos

The film *Idées Fixes / Dies Irae – Variations on the Same Subject* (1977) is governed by the principle of inversion: between word and image, depth and surface, and male and female. No element, visual, acoustic or written, appears in a state of self-affirmation without having already been distorted by another, also without contaminating another. The film incorporates conflicting claims, without favouring one or the other, maintaining for itself a position of inbetweenness. Each integrated element affects its host, tampering with its identity, haunting it with possibilities and voices. The figural layout of the film title, as it appears on the screen, breaks down the horizontal axis of two formulaic syntagms, 'idées fixes' ('obsessions') and 'dies irae' ('day of wrath'), reconstructing them vertically as 'IDEESDIES' and 'FIXESIRAE' – which would be vertical, were the two original syntagms to be written in two consecutive lines, welded into a continuous horizontal sequence, each resulting amalgamation evoking the components of a *locus communis*, a lost minimal 'isotopy'.[1] However, the fact that they are rebound horizontally does not necessarily mean that they should be read in this way. On the contrary, it signals that we are free to read not only vertically, as a kind of *parallelismus membrorum*, but also as 'ideas of wrath' or 'fixed days'. The change of order, discontinuing unidirectional time, standardises the chiastic coupling as a *modus operandi* of the overall direction of the film. The reversal of the spatial axes is established as a construction principle of the text, which will culminate, as we shall see, in the paradox of a vertical horizon.

The relationship between the theme and its variations, as indicated in the subtitle of the film, is the second constructive principle of the film. The shots form a network of variations, interchanging their components, complementing each other and cross-referencing throughout the film. The question is what the theme is: it is absent, a structural centre which lies elsewhere. It permeates the film, leaking into the details of its materials, but only the distorted 'Dies Irae' of the title gives its name away; it is Carl Dreyer's film of the same title (*Vredens Dag* ['Day of Wrath'], 1943). In a relationship of double exclusion, the short but dense essay that Angelidi wrote on *Vredens Dag*, entitled 'Two Heritages? (*Dies Irae*)', concerns equally, without mentioning it, her own film, an implicit confession of what remains unsaid in the film itself. Adopting Apollinaire's lesson, Godard once argued that the best way to review a film is by making another film. In her film, Angelidi re-writes Dreyer's film in the way in which she will read it, while, in her essay, she effectively reads it in the way in which she has already re-written it. It is logical, then, to begin our own reading from the same byway, revisiting her essay.

THE TWO HERITAGES

According to Angelidi, each of *Vredens Dag*'s lead characters is marked by a series of dichotomies, which divide her/his existence into opposite poles, such as body/spirit, desire/law, sensuality/moral consciousness, from which she/he must choose to reconcile with one only while defending it. This series is dictated by a dominant dichotomy, which implies symmetrical antithesis between the sexes in traditional terms of activity and passivity or power and submission. This legacy of gender differentiation as insurmountable and indelible preserves and perpetuates all kinds of alienation in the life and death of the characters. However, Angelidi demonstrates through the character of Ann that, if there are 'two heritages' (maternal/paternal), one is not the opposite of the other. The maternal heritage contains the possibility of overcoming both dichotomy and symmetry, by incorporating the symbolic opposites. While the paternal, in the interest of the reproduction of its ideology, holds fast to the reciprocal exclusion between the terms of each binary opposition, where one term corresponds bijectively to the other, the plurality of the maternal allows the affirmation of more than one choice, where no single signifier of sex difference claims the final meaning of any social discourse.

The invasion of the blood-stained Herlofs Marte into the rectory, persecuted as a witch, reveals to Ann the alternative of claiming pleasure, an unprecedented transgression for her, 'wild as her lust', which redeems her from guilt. Accepting the maternal heritage, the legacy of a mother who was also accused of being a witch, but not convicted, because she was saved by Absalon, Ann's husband, Ann recuperates her sacrificed desire and becomes 'dangerous for men's law': 'she becomes a *witch* because she *desires*'.[2] Here 'dies irae' stands as an anagram for 'desire'. Dreyer's *mise-en-scène*, through sets, costumes, lighting and colour palette, frames the characters between contending assertions, exposing their inner conflicts and limited options available. For example, the sets, unable to restore an individual's experience into a totality, distribute the 'two heritages' to separate spaces. Hence Herlofs Marte is privileged in outdoor locations, in the countryside where the forces of nature reside. When she enters the rectory, she is captured by her persecutors in the attic. In contrast, Absalon dwells indoors, in the rectory and in the interrogation and torture chamber. When he goes out into the countryside, on his return from Laurentius's home, the elements of nature take revenge on him, and the storm anticipates his demise. Herlofs Marte is burned in the countryside as a possessor of the forces of evil, of nature. Absalon dies inside the rectory from exhaustion or from the harshness of Ann's words, 'a continuation of Herlofs Marte's'. On the other hand, Ann

> chooses to die inside and / or outside, she chooses not to try to escape and whether she is a witch or not is of no importance. She is and she is not, she is both nature and spirituality. [. . .] The integration of nature and interior architectural space is ultimately realised onto Ann's face-landscape. Like Jeanne d'Arc [in Dreyer's 1928 film *La Passion de Jeanne d'Arc*], she claimed for her personal truth finding it in the final introjection of nature. Each set retreats and gives its place to pure white [. . .].[3]

Angelidi's last remarks are partly based on Philippe Parrain's observation that, in the course of the film, 'pure white and black are continuously in conflict, dividing [Ann] between them, forcing her to choose'.[4] In the final shot, with the internalisation of nature and the retreat of décor, comes the lifting of dichotomy, setting both her consciousness and sensuality free and allowing them to occupy visual space. On the other hand, Martin, Absalon's son from a previous marriage and the incestuous object of Ann's desire, 'like any repentant, former participant in a revolution', restores the dichotomy and inherits paternal authority through a treacherous act, the betrayal of Ann. He thus camouflages the indirect murder of the father being the fundamental violation of the law that establishes every law. Through the 'suppression of the flesh-pleasure', Martin restores the return to the order of an 'asexually incestuous family'. The cohabitation of the two heritages within that of the maternal opens up the prospect of abolishing the hegemony of any signifier that supports their difference, as the guarantor of truth, justice and ownership. Thus, the meaning of each discourse may remain open to a radical contingency.

Angelidi's reading of Dreyer's film in her essay summarises the *idée fixe* (theme) on which she orchestrates her own *dies irae* (variations). She re-imagines *Vredens Dag* and reshapes its visual and narrative patterns into the fabric of her own film. The chiastic intersection of the words in the title, as shown on the screen, suggests that what is an element of content (*idées*) in Dreyer will be transformed figurally in Angelidi, since *dies* indicates what comes to visibility, in the light of day; what is a figural element in Dreyer will be transmogrified into an element of content. In this dual-front processing, the ideological theme will unfold in a series of figural variations, while the figural espacement will be transformed into ideational values. As Lyotard demonstrated, the figure stages both a conflict between the visible line and the intelligible letter *and* an interweaving between spatial configuration and verbal speech.[5] What Angelidi calls the 'corporealisation of concepts'[6] presupposes the verbalisation of corporeality. This notion is exemplarily suggested in Angelidi's pointer to her actress, Josy Delettre, who plays the character of the bald woman:

> I had to tell her that she should move like a volume in the film, as if we had a square piece of paper in the middle of which a sphere comes in and then leaves. [. . .] What was important was that she be a sphere, not moving, let's say, her arm in a way that protrudes from the sphere. [. . .] 'Your movements have to be minimal [. . .] you must realise that you stand and move in a cube and your body is a sphere inside that cube'.[7]

This remark is programmatic for the 'redefinition of the actor in relation to the other elements [of image and sound]'[8] and applies to Angelidi's entire oeuvre. The bodies, losing their dramatic character, dematerialise into archetypal geometric shapes, abstract signs, symbols, sounds, gaps or blots on the surface of the screen. The spoken word pervades the image, folding into its graphic matrix; and, vice versa, the visual image filters through the word and impregnates it with spatiality. Accordingly, the image is disrupted by a discursive structure and imbued with a layer of 'opacity', while the figure installs a pictorial layout into the 'transparency' of language. Movement, colour, lighting, framing, scenery and performance coordinate with one another to produce machines of figural invention. The secret of the image, if any, lies not in the hypothesis of a meaning concealed within it, but in the transformations of the figure, in its movement and *peripeteia*.[9] However, nothing corresponds between the two texts in a one-to-one relationship. On the contrary, the variation may only be slightly reminiscent of the theme, yet it retains its essence in its details; the detail constitutes an unbroken line on the basis of which we can identify the theme. In the hermetic rhetoric of this collection of fragments, the standard becomes iconoclasm, epilepsy, a demon's entrance into the body of the normal. Therefore, by detaching the core of *Vredens Dag*, filtering it through its own obsessions and refolding the one into the other, *Idées Fixes / Dies Irae* dreams of Dreyer's film.

The logic of 'variations on the same subject' implies that the syntagmatic relations among the shots, in the sense of narrative transitivity and logical continuity, weaken. 'I could not write linearly', says Angelidi.[10] At the end of the film we are still at the beginning. The serial structure encourages us to perceive the images 'in a non-associative manner',[11] out of forward causality; the pattern of thematic repetition replaces one image with another by abrupt transitions and jumps, as if they were successive 'parentheses'.[12] Hence 'the production of different intensities'[13]: each 'intensity' emits an amount of energy, which is not transferred to the adjacent shot, but concerns the level of immanence, that is the series of materials, a 'series of parallel texts',[14] inside a single shot. However, as the suspension of a linear trajectory seals each shot from its neighbours, the enclosed 'parallel texts' are not necessarily synchronised with each other; on the contrary, the more each shot closes itself in its own content, the more its materials 'defect' and spread themselves within the whole through the paradigmatic axis. Each shot cannot trace itself to an overlying and all-encompassing totality, since the whole consists, precisely, of repetitions of the 'same theme'. Thus, the reading is legitimised to combine materials between different variations: to attach, as we shall see, a sound to an image that comes later or to put together two distant movements. In every shot, an endless gestation of all the rest takes place.

The *idée fixe* on *Dies Irae* should be understood literally; the same latent thought underlies every shot of the film: the theme of the 'two heritages', in other words, summarised by Walldén as 'the experience of the psychic and social construction of the woman' and, more specifically, 'the impasse of a revolution that ignored women, even though it was enthusiastically accepted by them'.[15] Dreyer's film, as read and re-written by Angelidi, hints at a way out by questioning dichotomy. In her struggle for a new kind of cinema, she engages with the subversive potential of Dreyer's legacy as a form of resistance to stereotyped representations of women's subjectivity. Her article is the ultimate variation on the Dreyer theme, but it is logically presupposed by the rest of the variations in her film. So, the last variation is the theme of the previous ones. And Dreyer's film becomes another variation on the Angelidian theme.

PHANTOMS IN THE MIRROR

In the fourth shot of *Idées Fixes / Dies Irae* we are introduced into the interior of a covered bridge of a railway station. By placing the vanishing point at the centre of the frame, the camera quadruples the isosceles triangle formed by the convergence of perspective lines and produces the ground plan of an inverted Albertian 'visual pyramid', with the top of the image mirroring the bottom and the left side mirroring the right. A large bald woman enters the frame following the trajectory of a couple of black silhouettes, of indeterminate gender, which walked away down a cemetery path in the opening shot (Figure 8.1). She is, according to Angelidi, a 'woman-man' or 'the symbol of a castrated woman'.[16]

Figure 8.1 Still, Angelidi, *Idées Fixes / Dies Irae* (1977).

The figure that travelled towards the background is withheld by the image; she is a hostage to it, as is the viewer. But this shot also introduces us into a time whirlpool, where a *katabasis*[17] is attempted, involving a confrontation with the legacy of gender. The woman makes a propitiatory offer to the three men who stand petrified at the entrance to the Underworld. Like most characters in the film, judging by their particular hairstyles, clothes and gestures, they do not own 'a single heritage', but are on the verge of an ambiguous, non-binary gender; in fact, the reversal of depth and surface extends to the figural refolding of gender characteristics. Yet, in this case, the woman does not offer libations to the dead to exact an oath from their souls to foretell the future, as did the epic heroes when they descended to the nether world to meet their parents; rather, it is a descent into the prehistory of childhood. The male figures are not so much guardians of Hades, a three-headed Cerberus,[18] as abandoned marionettes with identical bodies, totally mastered, reproducible images, just before they take on the oedipal roles that will be given to them in the 'family romance' of the next shot; to be sure, the plunge into the depths of perspective proves to be a move towards revelation, not deprivation, a *nostos*.[19] In the fifth shot, we are already in the tenebrous house of a childhood memory, and darkness here is a means of vision. However, if we accept that the bridge leads to the metro station of La Défense, that is, if we associate it with a Paris Metro sign in a persistent shot that comes, exactly in the middle of the film, to mark this woman's becoming retroactively, then what follows is the defence process of a screen memory blocking an unpleasant perception and denying through distortion the traumatic past.

Here is anxiety as disturbing as the way its motivation escapes us. The space of the station bridge has been morphed into a home interior. Due to the fact that the perspective depth is obscured, the room, although its door is open, does not reveal its secret. We need to look at René Magritte's *L'Assassin Menacé* (1927) to realise that what is most crucial is missing. In that painting, which this shot transcribes, hiding its most essential clues, two men, possibly detectives, armed with a club and a net, lurk on both sides of the foyer to ensnare the 'killer' who is listening to music on a gramophone in the room, while a blood-smeared naked woman is lying on a couch. In Angelidi's rendering, the lethargic marionettes of the previous shot take the place of the shadowy avengers of the murderer, while a voice is heard stuttering 'père . . . peur' ('father . . . fear'). Some commentators on the painting have linked the female figure to the painter's mother, who drowned herself in a river when Magritte was fourteen, and the killer to Fantômas, the anti-hero of popular novels and films who spread terror through a series of murders, robberies and abductions.[20] What better setting could be found for the staging of the *primal scene*,[21] the child's fantasy of the parents'

Figure 8.2 Still, Angelidi, *Idées Fixes / Dies Irae* (1977).

coitus as a heinous crime against the mother? We are not interested in the identity and motives of the killer: we already know. The two detectives, powerless to prevent the primary violence, re-enact an elementary situation, the desire to rescue the mother and get revenge for the paternal assault.

In this shot, the two pig heads, hung on the wall, recall the 'hole with the pigs', the fate of Herlofs Marte, especially her capture in the semi-darkness of the rectory attic (Figure 8.2). Along with the stacks of accumulated boxes and the rails on the floor, echoing the tracking shot in the attic, they remind us that intruding into an attic is the 'royal road' to the 'clutter' of the unconscious. They also allude to another witch, Circe, also *polypharmakos*, an expert on potions and herbs, *Odyssey*'s archetype of a sexually predatory woman, who, by subjugating most of Odysseus's crew to their primitive impulses, makes them lose both their self-control and freedom, in other words, transforms them into pigs. The 'supernatural' and, therefore, inscrutable cause of anxiety, violence and moral corruption of the male is supposed to be rooted in the abyss of the enigmatic desire of a sorceress. Evoking the blood-stained Herlofs Marte in the attic and keeping up with the Surrealistic interest in the imagery of female victims,[22] originating in the imagination of Romanticism, the mother lying dead in the room is an aestheticised sadistic version of the same primordial fear. As the painting is inspired by a shot from the third part of the *Fantômas* series, entitled *Le Mort qui Tue* (*The Dead Man Who Killed*, Louis Feuillade, 1913), in which two men wearing black hoods secretly wait outside a door to attack a man who is wielding a knife, Angelidi reterritorialises the figural where it originally belonged, giving it back to its cinematic matrix. Next we will try to find out what happened inside the room. Paraphrasing Magritte, the only way to capture Fantômas is to enter his victims' dreams.[23]

The crime scene of the painting is framed by the two detectives in the foreground and the three men at the window, who, according to some commentators, represent the painter as a boy and his younger brother, hidden in the background, peeking at what is happening in the room. The depth-to-surface correspondence brings these two groups of male figures together.

The detectives exhibit the features of the boys' idealised personality, grown-up and so raised to a level with their father. As Freud says, in the rescue-phantasy all the boy's instincts 'find satisfaction in the single wish to be his own father'.[24] The presence of the extra 'boy', matching the 'failed', murderous version of the father, balances the number of figures on both sides of 'spectators' and 'actors'. Thus the prospect of arresting the killer is suggested as the classic oedipal choice of transition from 'being' to 'having'. In Angelidi's *mise-en-scène*, the centre and the periphery are transposed; on the one hand, the three 'children' are in the place of the avengers; and, on the other, in the next shot, we watch the primal scene through the 'window' of a mirror, while in close-up the child becomes a woman. The aperture in the background of the painting, from where the voyeurs look at us, turns into a 'hole' through which we see what is happening 'behind' us, behind the point where the camera is placed. So we borrow the position of the window observers. Through the censorship of the mirror, the supposedly monstrous act that took place in the parents' bedroom is sublimated into a funereal ritual. But even if we are probably 'disappointed' at the enclosed spectacle, we see the same thing as the eyewitnesses in the painting: the bed sheets testify to that.

In a further reversal of the scenario of the primal scene, the father *protects* by enshrouding the mother, using the sheet that already covered the monument in the second shot, whereas the bald woman, in the guise of a white cloak, borrowed from the inquisitor's wardrobe, although she is clad in black on the bridge, *enjoys*, first eating a pineapple and, then, plucking a chicken while laughing deliriously.[25] The knife and the dead chicken eloquently represent the act that took place. The plucking hints at defloration; a promiscuous woman or a slut is the sexist connotation of the word 'poule' (hen) in French; and the pineapple ('ananas') figuralises masturbation ('onanisme') by means of phonetic affinity. Accordingly, the syntactically ambiguous phrase 'old women / who are burning / corpses / from masturbation', which is later heard in the 'big letter' scene, condenses the enjoyment of the bald woman and the fate of Herlofs Marte. However, her tropes of enjoyment are not stabilised in the genital zone; as Irigaray writes, '*woman has sex organs more or less everywhere*. She finds pleasure almost anywhere'.[26] The pineapple and the chicken comprise a pair of part-objects suited to an active oral stage.[27] This is reinforced by the phrase 'the handkerchief smells like mum and I eat it', also heard in the 'big letter' scene. To understand the connection between the handkerchief or the sheet and the screen we have to take into account the theorisation of the dual relation of the infant-spectator with the breast-screen, an object relation that 'feeds' the cinematic projection.[28] We see not only with the eyes, but also with the mouth. We suck the image and merge with the 'blank background', with the maternal flesh that supports it. In this case, the oral drive connects one Magritte painting at issue with another, *Le Plaisir* (1927), from which the scene with the chicken draws the full meaning of its multiple perversity. Death and feminine *jouissance*[29] converge on the image of blood, in one painting trickling from the mouth of the dead woman with a handkerchief over her neck, while in the other dripping from the mouth of a girl who eats a bird alive, staining her lacy collar. Later, driving Ann's 'dissolved sensuality' to the limit, at which Dreyer had attempted to arrive only in another film (*Vampyr*, 1932), particularly with the character of Léone, we see two extreme close-ups of Angelidi's mouth, one with a razor blade in it and another with her tongue licking her lips, both favouring an erotic devouring, a deadly embodiment. Reversing inside and outside once again, the piercing laughter of the bald woman and the monologue of the 'big letter' turn what has been devoured so far into a voice and then, by throwing it out, break away from it. The voice should be understood in its 'excremental' dimension, as a leftover of the symbolic process, a residue discarded from any linguistic meaning, a waste and, therefore, as an *objet petit a*, a cause of desire or anxiety *par excellence*.[30] The voice, 'solidified' in an acoustic block and separated from the other elements, works to undermine the image and, like the 'visual poem' that fills the screen, takes on the dimensions of the frame becoming a square. Thus, any illusion of complementarity between speech and image is rejected.

We should listen to the litany of dictionary entries, recited by Angelidi, in a similar manner. In this sequence of Greek words in alphabetical order, the broken-up delivery of the initial syllable of each one, always an alpha, accompanied by percussion sounds, sectioning it from the rest of the word, performs vocally the material remainder of the symbolic process, the *objet a* of the speech sound itself as a cause in the strict sense. The voice doesn't belong to a body; the gaze and the voice are adrift of each other. Angelidi apparently searches in vain for her name among these words. In Greek her name, 'Αγγελίδη', is located somewhere between 'αβαθής', 'shallow', and 'άγραπτος', appropriately, 'unwritten'. Since most of the cases begin with the prefix α-, which is an *alpha* privative, expressing a negation of identity or a lack of presence, she is unable to attain knowledge about herself or her sex from the signifieds through which a culture taxonomises personal experience into totalising forms. Even her own surname evokes an 'angel', a sexless creature. In view of the written words which appear in a previous scene, she inscribes herself into the film through an 'ellipse' and not a 'mimesis'. She cannot find a reference to herself, not only because the words are listed just in the masculine form, but also because language fails to guarantee any kind of existential bond with the things it designates. Unable to identify herself in language, she drifts away from this memorial service of bodies. So, if her name's irreducible singularity escapes the anonymity of common words, then language alienates as much as the advertising posters, which mockingly force one to make a choice between the left and the right, asking 'are you with the left or with the right party?' All that remains is to quote other people's sayings, as in the 'big letter' scene, to populate the shot with words, infest the image with speech and to soliloquise. Consequently, the recycling and the isotonic utterance reduces the richness of language to a clanging cymbal or a trembling string, even a monotonous beat, like the mechanical pace of women who, in a following shot, are crossing the room as if they are immune to words, as if they do not inhabit the house that 'is' language. So the film makes the voice visible, it shows it *falling* to the floor or *slipping* through the cracks of the editing cuts, between bodies and shots. 'Speech is, for me, a visible element',[31] says Angelidi. And Dreyer says: 'speech [. . .] must be a constituent part of the picture'.[32]

TEACHING THE REVOLUTION

We know from Cocteau that mirrors can benumb, captivate and lure human beings into a vertical transition to the Underworld, which is a hall of mirrors. In the shot of the 'primal scene' the phantoms of the ancestors appear in a mirror; in this mirror within a memory that is the Magritte painting from which they come, they are folding a sheet ceremoniously, dividing it into symmetrical parts. They split, bisect, partition, segregate according to sex and draw horizons; they distribute gender roles. Nevertheless, in every male 'protection', involving a transcendental hierarchy, a prison cell is looming. The bald woman, who is not yet a woman, but a becoming-woman, who revolts by enjoying unconventionally, for the time being seems to be unaffected by the imminent threat (Figure 8.3). But the very reflecting structure of this image predisposes us to anticipate the mutation of 'protection' into its reverse, its true self: our intimacy with a mirror is ambivalently founded on a blend of love and aggression, inseparable from each other. After the 'mother's' abrupt disappearance, the 'father' approaches the bald woman menacingly until a jump cut turns him into a woman. In a reversal of cause and effect, this woman, having torn the veil and come out of the mirror, naked now and in a state of madness, re-writes the original 'crime' that established 'protection'. The 'protected'/dead woman escapes the image,

Figure 8.3 Still, Angelidi, *Idées Fixes / Dies Irae* (1977).

restoring the archaic fear of the primal scene. However, the fear of the father is, at the same time, the father's fear. The flight of the woman from the place of violence is, at the same time, an invasion, an attack and a repression. With this gesture she comes out of one place and enters another, reiterating the dialectics of rebellion and submission. 'We convey the things they teach us / even the revolution they teach us', we hear in the 'big letter' scene. On the one hand, attacking a rebellious subject, a former revolutionary herself, with the turban on her head, we recognise in her image the figure of Marat in the bathtub, although we have not seen him yet, and, superimposed on it, the gesture of the dissident Charlotte Corday and her deadly attack. Through a work of figural condensation, the murderer fuses with the victim and the revolution is 'assimilated', transferred as 'heritage'. She wants to save the bald woman not only from the threatening 'father', but also from her enjoyment so as to suspend its inherently disruptive potential. Although it is difficult to distinguish what she is holding with her raised hand, we assume that this object will end up on the floor in the bathtub shot. But on the other hand, perhaps what Corday raises and, in some way, delivers to the bald woman is the hen, a 'sacred carcass', like Marat, when, in the next shot, she will knife it to death. In this way, she conveys the heritage of the *femme-homme*.[33] Therefore, the family *pietà* is transformed into Jacques-Louis David's 'pietà jacobine'[34] and the sacrifice of the heraldic animal presents a cover for the other murder.[35] Now, with the mediation of the mirror, David's painting *La Mort de Marat* (or *Marat Assassiné*, 1793) displaces Magritte's staging of the primal scene, reversing its gender roles.

The suppressed horizon, literally and figuratively, is a motif that does not retreat from any variation of the original theme. The absence of the horizon attaches an oppressive element, which precludes the prospect of revolt or transgression. The furthest we can see in the scenographic space, the edge of the covered bridge in the fourth shot, is just a dot, the opposite of a horizon. Later, its negation in the shots of the highway tunnel and La Défense metro station orientate towards a resolution through sublation in its concept by means of the written word 'HORIZON' above the bathtub of the dead/living Marat, in a recast of David's painting. The word 'HORIZON' where no horizon is possible, on the bathroom wall, the word indicating an opening where only an impasse is visible, tells us, firstly, something about the dead end involved in the representation of a revolutionary historical figure: 'the impasse is David's painting itself, the fact that David made this painting and not that he shows Marat killed in it'.[36] As the pattern of axis reversal has foreclosed the horizon, the film writes what it cannot show, it sublates into an idea what cannot be incarnated graphically, but is gestated as a possibility. Between the visual absence of the horizon and the word that restores it, as the horizontal arrangement of the letters themselves reinstates it, drawing a line somewhere in the 'background', between the earth and sky and between the accounting of practical politics and partisanship in the revolutionary passion, the choice is undecidable. On the one hand, the horizon, an 'invention' of Renaissance painting, is the opening, the denial of boundaries, the lack of obstacles and the possibility of even impossibility itself; but, on the other, horizon also means boundaries, borders, division, dichotomy and immutable impossibility of any possibility. Excluding what is beyond it, a horizon means a dead end, even if its limit is that of the earth's sphere. In this case, the revolutionary horizon of David's painting lies in the fact that he rejects the portrayal of the perpetrator of Marat's murder, painting her out of history, although Charlotte Corday, by all accounts, did not try to escape. Taking the pen from Marat's fallen hand, the same pen that had recently drawn on paper the limited horizon of a revolution, Angelidi re-writes it on the image as a horizon that includes the possibility of comprehending what David condemns to obscurity. Appropriately, Marat in the film is played by a woman, a woman like Angelidi, who happens to be Angelidi herself. The written 'HORIZON' assumes a temporal depth, a future moment of healing the historical trauma, where, as Marat wakes up as a woman, those that were two are united on one horizon, which is no longer a(n) (l)imitation. This unexpected 'resurrection' carries the ruins of paradise, of a wasted utopia.

But how does Marat come about in the first place? We should look for the emergence of the signifier 'Marat' in the work of figurality, where, on the one hand, it condenses the names of *Mar*tin and Herlofs *Mar*te and, on the other, displaces their role, a former 'revolutionary' who becomes a bearer of oppression and a woman-martyr who vehemently avenges her executioner, respectively, in a historical event that combines certain traits of both. This explains not only why Marat has feminine features, but also why (s)he is alive and dead at the same time.

With the coalescence of Marat and Corday, this archetypal *femme-homme*, the 'virgin with the knife', the film materialises the interpenetration of active and passive foreshadowed in the titles of Magritte (*L'Assassin Menacé*) and Feuillade (*Le Mort qui Tue*), culminating in the lyrics of the Dionysis Savvopoulos song heard at the end: 'the murderer and the victim hand in hand'.[37] The 'impasse' of David's painting lies in its depiction of a political revolution without leaving room for the woman, whose act has no power over the ideas represented by Marat. Corday is inscribed metonymically through the symptoms of her deed on the idealised body of a hero, a 'friend of the people' and a martyr of the revolution, who, with a pen in his hand, is still writing, while David is erasing. Since she is absent as the subject of history, the painting bears only the name of Marat. Similarly, the title of Magritte's painting focuses on the fate of the killer, forgetting his victim. The radical solution proposed by Angelidi is not just to make Corday appear, but to portray Marat himself as a woman. Or, more precisely, to let Corday take the place of Marat, recovering visibility after centuries of absence, and entwine the roles of the perpetrator and victim, seeing that

Corday was also David's victim in the incomplete representation that he produced. Certainly, the presumed coincidence of the perpetrator and the victim in the same character also contributes to the narrative closure of Dreyer's film.[38] The movement added to David's painting with Marat's disrupted arousal is aligned with the impetuous intrusion of Corday: it is as if two successive, albeit time-inverted, stages of the same uprise, have separated and been removed to different places along the film. Angelidi describes the interpolated movement as 'subversion' of the painting and 'self-irony'.[39] Actually, we would rather say that this concentrated, excessive burst of energy, this displaced cluster of affect, serves as a signature, affixing an irreducible stigma, not to be found in a dictionary and certainly not to be written on any horizon.[40]

Therefore, the lost horizon of the bathtub shot should be searched for right here: on Corday's back, rotated 90°, on the painted vertical black line separating two worlds, the revolution from the counter-revolution, the victim from the perpetrator and the man from the woman. In the next shot, through the division of the frame into two symmetrical halves, it becomes a line of fire, on which one image attacks the other. The collision between them causes the screen to establish a dichotomy in its structure, obscuring the left half, that of 'protection', and restricting action to the right one, that of *jouissance*. In this way, Dreyer's subtle gradation of tints and shades is polarised in raw materials of black and white and, at the same time, David's vertical two-part articulation of space is made horizontal. The splitting halves do not try to refold into each other, remaining separate; each seeks to circumscribe the woman into its own outline. In Dreyer, as we have seen, the décor recedes, absorbed in whiteness; in the close-ups of Jeanne d'Arc in *Passion* or Ann's 'face-landscape' in the last shot of *Vredens Dag* nature is internalised. By contrast, Angelidi shoots fragmented erogenous zones of the mouth and female genitals, remnants of a mythical whole, which, by eliminating the background, do not have the power to transcend the ruins of a prohibiting and restricting past. The closest we get to nature is the graveyard in the first shot. In the 'big letter' monologue, an extreme close-up frames her face so tightly that her hair remains unseen. The hair turns out to be a sacrosanct taboo for women. While all men have long hair, most female characters cannot untie their hair, as Ann does; in a sense, they are 'castrated'. Angelidi does her best to hide her own, wearing a turban as Marat. Here, both tight framing and the razor blade hint at Jeanne's shaved head, but without tears, hysteria or God. Pregnant with words, she is looking us in the eye. Both captivating and aloof, despite her restrained rage, she looks like an automated mechanical puppet, programmed to recite and repeat. Although she transfigures her face into a scene of the unseen, she is not an actress, because she does not forget who she is, but only remembers her proximity to the realm of the dead. Similarly, the shot of the female genitals becomes a mirror that trades with the invisible, namely with an unborn child, staging a sacred scene in the depth of this scene between perversion and initiation.[41]

Later, when the white walls of the apartment occupy the screen, evacuating it of images and exposing the white surface supporting the cast shadows, no human face mediates to project an interiority outwards. So, the divided image, the condition of juxtaposition and discrimination of its unhappy halves is the logic of patriarchy. It may free up space to show what has been suppressed and claim therein visibility; even so, as the bald woman's wild enjoyment cannot extend itself to the entire screen frame, it remains incomplete. It is a private enjoyment, an enjoyment of the same, the One. This 'One', however, like Plato's mythical ancestor of the human species, the spherical *androgyne*, contains both sexes of this 'woman-man'. In actual fact, it pays off a rather spectral debt and, therefore, it is soon 'domesticated' and normalised by adopting the prevailing norms.

In a following shot, an advertising hoarding promoting washing machines invades the 'family' home. Its command to 'enjoy', 'mum no longer needs to get tired, because it is so easy . . .', turns the bald woman into a simulacrum of its discourse and brings her body into alignment, remaking it in its image and according to its likeness; in the last shot of the film, the washing machine is in the kitchen so that the home and the advertisement become indistinguishable. The dead chicken will prove to be the offering for an unconditional surrender; it is the woman who acquires the status of a murdered object. The written word 'MIMESIS' reinforces the dominant image of the world, which may or may not be the outcome of a sophistic cheat. Likeness is the other side of mimesis, that is, emulation, assimilation 'even of revolution', as Angelidi says, submission. By contrast, a true ethical prowess involves the creation of something new. The word 'ELLIPSE' opposes repetition and possesses a kind of revolutionary persuasion. The fleeting revolt of the bald woman glides into reconciliation with the maternal figure of 'protection' and is tailored to 'enculturation'. Her blissful bodily self-affirmation is disrupted by gender-specific commodities, objects of anxiety; her laughter does not resonate anymore. However, for now, the verses of the 'visual poem', 'their husbands died young relatively',[42] followed by a series of possible variations, in which the syntagmatic displacement of words produces twenty-five understandable sentences, could resonate as an expression of an unacknowledged wish, namely Ann's, who, as soon as she announced it, caused her husband's death.

Let us now ask why the monologue is called 'the big letter',[43] and to whom it is addressed. Is it perhaps the same letter that Marat keeps hold of even in the throes of death, given by Corday to deceive him, but re-written in an inverted form, in order to reach its destination by revealing the violence of its true content? Since we can see Angelidi's face only up to her forehead, nothing precludes her still wearing the turban, literally or figuratively, and addressing us as Corday, using quotes from famous men and anonymous women, perhaps with the sole exception of Irigaray. Is the razor blade in her mouth, just before her monologue, a deadly bond between the voice and the body, a drying-up of enjoyment, equipping her with anger, or is it a guillotine that will decapitate Corday, like the frame limits 'sever' Angelidi's head?[44] And is the knife, used by the bald woman to ecstatically pluck the chicken, the same one that David removed from Marat's chest, because a knife would be inappropriate in a 'memorial stone'? The mouth with the razor blade succeeds the shot of the vulva, forming together that kind of figural continuum that Angelidi calls 'a big black hole' in her essay on Dreyer.[45] The phrase 'shut up' is not only a reaction to the lyrics of the preceding song, but it also functions as a sound equivalent to the razor blade; at the same time, the razor extends its threatening 'lack' back to the shot of the vulva with the same gesture as used to cut off the quotations in the monologue from their original context. The razor blade is not an aesthetic supplement; there is not any fetish, any 'mimesis' of the phallus, to veil the threat of difference, the 'ellipse', posed by the female naked form. By the same chiastic strategy, the pharmaceutical label 'usage externe', emblematic of *every* cinematic image, as long as it is not for eating, superimposed on the vulva, does not simply connote both objectification of the female body and autoeroticism, but it also comments on the shot of the mouth, implying its deprivation of a voice understood as an expression of interiority. More radically, a 'collage' of shop signs, 'Jouets' 'Organiques', is folded into both image track and soundtrack, producing the image of a female sex *organ* and the sound of a church *organ* respectively. Surely, we have come a long way from an *organic* concept of the artwork!

THE BEGINNING: BEYOND THE HORIZON

In the last shot of the film, we return to the beginning of *Vredens Dag*, to the potions and elixirs in Herlofs Marte's kitchen, just before the invasion of the soldiers to capture her, but she is no longer there; she has escaped, leaving the pot boiling over the fire. At the end of *Idées Fixes / Dies Irae*'s counter-initiation course, all that remains is the persistence of clichés, ruins of commodities of a pervasive sticky ideology. The transcendental elements of art have been flattened out, the *katabasis* has been domesticated and the oppositional forces of the lugubrious bedroom have been de-sublimated into the dishes in the sink and the football match on the radio or TV. Indeed, a very secular day of wrath! However, the home, which was initially linked to the idea of a tomb, remains a dystopia, an experience of the dominant, a décor for the 'traditional' suburban, consumerist, nuclear family. A female voice, uttering the paronyms 'usine – cuisine', triggers a transition from the spectacle of Chinese workers standing outside the patio doors, looking at us from the outside, while we look back at them from the inside,[46] to the kitchen, the 'factory' of the woman. A verbal displacement flows into a new figural setting. There is no human sight in it, but trivial actions continue, recurring on their own. In an advanced industrial society, the mother and wife as producer and reproducer of labour power have become spectral, as has capital itself. Eliminating visible bodies and assigning the performance of domestic labour and leisure, such as washing dishes and listening to football broadcasts, to the soundtrack, the shot substantiates for both wife and husband positions of pure virtuality, through a standardised set of mundane actions, which anybody could incarnate.[47]

However, this resignation is soon counterbalanced by a 'desecration' of the private domain through the invasion of a female soldier in the 'battleground' of the kitchen, making the 'little soldiers with wooden swords' in Savvopoulos's song materialise. This violation gives what has been separated from the community, namely the 'sacred' space of private enjoyment, back to the public sphere. It breaks the daily routine and hints at a possible intersection that remains to happen, which may bring about a restart or even initiate a new theme. The final shot revises the frontal 'planimetric'[48] compositions, which dominate almost the entire film, by rearranging space diagonally and removing the vanishing point out of frame, that is, *beyond the horizon*. Perhaps this change of point of view, engaging a potential political turnaround, with the co-articulation of the two heritages, the multiplicity within one and the rejection of both depth and surface, is the true horizon that the film traces.

NOTES

1. Algirdas Julien Greimas, *Sémantique Structurale* (Paris: Larousse, 1966), 96.
2. Antoinetta Angelidi, 'Two Heritages? (*Dies Irae*)', *Synchronos Kinimatographos* 79, 21–2 (July–October 1979): 93. Emphasis in original.
3. Ibid. Emphasis in original.
4. Philippe Parrain, 'Elements of the Image', trans. Antoinetta Angelidi, *Synchronos Kinimatographos '79*, 21–2 (July–October 1979): 94, 96. (The original can be found in Parrain et al., 'Dreyer: Cadres et Mouvements', 59). Angelidi's article is followed by her translation of excerpts from Perrain's essay and from Dreyer's *Verdens Dag* screenplay. Her selection highlights aspects of setting, lighting and clothing and, in a way, complements her own observations on the role of nature, black-and-white patterning and the relation between inside and outside.
5. François Lyotard, *Discourse, Figure*, trans. Antony Hudek and Mary Lydon (Minneapolis and London: University of Minnesota Press, 2011): 7–8.
6. Angelidi, 'Antoinetta Angelidi', *Film* 17 (July 1979): 172.
7. Angelidi, Antoinetta, and Frida Liappa, 'A Discussion with Antoinetta Angelidi and Frida Liappa', interview by Michel Demopoulos and Christos Vakalopoulos, *Synchronos Kinimatographos '78*, 17–18 (January–May 1978): 94.
8. Ibid., 95.
9. *Peripeteia*: literally, 'adventure'. Aristotle, in his *Poetics*, uses this term to define a plot's turning point, a change of circumstances by which the action veers round to its opposite, such as the reversal of a character's fortune caused by the occurrence of an unforeseen incident.
10. Ibid., 90.
11. Angelidi, 'Antoinetta Angelidi', 171.

12. Ibid.
13. Ibid.
14. Angelidi and Liappa, 'Discussion', 89.
15. Rea Walldén, 'Poems or Essays? The Films of Antoinetta Angelidi', in *Antoinetta Angelidi*, ed. Stella Theodoraki (Athens: Aigokeros, 2005): 79.
16. Angelidi and Liappa, 'Discussion', 94. The latter perhaps evokes Germaine Greer's *The Female Eunuch*.
17. *Katabasis*: literally, 'descent'. The theme of the classical hero's journey to the Underworld, his entry into the realm of the dead while still alive, and his return. Odysseus, Aeneas and Orpheus, among others, accomplish this exceptional task.
18. Cerberus: in Greek mythology, a monstrous creature that guards the gate of the Underworld, usually described as a three-headed dog.
19. *Nostos*: literally, 'coming home', 'repatriation'. A *topos* in ancient Greek literature which refers to the epic hero's journey back to his homeland, usually by sea, as in the case of Odysseus.
20. J. C. Harris, 'The Murderer Threatened (L'Assassin Menacé)', *Archives of General Psychiatry* 64, 8 (2007).
21. According to Laplanche and Pontalis, '[a]nalytic experience was to cause Freud to attribute an increasing importance to the scene where the child happens to witness sexual relations between its parents: "Among the store of phantasies of all neurotics, and probably of all human beings, this scene is seldom absent." It falls into the category of what Freud calls the primal phantasies (*Urphantasien*). It is in his account of the case of the "Wolf Man" – "From the History of an Infantile Neurosis" (1914) – that the observation of parental intercourse is called "the primal scene". Basing himself upon this case, Freud brings out different aspects: first, the act of coitus is understood by the child as an aggression by the father in a sado-masochistic relationship; secondly, the scene gives rise to sexual excitation in the child while at the same time providing a basis for castration anxiety; thirdly, the child interprets what is going on, within the framework of an infantile sexual theory, as anal coitus.' (Jean Laplanche and Jean-Bertrand Pontalis, *The Language of Psychoanalysis*, trans. Donald Nicholson-Smith (London: Karnac Books, 1988): 335.
22. Robert Belton, *The Berriboned Bomb: The Image of Woman in Male Surrealist Art* (Calgary, Alberta: University of Calgary Press, 1995): 131–2.
23. René Magritte, 'Notes sur Fantômas', in *Écrits Complets* (Paris: Flammarion, 1979): 49.
24. Sigmund Freud, 'A Special Type of Choice of Object Made by Men', in *The Standard Edition of the Complete Psychological Works of Sigmund Freud, volume XI*, ed. James Strachey (London: Hogarth Press, 1957): 173.
25. This sequence visualises verbal ideas provided by three of the four phrases, written into cloudlike white shapes, in another painting by Magritte, appropriately titled *Le Miroir Vivant* (1928): 'personnage éclatant de rire', 'cris d'oiseaux' and 'horizon'. Given that a verse by Mayakovsky referring to a bird ('notre potage d'amour et de rossignol') is later heard, 'rhyming' in a sense with Magritte's *Le Plaisir*, it might not be entirely inappropriate to let some other famous verses of his accompany the scene with the pineapple and the chicken: 'Eat your pineapples / Chew your grouse / Your last day is coming / You bourgeois louse' ('To the Bourgeoisie', 1917).
26. Luce Irigaray, *This Sex Which Is Not One*, trans. Catherine Porter with Carolyn Burke (Ithaca, NY: Cornell University Press, 1985): 28. Emphasis in original.
27. According to Laplanche and Pontalis, the *oral stage* is '[t]he first stage of libidinal development: sexual pleasure at this period is bound predominantly to that excitation of the oral cavity and lips which accompanies feeding. The activity of nutrition is the source of the particular meanings through which the object-relationship is expressed and organised; the love-relationship to the mother, for example, is marked by the meanings of *eating* and *being*

eaten. [Karl] Abraham suggested that this stage be subdivided according to two different activities: sucking (early oral stage) and biting (oral-sadistic stage)'. (Laplanche and Pontalis, *Language of Psychoanalysis*, 287). The oral drive activated in this phase is directed towards a type of object manifested fragmentally, detached from the whole of the body, a *part-object*, namely the maternal breast, real or phantasised, and its symbolic substitutes. In the sequence discussed above, the pineapple, the chicken, the handkerchief, the white sheet and the screen comprise a chain of equivalent signifiers that the subject takes as objects of her desire.

28. For the relationship between cinematic perception and the oral phase, see the discussion of Bertram Lewin's notion of the *dream screen*, 'the dream's hallucinatory representation of the mother's breast on which the child used to fall asleep after nursing', and its connection to film projection in Jean-Louis Baudry, 'The Apparatus: Meta-psychological Approaches to the Impression of Reality in the Cinema', trans. Jean Andrews and Bertrand Augst, in *Narrative, Apparatus, Ideology*, ed. Philip Rosen (New York: Columbia University Press, 1986): 310–11.

29. *Jouissance*: a Lacanian term, designating an excessive enjoyment, with connotations of orgasm, indiscernible from pain and suffering. Prohibition of *jouissance* is inherent in the symbolic structure of language. The entry in the symbolic requires that enjoyment is discharged from the body, a 'devitalisation' accomplished through the castration complex. On the one hand, the subject seeks to derive maximum satisfaction transgressing the 'pleasure principle', the limit of allowed pleasure imposed by the 'protecting' symbolic law. On the other, the greater the enjoyment the subject gains, the more this enjoyment carries pain and suffering with it. *Jouissance* describes the paradoxical situation in which the symptom may become a bearer of enjoyment or, vice-versa, satisfaction may bring about suffering. It is closely linked to death, since the death drive is an aspect of every drive that seeks to break through the 'pleasure principle' and attain the realm of *jouissance*. In the context of the sequence discussed above, let us point out that Lacan's earliest remarks on the death drive describe it as a desire to return to the pre-oedipal fusion with the mother's breast. See Dylan Evans, *An Introductory Dictionary of Lacanian Psychoanalysis* (Hove and New York: Brunner-Routledge, 2003): 32–3 and 91–2.

30. *Objet petit a*. For Lacan, the voice is the partial object of the invocatory drive, an element imagined as separable from the rest of the body. When a signifier is materialised vocally, that is when the symbolic enters in the real, the gap between the linguistic meaning and the physical articulation of the speaker produces an irreducible leftover, a 'grain', which is a surplus of *jouissance*. The voice as *objet petit a* is this remainder that causes desire but can never be attained by the drive.

31. Antoinetta Angelidi, 'Light May Be a Sound and a Word May Be Light', interview by Eleni Machaira, in *Antoinetta Angelidi*, ed. Stella Theodoraki (Athens: Aigokeros, 2005): 87.

32. Carl Dreyer, 'A Little on Film Style', in *Dreyer in Double Reflection*, ed. Donald Skoller (New York: Dutton, 1973): 137.

33. Drawing from Peter Gay's analysis (in *The Education of the Senses*) of 'an international phenomenon that came into full bloom during the middle of the nineteenth century' (34), Nina Corazzo and Catherine R. Montfort (in 'Charlotte Corday: *femme-homme*') discuss the prevailing male position 'which castigated female activists and intellectuals as *femme-hommes*': these women were considered neither physically attractive, nor gentle, but rather coarse and violent in their emotions and their actions. They did not envisage themselves as goddesses of the hearth, but instead as co-frequenters of the male-dominated political, intellectual and cultural spheres so long kept closed to them (34). They argue that this caricature of educated and independent women as sexless and cruel predated the nineteenth century and use it to describe the dilemma Corday posed for most of her

contemporaries: although she possessed the physical attributes of a woman, she had not acted like one. Therefore, she was characterised as a loathsome amalgam of the two sexes, the *femme-homme*, the unnatural woman (33–4).
34. Jan Starobinski, *1789: Les Emblèmes de la Raison* (Paris: Flammarion, 1979): 81.
35. The resurgence of *le coq gaulois* (the Gallic rooster) as a national personification during the French Revolution enhances the correlation of the chicken to the 'Marat theme'.
36. Angelidi and Liappa, 'Discussion', 98.
37. A similar figural conflation is to be found in Magritte's painting *Les Jours Gigantesques* (1928), in which a naked woman repulses an assailant, a dressed man embedded in her, thus pushing herself. This painting appears in Angelidi's short video *L'histoirécrite* (1975).
38. This motif is to be found in Dreyer. Herlofs Marte is burned to death, but takes revenge by cursing Laurentius and, indirectly, Absalon; Ann kills Absalon with her own words, but is then betrayed by Martin and accused of sorcery by Merete.
39. Angelidi and Liappa, 'Discussion', 98.
40. All of a sudden a figure breaks off rupturing stillness or bursts into the frame, crossing the visual field abruptly. If we also take into account the soldier's invasion into the deserted kitchen in the last shot, we can identify a triptych of excessive kinetic expenditure. A part reacts with an Epicurean swerve to the stasis of the tableau centrifugally. This is an *acinéma* (see François Lyotard, 'Acinema', trans. Paisley N. Livingston, in *Narrative, Apparatus, Ideology*, ed. Philip Rosen ((New York: Columbia University Press, 1986)): 349–59) of abrupt convulsion of limbs, unpredictable aberration, lateral deviation and genetic entropy.

More radically, it is a trio of *passages à l'acte*, which rips the scene of the Other seeking asylum in the realm of the Real. The subject is derailed from the symbolic network (respectively, from the compromising formation of the mirror *pietà*, the 'neoclassical' harmony of the painting and the family 'pleasure principle') and, interrupting the social bond, identifies herself/himself with the object. For Lacan, a *passage à l'acte* is the point of failure of speech to support the semblance of truth, resulting in the appearance of the Real behind it (Jacques Lacan, *Le Séminaire. Livre XVIII. D'un Discours qui ne Serait pas du Semblant, 1971*, ed. Jacques-Alain Miller ((Paris: Seuil, 2007)): 32–3). We would argue that this triple kinesiological puncture of the 'homeostasis' of representation, tearing the veil of the 'impression of reality', nods primarily to the Real of the sex.
41. Cf. Ann's tambour, her embroidery frame, a *velum*, which is inserted between the eye and the object regarded, mapping the scene of desire for childbearing, for the creation of a presence not yet visible.
42. This could be a kind of idiosyncratic synopsis or a seemingly irrelevant moral of *Vredens Dag*, although in Martin's case death is meant to be symbolic.
43. Angelidi, 'IDEESDIES FIXESIRAE', 113. This is actually Angelidi's *re-writing* of the film's visual and soundtracks after the shooting, a description and commentary using printed images and words. In the 'big letter's' 'montage of citations', a notion of resignation, in the sense of an ahistorical return to the 'imaginary museum' of *dicta* from the past, and the aggressive discourse of the avant-garde cohabit with one another.
44. Similarly, in Dreyer's film, the ruff worn by Absalon and the inquisitors, as well as Martin's large white collars in the last scene, are reminiscent of instruments of torture, as they convey the idea of the head's disjunction from the body and, consequently, visualise the motif of insurmountable difficulty in reconciling the mind and the senses.
45. Angelidi, 'Two Heritages?', 93. In the context of Dreyer's two witch-themed films discussed in the article, we may identify the 'big letter' scene's ritualistic and mildly aggressive recitation and the display of the vulva as a double apotropaic act to ward off the enemy or the devil.

46. This shot alludes not only to Erró's *American Interiors* series (1968), a reference acknowledged by Angelidi in the film's 'scenario', but also to Magritte's *Le Moi des Vendages* (1959).
47. In this respect, the topology of the kitchen shot aims further than some of the films it hints at, such as *Jeanne Dielman, 23 Quai du Commerce, 1080 Bruxelles* (Chantal Akerman, 1975) or *Nathalie Granger* (Marguerite Duras, 1972).
48. David Bordwell, 'The Art Cinema as a Mode of Film Practice', in Bordwell, *Poetics of Cinema* (New York: Routledge, 2008), 163.

BIBLIOGRAPHY

Angelidi, Antoinetta. 'Variations on the Same Subject: IDEESDIES FIXESIRAE'. *Synchronos Kinimatographos '78*, 17–18 (January–May 1978): 99–115.
Angelidi, Antoinetta. 'Two Heritages? (*Dies Irae*)'. *Synchronos Kinimatographos '79*, 21–2 (July–October 1979): 93.
Angelidi, Antoinetta. 'Antoinetta Angelidi'. *Film* 17 (July 1979): 171–2.
Angelidi, Antoinetta. 'Light May Be a Sound and a Word May Be Light'. Interview by Eleni Machaira, in *Antoinetta Angelidi*, ed. Stella Theodoraki. Athens: Aigokeros, 2005, 86–7.
Angelidi, Antoinetta, and Frida Liappa. 'A Discussion with Antoinetta Angelidi and Frida Liappa'. Interview by Michel Demopoulos and Christos Vakalopoulos. *Synchronos Kinimatographos '78*, 17–18 (January–May 1978): 89–98.
Baudry, Jean-Louis. 'The Apparatus: Meta-psychological Approaches to the Impression of Reality in the Cinema', trans. Jean Andrews and Bertrand Augst. In *Narrative, Apparatus, Ideology*, ed. Philip Rosen. New York: Columbia University Press, 1986, 299–318.
Belton, Robert. *The Beribboned Bomb: The Image of Woman in Male Surrealist Art*. Calgary, Alberta: University of Calgary Press, 1995.
Bordwell, David. 'The Art Cinema as a Mode of Film Practice', in Bordwell, *Poetics of Cinema*. New York: Routledge, 2008, 151–69.
Corazzo, Nina and Catherine R. Montfort. 'Charlotte Corday: *femme-homme*', in *Literate Women and the French Revolution of 1789*, ed. Catherine R. Montfort. Birmingham, Alabama: Summa, 1994, 33–54.
Dreyer, Carl Theodor. 'A Little on Film Style', in *Dreyer in Double Reflection*, ed. Donald Skoller. New York: Dutton, 1973, 122–42.
Evans, Dylan. *An Introductory Dictionary of Lacanian Psychoanalysis*. Hove and New York: Brunner-Routledge, 2003.
Freud, Sigmund. 'A Special Type of Choice of Object Made by Men', in *The Standard Edition of the Complete Psychological Works of Sigmund Freud*, Volume XI, ed. James Strachey. London: Hogarth Press, 1957, 163–76.
Gay, Peter. *Education of the Senses. Vol. 1. The Bourgeois Experience: Victoria to Freud*. New York: Oxford University Press, 1984.
Greimas, Algirdas Julien. *Sémantique Structurale*. Paris: Larousse, 1966.
Harris, J. C. 'The Murderer Threatened (L'Assassin Menacé)'. *Archives of General Psychiatry* 64, 8 (2007): 882–3.
Irigaray, Luce. *This Sex Which Is Not One*, trans Catherine Porter with Carolyn Burke. Ithaca, NY: Cornell University Press, 1985.
Lacan, Jacques. *Le Séminaire. Livre XVIII. D'un Discours qui ne Serait pas du Semblant, 1971*, ed. Jacques-Alain Miller. Paris: Seuil, 2007.

Laplanche, Jean, and Jean-Bertrand Pontalis. *The Language of Psychoanalysis*, trans. Donald Nicholson-Smith. London: Karnac Books, 1988.
Lyotard, Jean-François. 'Acinema', trans. Paisley N. Livingston. In *Narrative, Apparatus, Ideology*, ed. Philip Rosen. New York: Columbia University Press, 1986, 349–59.
Lyotard, Jean-François. *Discourse, Figure*, trans. Antony Hudek and Mary Lydon. Minneapolis and London: University of Minnesota Press, 2011.
Magritte, René. 'Notes sur Fantômas', in *Écrits Complets*. Paris: Flammarion, 1979, 48–9.
Parrain, Philippe, Barthélemy Amengual and Vincent Pinel. 'Dreyer: Cadres et Mouvements'. *Études Cinématographiques*, 53–6 (1967).
Parrain, Philippe. 'Elements of the Image', trans. Antoinetta Angelidi. *Synchronos Kinimatographos '79*, 21–2 (July–October 1979): 94, 96.
Starobinski, Jan. *1789: Les Emblèmes de la Raison*. Paris: Flammarion, 1979.
Walldén, Rea. 'Poems or Essays? The Films of Antoinetta Angelidi', in *Antoinetta Angelidi*, ed. Stella Theodoraki. Athens: Aigokeros, 2005, 78–81.

CHAPTER 9

Antoinetta Angelidi: The Visual Gaze

Calliope (Pepy) Rigopoulou

This is a quest for Antoinetta Angelidi's gaze beyond her films; her relation to the visual arts, and painting in particular, through her life and works, her drawings and installations, and – yes – her short and feature films, the known and the lost ones.

Antoinetta Angelidi has painted obsessively since she was a child. In her words,[1] painting for her is a place of concentration and salvation. As she heads for adolescence, the art books her father gives her come to mark her way. Painting, the most silent of the visual arts, gives her discourse a new voice. This dialogue with painting has been a component of her work ever since.

During this same period when the art books she is given by her father cultivate her artistic gaze, she paints her mother's naked body with its hidden secrets. And not only that: She paints the 'rotten life' which, alongside that other life, the still or dead life (*nature morte*) of academic painting, vies for a locus of decay within and beyond the person. She paints cobwebs, which have this to teach: the secretions of a barely-there body are strong enough to lay traps for stronger prey. In this way, the microcosm undermines the certainty of the macrocosm. Or, more correctly, it reminds us that 'the random can be a powerful compositional principle'.[2]

These first drawings have not survived. Which is true, too, of a good many of her later works: like the photo series of a naked pregnant woman doing housework, made in 1978, a year after her return to Greece, which so shocked the organisers of the left-wing youth organisation festival it was intended for that they refused to accept it. Equally lost is a work she made with menstrual pads and tights in the context of a subsequent feminist action. 'We didn't believe in archives then. There was only the here and now!', she says. It is true that the

60s, 70s and 80s didn't seek to cocoon memories spider-like in archives; they were lived instead for their own expanded present. Action, gesture, provocation, the quest for the new, the relationship between art and life, in different ways and via different paths of thought and experience, were all reminiscent of some of the early twentieth-century art movements, such as Dada, Futurism and Surrealism: Dada with its sense of the present and the ephemeral, of the random and of here-be-dragons playfulness; Futurism with its adoration of the future and contempt for the outdated, the passé, even when its passing was just a minute old; and Surrealism, with its rights to the rocky paths of the unconscious, for World War Two had again validated Goya and the phrase he painted on his *Caprichos* (1799, no. 43): 'the sleep of reason produces monsters', but also for its links to the socio-political via and from the right to choose its ancestors, and hence another, different cultural memory beyond the bounds of official history – that of a labyrinth inhabited by Minotaurs.

Yet, in a sense, the paths of these lost images cross with the more recent ones in which Angelidi, in her 2012 installation *Stitches Without Thread*, herself becomes the weaver-in-the-spider's place, persistently delimiting 'spaces of freedom' with her harsh visual materials, but also with the totality of her work and life.[3]

During this same period, her adolescence, Angelidi persistently draws her face in the mirror. At this precious age at which one resorts to the mirror once again, she says she discovered traces of other, unknown faces upon her own. In these sketches (1966) which tend towards abstraction, one can make out different ages and a forcefulness in the line which tends towards the gestural. The abstract tendency which has its beginnings here is evident in her later visual work: in *Labyrinths* (1980), which she made when pregnant with her second child, Petros, I discern a kinship of sorts with Klee's 'magic' squares, which end up organising his topoi/utopias.[4]

This is when she films the material that she later used in *121280 Ritual* (Angelidi and Walldén 2008): 'Ritual in the home. You die giving birth, you are born dying'.[5] A ritual to exorcise the fear of childbirth, a ritual to welcome a life that's ready to cross the threshold, to move from the positive or the negative, but in any case, familiar, labyrinth of the womb into an unfamiliar new space.[6]

Rites of passage – the rituals of a transition which is guaranteed as a quality by nothing but the procedure followed on each occasion – also feature in the rest of Angelidi's cinematic oeuvre. In fact, we could say that this ritualistic element, which is both an abstraction and pregnant with the uncanny, having revealed the hidden familiar, is characteristic of Angelidi's entire body of work in both visual art and film. Abstraction, too, which is largely a mode of *oblique* depiction, also points to a principle common to both oeuvres. But what we have here is an abstraction *with* memory; the memory of the human, the *very human*. A memory which dwells in every transition, which inhabits every point. Something is incubated, something is becoming fluid, something is fraying. Memory like the Potnia Theron, a primeval mistress of the beasts who saves and kills them; a savage memory that persists. Sewing and unpicking, while the uncanny continually renews its relationship with the intimate.

This happens, too, in her *visual essays*, as I prefer to call her short films, to add another dimension to Angelidi's overall oeuvre. Essay in the sense of a somatic *essaie* rather than a scholarly form of disembodied expression; an attempt which embodies the element of fluidity along with that of a personalised *ordeal*: with both these words – attempt and ordeal – forever touching upon the framework of the real, the performative element, to reveal a *memory stage*.

As an example of an essay of this kind, I shall dwell on the short film *L'histoirécrite* (1975), another lost work, which engages with Magritte's *The Titanic Days* (1928) and the glove/fetish from Max Klinger's *Paraphrase on the Finding of a Glove* (1881), in combination with Marx's 2nd and 3rd theses on Feuerbach (1845), as these state, respectively, the need to educate the educator and the concept of revolutionary practice; a practice that gives a new content to issues of violence.

This work by Magritte, as the rest of his oeuvre, seems uncanny – *unheimlich* – in the sense Freud (1919) attributes the word in his essay on the subject. While you recognise it in his stated terms of representation, it nevertheless seems bizarre. You don't know quite how to get a handle on it, or whether you can actually view it as something natural. Here, the titanic relates to elements that are disproportionate, like the man's hands in relation to the rest of his body, which is no more than his shadow incorporated in turn into the outline of the female body. 'There is in the woman's body', Angelidi says describing the painting, 'the body of a man, and in her efforts to get it out of her, it's like she is uprooting her self'. The titanic is also connected with the mythic as passed down to us via ancient theogonies, including that of Hesiod, with the savage battles between generations and families. The kidnapping and rape of – in the main – women and children by men, plays a central role in these battles (as it does to this day). Rape is a thread running through Magritte's visual mythology: for example, in his celebrated *Le Viol* from 1945, in which death remains the great kidnapper and rapist – perhaps a reference to his mother's body, raped by the waters and plants of the lake she drowned herself in, a body he saw dredged up from the depths at the age of thirteen or fourteen.

In Angelidi, Magritte meets the work of Klinger, as this is developed over ten etchings. A work surreal before Surrealism, which tells a story whose protagonist is the symbolist painter himself. A glove a lady lost as she was skating connects the world of this playful activity for young and old with an off-balance balance – it is this second image of the ten which Angelidi uses. But it is also a link to the emergence of a fetishistic world, since the gentleman who is also skating, and is the artist, bends down to pick the glove up off the ground, losing his hat in the process. Which is the start of a story of the glove's delivery to its owner by its 'thief', which will never come to pass. In this context, the glove acquires a powerful symbolism, replacing the person to whom it belongs and ultimately inhabiting the artist's dream world, too, in which things are just as brutal as they are in reality, or more so. As a result, the glove ends up in the hands of a person/bat who snatches it out of the artist's dream.

Angelidi describes:

> Between these two works, there were two sustained shots: one in close-up, one a long shot. In the first, there was a woman's face shot so close up it was coming out of the frame. [A consequence, perhaps, of intimacy, when in a closed group like a family, for instance, people are treated as things?] The second, overhead, shot featured the title L'histoirécrite written diagonally across it. A woman was walking up and down this diagonal, dressed in a man's suit.

In 1976, taking one of the images from Max Ernst's *Volume II: L'Eau* (Volume II: Water) from *Une semaine de bonté ou les sept éléments capitaux* (A Week of Kindness or the Seven Deadly Elements), Angelidi made her own *L'eau*, a short film which is also now lost. Ernst's work was exhibited in Paris at the Musée d'Orsay in 2009, and in other countries[7]. It consists of 184 collages made from images taken, in the main, from diverse books and catalogues; Ernst published it himself in book form in 1934. Its title is borrowed from a French charity that ran a campaign promoting prosperity; given the world of violence, destruction and intolerance which emerges out of these images, its use may be sarcastic. In the seven thematic sections of this illustrated book, one for each day of the week, water, an element linked to mythic floods, corresponds to Monday. The particular image Angelidi selected shows a bare-breasted woman reclining as water flows in such a way that the inner opens outwards. Or the outside penetrates within.

Angelidi describes:

> The waters are turbulent. They reach the edge of the bed on one side, and on the other, behind curtains and a chair, there is a male figure dressed in black. The lens makes circular movements above the painting, revealing just a part of it each time: first the water, then the man, and finally the woman's bare breasts. The next shot [which Angelidi added] was an extreme close-up of a baby's bottle standing upright full of milk, which ended in a mouth on the edge of the frame. The movement of feeding was jerky and compulsive, like a sexual act. Behind the shots, a violent and bloody little song in French of my own making was heard.

On the unexpected encounter between the three painters and the philosopher around her cinematic table, Angelidi says:

> I made the two short films before *Idées Fixes* before I had my first child, Rea, I was pregnant during the second and worked on the script in the clinic I'd gone to because I had contractions. In both these films, I use images of pictures as they are, without manipulation, which isn't something I did in my later films. I've had a complex relationship with the paintings I use ever since.

If we recall that her father was the first supplier of images, we can also view her words as an evolution in her relationship with him: from the untouched image, the untouched *Word of the Father*, or of the painters who return as substitutes for the Father in other works of hers, too, we arrive at an emancipation that permits her to use the image freely. Angelidi moves on to an assimilation of the image, calling into question the undisturbed patriarchal discourse which exists beyond historical and psychological time.[8]

An example of an image being assimilated so that the *seam* isn't even visible can be found in her most recent work, *Noon Hour* (2006), which was made in collaboration with Rea Walldén, inspired by the late afternoon light in De Chirico's squares. With dizzying perspective – it's that time of day when shadows lengthen – it is in conversation with Gradiva's 'shadow', which is simultaneously memory and sculpture in Jensen's novel (1902). Jensen's *Gradiva* is a work which would not be so well known if Freud (1907) had not identified in it the meeting of the psychic and the cultural through both the mechanism of repression and of the return of the repressed. Angelidi and Walldén are here 'performing surgery' on the shadows with the help of the blinding light that 'burns' them; replacing them with people clad in black, like shadows. A different temporality breaches the everyday of the people's market and the emptiness of the road. The broken recurring speech is another tool with which to construct a sense of alienation.[9]

Angelidi's dialogue with painting is also made manifest in her references to works by Renaissance and contemporary artists in her films. Alberti (1450) considers Narcissus the inventor of painting because, as he says: 'What is painting but the act of embracing by means of art the surface of a pool?'[10] And G. Kernodle[11] argues that Renaissance painting in particular, which borrows elements from the structures erected at the entrances into medieval cities to receive the ruler of the day, which were *tableaux vivants* of a sort, in turn lends elements of space, as it is processed using the different versions of perspective, to the theatrical stage. Painterly and theatrical space exchange data thus and interact. Angelidi revives the sense of stage space in her films through her painterly quests, too. Of a space imbued with theatrical ritual. So, it's as if she's holding on to the staged/performative element of the – chiefly early – Renaissance as a privileged locus of her ritualistic cinematic style.

Her dialogue with artists of the early Renaissance is especially central in her film *Topos* (1985), perhaps because Angelidi discerns something transitional in their conception of space which she also seeks; a space that's strictly structured, but which also opens up a cultural memory that expands time. In the relationship between the emergence of a Renaissance perspective and medieval representations of city entrances, whose discovery Kernodle discusses, we can discern this sense of a stage constructed with the architectural material of real Italian cities to host the figures of the biblical drama in Simone Martini, Ambrozzio Lorenzetti, Fra Angelico and Paolo Uccello, as well as in Pierro Della Francesca and Carpaccio – all painters whose remembrance is also commemorated in the film's final credits. Alongside this general sense, the film includes an extract from Uccello's painting *St George and the Dragon* (1470), while the same work becomes a source of inspiration both for the film's costume design and the 'monster's' movements. Pierro Della Francesca's work *The Queen of Sheba* (1464) is another source of inspiration for the costumes and kinesiology, as well as for the film's singular hairstyles, while Carpaccio's *The Dream of St Ursula* (1495), a dream we might describe as penetrating the saint's body, but doing so without forfeiting its right to the scenic space, which it thus divides in two, comes to guide the scene played out by Mary and the Angel.

Angelidi's choice of particular artists such as Jan van Eyck, Cranach, Pontormo, De Chirico, Balthus, Carrington and Breughel for this film is 'surgical' once again. She takes elements from the women, as they are portrayed by Cranach, who also contributed through his relationship with Luther to religious images not being banished by the Reformation. The De Chirico girl with the hoop who crosses the film's locales has once again abandoned her shadow, which followed her in the *Mystery and Melancholy of a Street* (1914). But this work plays a part as an overall feeling in the dramatising of the mystery and the melancholy of the painter's cities in Angelidi's own work, through the cities' dizzying silence.

The allusion to Balthus inspires the velveted feel of the space along with the characteristic stretching of these bodies between child's and woman's. What is interesting is that these two modern painters serve, in Angelidi's cinematic writing, as reference points at one with the artists of the early Renaissance, perhaps because they insist in their work on a Renaissance lineage – De Chirico by taking perspective as far as it will go, so that real space is so extended it becomes unreal, oneiric; Balthus through his insistence on the interior of everyday spaces, which is thus transformed into something non-quotidian, as his figures are focused on their spatially elongated actions, which acquire a ritualistic dimension. The movement of Angelidi's lens, which is always a conscious choice, shakes up psychic places with its strong organisation, parallel or oblique but always in touch with the real.

Something shared, apart from their visual virtuosity, by the artists who inhabit Angelidi's films both tangibly and intangibly – Giotto, Simone Martini, Lorenzetti, Piero Della Francesca, Fra Angelico or Balthus – is their focus on the tactile. Their works exude a velvety, tactile feel. They invite the viewer to touch, to co-exist whole-bodily in their spaces. Spaces in which the sacred is diffused in various ways.[12]

Squares persist in her work: remember that her film *The Hours* (1995) she also called *a Square Film*. In the architecture and city planning of various civilisations, pre-eminent among them the Greek, there is something more earthy about the square than the cosmic circle. Starting with the city blocks which Hippodamus introduced in Piraeus, the square seems to seek to organise inspiration into a shape delimited by the conscious mind. Though, if one considers Malevich's *Square*, this programme may never reach complete fruition.

In Angelidi's visual work *Hanging Waters* from 1988, the squares into which the image is divided organise its vibrant action. However, the dynamics that determine this action escape the frame. Having banished colour, they dynamically take its place. An austere fluidity permeates this landscape, which is simultaneously interior and exterior. Places/soulscapes emerge from her visual and cinematic work. There can be no body without them. Even though we now know that everything is the brain, that every thought, every sensation, every emotion is set in motion there, we still indicate the seat of our soul by touching that part of our body close to the heart. Because the places of the soul reside in the body even for those who do not believe in souls and their journeys. Even if they do not travel willingly to Hades to speak with the souls, as Odysseus does in the Nekyia (Book XI) of the *Odyssey*, the souls visit them uninvited and lay siege to them until they converse. This is also the case with Freud who, despite the justified critiques of his work, by the feminists in particular, defines a topography of the soul.

The Hours, that square film which defines the not-made-by-human-hand stages of a ritual is in conversation, as Angelidi tells us, with the *Book of Hours*, which regulated the times of monastic prayer in both Eastern and Western traditions. These times must be strictly observed, with no allowance for the 'approximately' of physical time. The greying of *in between*, the uncertainty of dawn rising, the indolence of dusk falling, are translated into minutes and seconds. The systematic measurement of time laid down for monks' work and prayer in medieval monasteries has been linked with the emergence of capitalism.[13] We will recall that in the film *Metropolis* (Fritz Lang, 1927), the huge clock defines the people's very existence, being central to the film's thought and action. The raw material for her *Hours* was woven, Angelidi tells us, out of a series of childhood and cultural memories and dreams.

A small part of this material, together with elements from the artworks *Boat–Matrix* (1988) and *Fall* (1988), became the matrix for her visual artwork

Screen–Matrix (1991), before the completion of the film. The names of the projects serve as guiding points: The *Boat–Matrix* and the *Fall* are projected onto *the Screen–Matrix*. The artist describes the *Screen–Matrix*, which she has worked with pastel and iron nails, as consisting of a prismatic dark space and two suspended metal surfaces – a forest consisting of nails with their sharp ends pointing upwards. This is a hard material to work; a hard material to contemplate. Is it a *matrix dentata*, a uterus with teeth? Is it a place for an initiate to meditate? Or a place of martyrdom? The revival of the experience of the womb, with or without the use of psychedelics, was central to the quests of both artists and psychiatrists in the 1970s. Still, intrauterine life, with all its measuring and imaging techniques, continues to remain a mystery.

The use of nails returns in *Father, Chair* (2011). Angelidi participated in the 'Stranger in a Strange Land' show in Kerameikos with this work, as part of the ReMap 3 programme of the Athens Biennale. The title puns on the Père Lachaise cemetery in France, which becomes *Père La Chaise*, i.e., *Father, Chair*.

From one cemetery to another, the ancient one, Kerameikos and the neighbourhood of the same name where the exhibition is staged, allusion becomes the connecting thread. The work is a tombstone in memory of her father. Angelidi describes it:

> An upright black wooden box 180x45x45, open at the front, divided into three unequal parts. Worked in nails and lit by LED lines. A half-burnt book in the bottom section is for revelations and exploration. Beside a looped projection of my film *Idées Fixes / Dies Irae*. The film's opening image is of the Père Lachaise cemetery [. . .] The work is a funerary column in memory of my father who, when I was 10 years old, making texts into images, helped me find the words again.

Maybe one of them is written in nails on its inside: *a-rhythmic*. The old yellowed book in the bottom part is a clear allusion to the journeys her father gifted her through art books. It is encased in the rectangle that holds it in place, but lets it breathe with the gaps she leaves between the nail-inhabited surfaces. And the chair? Does it only exist as a pun? Perhaps not. The mind goes to the Buddha, represented solely by an empty chair. The image is of a precise absence: that of the only head of a religion who explicitly forbade his followers to make him a god after his death.

Angelidi's visual gaze relates not only to her visual art, but to her oeuvre as a whole. Her father's art books helped her find the lost words. 'Eikona' – the 'image', a word which in Greek also always means 'conjecture', which is to say something fluid which assumes a different form in the gaze of each of us – once served for Angelidi as equal to the word. Since then, the image has served in her work as generative of rhythm and form.

NOTES

1. For this text, I have used Angelidi's archive, as well as our conversations in spring 2020 (and before). I have also used a series of notes that Rea Walldén entrusted to me. I thank them both.
2. Rea Walldén, '[Stitches Without Thread]" (Thessaloniki 2012), text that accompanied, as a parallel discourse, Angelidi's exhibition *Stitches Without Thread*, Thessaloniki Film Festival, chOros18, November 2012.
3. On this installation, see Walldén, '[Stitches Without Thread]".
4. See Calliope Rigopoulou, 'La scene chez Paul Klee' (doctoral thesis, Institut d'Art et d'Archeologie, Paris 1, Sorbonne, 1984).
5. The short film which resulted from this material was composed in 2008 and screened for the first time at the Greek Film Archive's 5th Avant-Garde Film Festival, where I saw it.
6. Arnold Van Gennep, *Les Rites de Passage* ([1st edn 1909] 2nd expanded edn, Paris: A. and J. Picard, 1981).
7. Exhibition catalogue *Une semaine de Bonté, Les collages originaux* (30 June–13 September 2009, Commissaire: Werner Spies).
8. According to Walldén's notes, references to Ernst, Klinger and Magritte are found in *Idées Fixes* (1977): Magritte, *Les Promenades d'Euclide* [this work declares her stable relationship with an unstable space of subjectivity C.R.], *L'assasin menacé*, *La Voix du silence*, *Le plaisir*, *Le bouchon d'epouvante*; Ernst, *Les malheurs des Immortels*; in *The Hours* (1995): Ernst, *Une semaine de bonté*, Klinger, *The Dreams*; in *Thief or Reality* (2001): Ernst, *Une semaine de bonté*, Klinger, *Le gant, La plague*.
9. Rigopoulou, Αυτοματοποιητική Ένας λόγος για την Τέχνη και την Τεχνολογία [Automated: A Discourse on Art and Technology] (Athens: Apopsi, 1988) and *Ο τρελός Πρόεδρος και η γυναικεία ηδονή* [The Mad President and Female Pleasure] (Athens: Topos, 2008).
10. In his *De pictura* [On Painting].
11. G. Kernodle, *From Art to Theatre*, Fifth Edition (Chicago: The University of Chicago Press, 1970).
12. Once again, Walldén's notes on the dialogue between particular artists and works and Angelidi's films provided valuable data.
13. Lewis Mumford, *The Myth of the Machine* (in Greek), trans. Zisis Sarikas (Athens: Ypsilon, 1985).

BIBLIOGRAPHY

Exhibition catalogue *Une semaine de Bonté, Les collages originaux*. 30 June– 13 September 2009. Commissaire: Werner Spies.

Kernodle, G. *From Art to Theatre*. Fifth Edition. Chicago: The University of Chicago Press, 1970.

Mumford, Lewis. *The Myth of the Machine* (in Greek), trans. Zisis Sarikas. Athens: Ypsilon, 1985.

Rigopoulou, Calliope. 'La scene chez Paul Klee' (doctoral thesis). Institut d'Art et d'Archeologie, Paris 1, Sorbonne, 1984.

Rigopoulou, Calliope. *Αυτοματοποιητική Ένας λόγος για την Τέχνη και την Τεχνολογία* [Automated: A Discourse on Art and Technology]. Athens: Apopsi, 1988.

Rigopoulou, Calliope. *Ο τρελός Πρόεδρος και η γυναικεία ηδονή* [The Mad President and Female Pleasure]. Athens: Topos, 2008.

Van Gennep, Arnold. *Les Rites de Passage* [1st edn 1909] 2nd expanded edn, Paris: A. and J. Picard, 1981.

Walldén, Rea. '[Stitches Without Thread]'' (Thessaloniki 2012), text that accompanied, as a parallel discourse, Angelidi's exhibition *Stitches Without Thread*, Thessaloniki Film Festival, chOros18, November 2012.

Interview with Antoinetta Angelidi

Giving Birth to her Films: Wandering with Antoinetta Angelidi

Rea Walldén

Antoinetta Angelidi takes us on a walk through the forest. She discusses how she makes her films: her constructive principles and her method, as well as the particular realisation of her films. She offers keys for understanding, leading us through theory and practice, her work and her life. She returns again and again to the same concepts and experiences, adding different levels of meaning, like a spiral leading deeper and deeper into her magical world. She presents her views on what cinema is, heterogeneity and timing and cinematic space. She speaks about her work with actresses and actors, on kinesiology and speech enunciation. She recounts her conception of film 'schema' – a notion that combines the senses of idea, shape, form, and structure – and the 'schemata' of her films. She discusses her perception of film sound, as related to timing and heterogeneity, and the work on the sound of her films. She muses about her relation to real places and shooting locations. She analyses at length the inspirations and references, and the beginnings of each of her films. The conversation ends with a meditation on life, death and art.

This exchange cannot but bear witness to the interviewer's very long and intimate relationship with Angelidi. It cannot be avoided. Our words are interwoven with each other, as are our lives. The conversation took place in Greek, in Athens, in August 2020, in the short respite between two Covid-19 lockdowns.

On her conception of cinema

Rea Walldén *(RW) – Where do you begin?*

Antoinetta Angelidi (AA) – For me, cinema begins with the distortion of images by timing; there is something programmatic about it. The process of de-composing the complexity of images through the introduction of time is determinative for my conception of cinema as a means of expression. Timing is a composition of the movements inherent in the image, where movement is rather a distortion than a transportation, and each element of the image may move independently. And inversely, I started perceiving images as a raw material for their decomposition. Therefore, I could extract an element from an image and connect it with an element from another image. Moreover, since the beginning, I realised that this decomposition of images should be done according to different codes.

Through this initial conception of timing, I formed my own peculiar conception of space. The passage from two to three dimensions, which had appeared difficult during my studies in architecture, was solved on a different level. Images were no longer two-dimensional. They became the synthesis of many linearities, which could be re-composed and combined with elements from other images. That is why I so often refer to the dream I saw after visiting the 1972 Documenta exhibition at Kassel: an image recalling Magritte, where a just perceptible movement was introduced. It revealed to me a new compositional principle, which led me to abandon architecture and reach towards cinema.

This conception of images as raw material, not to be copied, but to be decomposed and re-composed as a synthesis of signs of independent existence, functioned as a bridge for me from painting and architecture to cinema. In my new means of expression, I re-discovered geometric tracings, that is, the structural organisation underlying apparent form. Moreover, this concept of de-composing, of fragmenting, became my leading principle for approaching all the elements of a film: images, spoken and written speech, music, noises; even the actresses and actors' bodies and voices can be fragmented the same way as an image can. I was thus prepared to receive Christian Metz's concept of cinematic heterogeneity as almost obvious. It became a primary principle for the entirety of my work.

Another feeling I have had since the beginning was that cinematic time is another kind of sound. I had this feeling of film as a dark landscape that breathes in the theatre. That is why I believe that sound in cinema is like the sound of the universe, just perceptible and yet defining of our timing. I was very interested in the experiments by John Cage. It is not just the fact that noises become a part of music; all sound and music become one. At the same time, speech is dissolved in the timbre of the sound of the words; so, words are important to the musical composition, and therefore to timing. Then again, there is the heterogeneous use of texts, with which I have experimented since my first year at IDHEC (Institut des Hautes Études Cinématographiques,

Paris): the co-existence of different texts, which by themselves may be uncritical, and yet their juxtaposition gives rise to a sharp critique.

This multi-levelled space is cinema for me. I had begun with two-dimensional space. I have been drawing ever since I remember myself and it was through painting that I first felt this 'thing-condensation' that nourishes our lives. Painting saved me. Yet, I enter cinema with this rupture: space no longer has two dimensions, or even three. The peculiar space of cinema is a synthesis and a dialogue of the multiple linearities of different codes. A movement, a colour, a light, darkness, a camera movement, actresses and actors' movements, speech, bodies, texts – combined together create the multidimensional space of cinema. It is a serious mistake to reduce cinematic space to shooting locations. It is a synthesis that even exceeds frame composition, and the relations between, in and out of shot. Space in cinema is in a peculiar continuity with time.

I can even say that space in cinema is a living body. I had this realisation when working on *Topos*. This film's space is the body of a woman, the troubled field of a human body on the threshold between life and death. Space speaks in this film, aches, weeps, breathes. Here, we have a literalisation of the breathing of the film's body. And I understood that every film is a living body.

On directing actresses and actors, kinesiology and enunciation

RW – How about the bodies of actresses and actors; and their kinesiology and speech articulation? How do you direct them?

AA – Actresses and actors don't act, don't reproduce, don't imitate; they are vibrating soundboards. We work on their voices independently from their body movements, and on their sounds independently of their meanings. The principles of their kinesiology are inspired either from paintings or from non-human living creatures.

In *Topos*, the stretching bodies are inspired by Balthus, while the passage from immobility to sudden movement and the sudden change of movement-flow are inspired by birds of prey. The aim was to produce through the bodies a feeling of abruptness, which was important for the film as a whole. This sudden movement after complete immobility begins from the relation of the bare feet with the earth on which they stand. It is as if the actresses are linked with Earth by an umbilical cord, which creates a tension in waiting to move. And then they pounce, by an effort that involves their entire body, starting from their earthbound feet, gaining strength from their clenched stomach, and finally giving breath to their upper body.

Speaking of actresses and actors, casting is important. When casting, I observe the expressiveness of their hands, the way their hands move in relation to their bodies, and their ability to move them in a distorted way, as well as their timing in responding. To give an example, I chose the little girl that played in *Topos* because she contemplated before responding to my questions and directions.

Then, I cultivate a personal relationship with each actress and actor. I don't do a collective initial reading of the script, as is common in theatre. I approach each of them separately and in a different way, aiming at their individual body's overall expressiveness. We do exercises of combination and dissociation of their movement and speech, attempts at different variations of these possibilities. We often use books with images from paintings; but also animals, such as eagles and snakes. Through this personal relationship, we are led to an individual expressiveness, which should then remain distinctive when the actresses and actors come to work together.

RW – You do a lot of preparation and rehearsals for a long time before shooting. I remember you rehearsing in our home . . .

AA – When making *Topos*, I found *Les démoniaques dans l'art* by Charcot, where he compares the poses of hysterical crises that he had photographed to the representation of possessed women in art. These different types of crisis were nothing other than different ways to stretch, to open up one's body. In *The Hours*, we did a lot of rehearsals with Evri Sofroniadou using elements from this book. Her delirium in *Thief or Reality* is also based on the possessed women in art. Speech is dissociated from her movements and from its context. It is a continuous variation of a single phrase, on the concept of distinction, in its many meanings.

RW – In Thief or Reality, *there is also Parthenopi Bouzouri's delirium . . .*

AA – Bouzouri moves her body in a circular way, not in spasms as does Sofroniadou. This kind of cyclical body movement adheres to her speech in her delirium. They are two different kinds of delirium in this film; one could say complementary to each other.

RW – These two characters are definitely complementary in the way they speak and act. They were written this way.

AA – Yes, and their bodies also function complementarily to each other. They reach their peak at their moment of delirium. The Sculptress (Sofroniadou) peaks in her delirium on distinction, while the Scientist (Bouzouri) in her delirium on speech, in her immersion into the black waters with her dead child.

The direction of the mother's delirium, which you wrote under the title of 'The Water Libretto', required special preparation. I worked it in two separate phases: the voices' acting on the one hand, and the bodies' acting on the other. The first phase comprised the work we did in order for the bodily quality of the voices to be expressed. We worked very closely with Bouzouri, the mezzo soprano Maria Georgakarakou and the composer Thodoris Ampazis, to create this bodily quality of sound and the echo between the voices; this peculiar echo, as if the voices belong to the same split body. So, we recorded this text. A different phase was the shooting, where I shot Bouzouri and the child (Philippos Intzes), completely independently from the sound. This co-existence of mother and son in a bathtub was like a realised Oedipean relation. These two bodies were interwoven in a game that was shot from above, in a bathtub like a tomb, filled with water like amniotic fluid. And then, in editing, the game of the two bodies was interwoven with the game of the two voices. Yet the voices were women's voices . . .

Before the shooting, we had done a lot of rehearsals in the bathtub of my home, with Bouzouri and with Intzes separately. Particularly with Bouzouri, I took a lot of photographs in the bathtub, when I was telling her to turn or place her hair in one way or the other. Having worked on their kinesiology separately, when on set they had to navigate their bodies together, in a dance between communication and conflict. It is not clear whether the one body tries to eat the other; both sides play in a carnivorous way.

RW – You have also worked a lot on the way Sofroniadou walks in The Hours . . .

AA – In *The Hours*, Sofroniadou is a condensed pillar with a slope. This repeated slope of her body produces the characteristic limp of the character of Sophia, the governess, and is modelled on the leaning tower of Pisa. In *The Hours* the problem of the main character's inability to communicate is central. It was inspired by my own experiences and incorporates a moment of deep revelation that I had in front of a Bruegel painting in Rotterdam. It was the tower of Babel and I wanted to kneel and cry. So, this film is a building.

RW – As you always say, many characters in The Hours *function as bipolar couples. In the case of the governess and the mother, Sofroniadou played both roles and it was her acting and kinesiology that distinguished the one character from the other.*

AA – These bipolar couples had an appearance of positive vs negative, as we usually understand bipolarity, but in reality, they constituted different degrees of negativity. While they opposed each other, they combined with each other in increasing the dead end of no communication with the child. Sofroniadou plays both the mother and the governess, wearing the same dress in a different colour.

While the costume designer of the film was Anastasia Arseni, this particular dress was designed by Lily Kentaka, with whom I had collaborated in *Topos*. It is a dress inspired by Max Ernst. A black version of it is worn by the governess and the grandmother, and a white version by the mother. So, we have a black and a white version of the same dress, worn by the same person to play two different characters. And this is precisely what happens with the characters themselves: they appear opposite, and yet both are negative.

RW – They are facets of the same person. These two versions move differently, though; Sofroniadou plays the mother and the governess differently.

AA – Indeed. As I said, the governess is the leaning tower of Pisa, and this determines the way she walks: slowly and with a limp. The mother, on the other hand, has much more body flexibility and lightness, and she moves in a way that accentuates her femininity.

On the 'schemata' of her films

RW – You have often said that when you begin a film, a form sucks you in, a 'schema'. Tell me about this process, and also about the schema-structure of your films – you have just called them buildings and bodies.

AA – When I begin a film, it is as if I am sucked in by a schema, a matrix, a time-condensation. What is important to me is that this condensation lasts for the entire duration of the film's production, through all its phases. The initial conception re-emerges in different ways and degrees during the entire process. I have developed several techniques to keep myself concentrated on this matrix, this timetrap, such as meditating on a painting. A film is indeed a building, a big schema-structure, which re-emerges in every phase of its composition as it includes the new elements, until it is finally completed. It is important to always have in your mind the initial conception: in shooting and in editing, in choosing and forming the shooting sets, in directing the actresses' and actors' movements, and the camera. In post-production the initial conception re-emerges through new discoveries and bursts of illumination, where you realise that your initial schema gets a new form.

Idées Fixes / Dies Irae begins by posing the question of the relation between two and three spatial dimensions, as well as the difference between a fixed image and the introduction into it of a just perceptible movement: this slight difference that makes such a huge difference. I remember that I had read that the slight movement of leaves had caused an immense impression on the viewers of early films. It is also significant that I use a cemetery as introduction: the first shot of my first feature-length film is the cemetery of Père Lachaise in Paris. At the time, I was thinking about the deadening of the gaze and, simultaneously, about the awakening of the dead. I was thinking that by getting involved in filmmaking, we start a relation with the present, the past and the future, while always being on the edge of a razor, on the threshold between life and death. I perceived filmmaking as a preparation for death. The final result of my films – no matter how prepared and worked in advance – always surprises me.

The schema-shape of *Idées Fixes* is divided into two parts. Both begin with very long shots, followed by fragmented shots. In the first part, after the long shots dealing with the fundamental questions of the arts of painting and cinema, we have what I call a 'parenthesis'. It is a series of shots that opens with the enunciation '*père-peur*', father-fear, and closes with '*père encore*', still the father/ father, more! It criticises, through a fragmented construction, the concept of Aristotelian narration in its relation to patriarchal dominance. The second part of the film starts with a long static shot of the sign of La Défense metro station in Paris. It alludes to the military term but also to the psychoanalytic concept of resistance to analysis, as well as to the spectators' resistance to the film. The way of its filming is a reference to the Hyperrealist movement. It opens a series of shots that take us on a journey through the different movements of contemporary art, which are refuted and re-constructed until we arrive at my own body. The film involves and implicates my body in different ways, and inverses me, my own existence, as an actress inside the film and as its creator.

At the time of making this film, I was obsessed with a schema that included me, the schema of women's bodies as represented in art, and the feeling that I am not satisfied with it. I was not satisfied with any woman's body in any kind of cinema, whether mainstream, *auteur* or avant-garde. I tried to inverse the codes: thesis, antithesis, and then reversing both thesis and antithesis. I was in a rage; I had an immense anger. I defined cinema the way I wanted it, anew. While studying at IDHEC, I was infuriated by every kind of cinema. I didn't want to follow anyone. I did have great loves, like Dreyer and Murnau, but I didn't want to copy them. I was obsessively enraged.

Topos was made in completely different circumstances, after my return from Paris to Greece and my second pregnancy. It speaks of women's experience but in the way I felt the embodied life of images. I felt my body as a field through which images pass. I was the place in between inspirations and visualisations. *Topos* is an assemblage of bodies that function as in-betweens for the film to exist as a body. In this way, the body breaks up into many signs, the film becomes an agitated field, it fragments into multiple faces and speeches of this same woman, who gives birth and dies. It transfigures my own experience of pregnancy, an experience which is similar to filmmaking, a time trap where your body co-exists with another body, where two are one.

While pregnant for the second time, I started listening to what people around me said. It was as if I opened my ears for the first time. In the past, I closed my ears to everyday speech in order to keep alive my own desires and my own plans with regard to the art of painting initially and of cinema later. So, when I opened my ears and listened to the buzz around me, I heard the most diverse and curious things about what people thought of pregnancy and of being pregnant and of giving birth, and their thousand little nastinesses.

Topos is clearly structured in three parts (and a Prelude). The first part is 'the Moment', which is fragmented in multiple facets. The second part is 'Mourning'; it has almost no speech but a silent repeated chord of pain. There are very few words – 'tomb', 'I bury', 'burial' – and they are spoken in the unclear articulation of Greek by Martine Viard. The third part is 'the Game', which opens with the end of mourning and the return to the 'Prelude', before 'the Moment' of death-birth. In the Prelude, over the character of Maria (Janny Gastaldi), Dante's words are spoken (by Maya Limberopoulou), in a dialogue with his teacher. The teacher says, 'I will lead you where people die for a second time', and Dante tells him to look at the monster that prevents him from moving on. This obstacle won't be surpassed until she is immersed in mourning and she remembers the knowledge of the dead who mourn their second death. In the third part, the teacher is invoked once more and leads to a reshaping of the given, to an outrageous topos-place, a topos where the dead and the living co-exist.

Similarly in *Thief or Reality*, there is a table at the end of the film, where both the dead and the living are sitting. This co-existence can be found in all my films because in our heads we can't distinguish the living from the dead, in the same way that we can't distinguish the present from the past and the future.

RW – One could observe that the triadic structure of Topos *is in a way interrupted by the sequence of another table, around which sit the men discussing the moon, and women . . . Let us move on to* The Hours.

AA – *The Hours* is a swinging back-and-forth between the past, the present and the future. Its shape is as if it opens and closes, like an accordion. In *The Hours*, the voices I had repressed return. Those voices to which I was deaf, which I had repressed in my childhood so that I had almost ceased to hear the sound of the world around me. These voices came back to weave their meshes of bipolar oppositions, where both sides were negative. Through the immersion into the repeated negative experiences, I discovered the experience of my inner voice; that voice that can transform a mute child into a visionary. I discovered the road from the silence of oppression to the silence of meditation, and the transformation of the experience of a life into a lucid dream. My silence was resistance.

RW – Towards the end of the film, the inner voice says, 'And thus the framework of the void collapsed'. 'Skeleton' (the word used for 'framework' in Greek) adds to its structural sense connotations of both 'body' and 'building'.

AA – Babel are the voices of the environment. Family, school, lovers, politics – they are all part of the tower of Babel. And in it, determining, is the leaning tower of Pisa, the governess and her perverse religiosity. This character organises the others and is mirrored in them. She is in a way the leaning axis of the entire Babel building.

And thus, we arrive at *Thief or Reality*, which is again a fragmentation into three characters, all three of whom are versions of Antigone. They make together a house of fire, water and earth, which is traversed by the blowing wind, the character of the Thief, who breaks and mirrors their inner contradictions. Gender is disseminated to the characters in unconventional ways. The film comprises three versions of the same day. Each is a reference to a different phase in the history of cinema.

RW – They also represent different philosophical viewpoints: fate, randomness and free will; while the Thief is death, and reality.

AA – We have connections with multiple paintings and texts, as is the case with my other films, but here I am haunted by the memory of the actor Nikos Skylodimos who committed suicide while rehearsing for the role of Antigone. I put the text I wrote when I completed my psychoanalysis in his mouth as a post-mortem speech. And the film closes with the post-mortem table where the dead and the living co-exist, putting questions to each other about the meaning of human passion or its lack.

On the sound of films

RW – Will you tell me about the way you perceive and work on sound?

AA – Film sound for me was born out of timing. It all began with the realisation that images have timing and with a conception of sound as silence. Film sound begins with silence for me. The images of my films include timing. Timing is a very personal relationship with image and is created during shooting. Timing is therefore crucial for the musicality of a film's images. Film's initial form could be perceived as completely silent, because the sonar and musical dimension is already embedded in timing. Film sound is always a synthesis, an overall design, which includes music, speeches and noises. It has an antithetical and complementary relation to image. It is not just that the sound functions as a counterpoint to image, as Eisenstein would say, it is that sound can be image and image can be sound. We can see sound like a strip that exits people's mouths and moves in the space around them, in the same way that, in medieval illuminations, speech was depicted as a ribbon that comes out of the mouths and encircles the image. Sound can also fall on an image and break it, or wound it like a razor.

L'histoirécrite, the first film I shot, was very short, just 7 minutes, and is now lost. It was then that I first combined three different parallel texts and realised that when texts co-exist, the result is a strange synthesis of words with a very acute critical dimension. The co-existing texts in this film were the conjugation of the verbs 'to be' and 'to have', the first lesson of French for foreigners, which was full of gender stereotypes, and Marx's third thesis on Feuerbach about the need to educate the educator.

When I made *Idées Fixes*, I worked with Gilbert Artman of Urban Sax for the composition of the sound of the film. We agreed that we considered music to be a part of the overall sound design of a film. We thus started by multiplying the words of a poem that I wrote as part of the film's speech; and we accelerated the recording until it became similar to the song of the cicadas. We created sounds by processing speech. We used different materials and words in order to create a jazz composition. For example, we used words beginning with the negative prefix 'a-'; we separated the initial alpha as upbeat; and then left the rest of the word as downbeat. We used metallic objects from his yard as instruments, among them an old empty bathtub. He also gave me the musical piece that is played over the first part of the film at the cemetery. It is a sound made by the sixteen saxophones of Urban Sax; one instrument after the other begins emitting the same sound with a small distance from each other.

RW – A musical canon.

AA – Yes . . . In *Topos*, I collaborated with Georges Aperghis. At our first meeting, he told me that 'we will begin with silence' and he gave me the score of his *Recitations*. Martine Viard and I created all the sounds of the film, using parts from the score of the 5th *Recitation*. We watched a first editing of the film together, which was completely silent, and Viard made all the noises and sounds using her voice, improvising on the musical score. We chose where to add sound; not every object or movement in the film produces a sound. Apart from the sounds made by Viard's voice, *Topos* is also traversed by the speech of Annita Santorinaiou. Her voice speaks through the bodies of all actresses, as well as of the actor playing the Juggler. The voice passes through the bodies. In Aperghis's words, '*elles se sont dites*' (they are spoken, they speak themselves). A third voice is that of Maya Limberopoulou, which is heard in the Prelude over the body of Gastaldi, reciting in Italian the first canto of Dante's *Hell*. In all three cases, enunciation functions more as sound than speech. There is one exception; a parenthesis of 'realistically' enunciated speech, in the sequence of the table in the middle of the film, where men speak with their own voices. They exchange false theories and inanities in all seriousness.

RW – Your own voice is also heard in the film.

AA – Yes, in the same sequence, through the body of the little girl.

The musicality of *The Hours* was born when I heard Maria Georgakarakou singing Purcell's 'Music for a While' in the Conservatory. It moved me deeply. I said to myself that this musical piece will dominate and permeate my film. It is symbolic for me. It is in music, unfortunately, that I met castration and the destruction of my childhood, in an experience with my violin teacher that deprived me of speech for a time. And it was in music, with this song, that I would speak of re-discovering speech. For *The Hours*, along with Georgakarakou, I collaborated with the composer Dimitris Kamarotos. The initial idea was to disperse the song through the entire film. In the final work, the song appears in the crucial sequence with the violin teacher. The sequence is preceded by the song sung by Georgakarakou, and is followed by a complete fragmentation and disorganisation of the piece. 'Music for a While', the moment of music, is given as a moment of illumination and communication with the divine, which is then broken into pieces, like the child's reality. A unified gaze becomes devoured and destroyed. In the fragmented and distorted song, speeches from the film are intertwined, turning into a devouring space of little Spendo's reality.

Thief or Reality, I wrote with Rea Walldén, you that is. The sound of this film is once again a total feeling, a total design, with as central point the 'Water Libretto', where the ability of speech is lost and found again. It is the delirium of a woman who destroys her body because she has lost her child. For the sound of the film, I collaborated with Thodoris Ampazis.

RW – Before describing your collaboration with Ampazis, you could say a bit about how some significant choices regarding sound are already inscribed in the script; such as the different approach to sound in each part of the film, the way speech is composed, elements of articulation . . .

AA – Of course, a lot is already written in the script . . . There were the choices that sound will be a score made by the speeches, that the first part will have no speech at all and the only sound will be the buzz of action . . . The second part was expressed through the delirium. You wrote it; talk about how the form of your writing includes enunciation.

RW – The 'Water Libretto' was written in three vertical columns, to be read horizontally, each of which is constructed differently, as a different kind of speech, with a different subject – although it happens inside the same person, of course. The text contains immediate indications about enunciation but also implies it by its structure. I would argue, though, that while it does function as a turning point for the second part of the film, it does not give us the logic of speech construction for the entire second part. There is the principle of what is heard and what is not in each part of the film: the first part is silent; in the second, we can hear what is said; in the third, we can hear both what is thought and what is said; while the coda is meta-linguistic. This has consequences for their sonar universe in general. Moreover, each part has a key moment. For the second part, this is indeed the liberating delirium. For the third part, it is this long post-mortem monologue that you wrote, Antoinetta, which is then followed by the table sequence. This sequence can be perceived as a separate fourth part, a coda as I said, where meta-language reigns. Once again, we have a composition of different kinds of speech, which imply, invite, different enunciations.

AA – As we said, the first part is silent, a buzzing silence – what I call the buzz of the universe. In the second, the speech is closer to the everyday, passes through the delirium, and then is formed into a composition of three presences, to be compared, finally, to the sung text of 'Oh, my sweet spring'.

RW – The mourning of the Mother of God (hymn sung on Good Friday in the Greek Orthodox churches) . . . When speaking of directing the actresses, you described quite extensively how you worked with the singer, the actress and the composer on the delirium. What was interesting for me when I saw the finished version of the sequence was how the passage from words to film was both faithful and unfaithful to the initial text, adding and erasing levels of meaning. Something completely new happened there, a multiple reflection of voices and images, as if the one pulled the other into a dance. I think that this is a moment of opening for the film.

AA – Exactly. That is why when I am asked to give a significant extract of the film, I always choose the water delirium.

In the third part, we can hear the characters' thoughts. A lot of it comes from my own thoughts, and yours, and texts by Thomas Bernhard, and the text of Sophocles' *Antigone*. It concludes with the Actor's long post-mortem monologue, the text I wrote when I finished my analysis, about the realisation that there has never been a lost paradise. It was worked as a monochord enunciation, like a ribbon out of the mouth that surrounds space, a continuous flow, a wave. At the end of the third part, we arrive at what can be perceived as an independent part, an epilogue, the co-existence of all the characters of the film who discuss their roles in a metalinguistic canvas. There, there is an instance when two speeches are enunciated simultaneously: the Thief speaks about the art of acting, a text of mine; while the dead Actor speaks of his experience of acting, a text taken from Bernhard.

RW – Indeed, this is an interesting instance with regard to both meaning and sound, but also as a visual composition. The Thief, who is death, and the Actor, who is dead, speak about the human condition as a form of acting; the one speaks from without, the other from within; the one is en-face with open eyes, the other in profile with eyes closed. Moreover, they speak completely simultaneously, something that happens very few times in the film. To all this, one should add that in the film, the Thief is addressed as a 'he', yet played by a woman; while the Actor, played by a man, plays a woman's role, that of Antigone.

AA – About the sound in *Thief or Reality*, I should also say that Ampazis used a lot of delayed sound, out-of-phase with its presumed corresponding cause. For example, when the Scientist falls on the glass tubes and bottles, and throws them off her table and the screen, Ampazis put the sound of breaking glass much later than the time realistically needed for them to reach the floor. This created a deepening of space; it changed the dimensions of space.

It is you who made the soundtrack of *121280 Ritual*, without the help of a composer. The shooting took place in 1980, the day before I gave birth to my son. I re-discovered the raw visual material in 16mm in 2008, and we edited it together into its film form. And you added this speech of a child who is both inside and outside of her mother's womb.

RW – The shooting is yours, and the acting is yours. It is you who are the heavily pregnant woman who performs the ceremony on her body in the bathtub. Literally, it is you who are pregnant, and the child inside you is my brother, and the child outside is I; and yet I am not. I wrote the text twenty-eight years after the shooting, placing myself in the position of the child, the one outside and the other inside, at an age when I could also be the mother. I gave voice to myself of that past time. This is the text: a love poem to my mother, you. The work on sound turns this chanting into music. By repeating sounds, by superimposing different enunciations of the same words, by changing the speed of sound, a musical piece is created.

AA – It is very interesting the way you recorded it. You spoke the text with different intonations, different sonorities, and sang it in different ways.

RW – I think that one of those times, you too read the text.

AA – Yes. We played in many ways while making this film. We worked in a way that I hope we will use again in the future, incorporating the creation process into the final project, as well as the element of *in situ* improvisation. We had decided to use this method of sound composition in our next feature-length project, *Medea / Kore*, which was planned to be shot a year later, but was postponed for lack of funds. We have worked a lot on it since but we haven't managed to complete it.

Then, there is my *Tears Sins*. Its sound is a seamless, one-piece speech. It is again a film-performance. Both the act and text I conceived and performed during sleepless nights of great tension, in 2013. And you recorded them during these same nights.

On spatial experiences and shooting locations

RW – Earlier in this conversation, you spoke of your conception of cinematic space, and that it should never be confused with the shooting locations. Now, I will ask you precisely about your relation to extra-cinematic space: how your experiences of places have affected your filmmaking and how you choose your shooting locations.

AA – Three experiences are, I think, significant. First are the magical locations of my childhood: the sleeping factories. My father was a chemical engineer and worked as a technical manager in different factories. From a very young age, from when I was three years old, he took me with him to the factories on Sundays, when he went to work, while no one else was there. I would wander freely in the empty factories. I had this feeling of magic, this magic of empty spaces condensing human labour, this presence of human labour in the bare spaces. My magic places have never been domestic. When I visited the Gazi factory for the first time, looking for shooting locations for *Topos*, it had just been closed down and emptied of workers. This floor, smeared with industrial residue, I felt it like moving sand. I felt as if entering into a sacred place. I was deeply moved, and remembered the magical industrial spaces of my childhood.

The second significant spatial experience was when I visited the 1972 Kassel Documenta. And I don't mean the dream that opened my way to filmmaking; I mean the exhibited environments. These spaces seemed to me to bear memories of a primal architecture, an architecture connected to the universe, similar to the dream architecture of the Australian aborigines or Stonehenge. I felt that human-constructed space is a shamanic response to and conversation with the space of night, the deep darkness of the universe and the Milky Way . . .

The third experience is the one that led me to study architecture. In school, during the breaks, I used to make very fine and detailed drawings of dry leaves and spider's webs. In the final year of high school, I visited Paris and entered Gothic cathedrals for the first time. I felt enchanted by the stained-glass windows of Sainte-Chapelle. So, I dreamt of a cathedral made of spider's webs, a gigantic weightless three-dimensional structure illuminated by the sunlight. This dream led me to architecture. Yet I didn't find in the practice of architecture the secrets and mysteries that were later revealed to me in filmmaking.

I think that my relation to space was very insightfully encapsuled by Christos Vakalopoulos, when he said of *Topos* that it was as if human situations were inserted into the darkness of the universe. I would place a sofa or the surface of a table, and my characters, in the dark void of industrial spaces.

On the references and genesis of her films

RW – *Among the most recognisable characteristics of your films are the multiple references to the history of art. Would you like to speak of the ways in which you use these references?*

AA – In my first and lost film, *L'histoirécrite*, I used two works: René Magritte's *The Titanic Days*, where a man's body is enclosed in a woman's, and the woman tries to get it out of her but can't because they are a part of each other's body; and an image from Max Klinger's *Paraphrase on the Finding of a Glove*. In my second lost film, *L'eau*, I used an image from Max Ernst's *Une semaine de bonté ou les sept éléments capitaux*. After these two films, I have never filmed again an image as such. Because in the meantime, I had given birth to a baby girl who, for the first time, looked at me and saw me.

For the rest of my films, the relation with painting relied on a de-construction and re-construction of images, which I made my own. I took elements from the history of art, from paintings, and then I re-made them. For example, in the first shot of *Idées Fixes*, I combined *The promenades of Euclid* by Magritte with the Père Lachaise Cemetery. As I said earlier, I chose to shoot a cemetery as the first image of my first feature-length film; I was very interested in the liveliness of the places where the dead lie. So, I framed a path centrally, so that it would appear like a cone and therefore to introduce this indecisiveness between depth and height, to reveal that depth in a two-dimensional image is an illusion. In a way, I superimposed the two cones of Magritte's painting.

RW – In a way, you used a compositional principle that reproduces the same theoretical question with the painting, without reproducing any element of the painting as such.

AA – Yes. In other cases, I use my references in different ways. For example, in *Topos*, I took the little girl with a hoop from Giorgio de Chirico's *Mystery and Melancholy of a Street* and detached her from the painting; and she wandered through the entire film. She was played by Clairi Mirtseki. This same De Chirico painting, I used in another way too. If you look at the painting carefully, you will observe that it also depicts a construction like a wooden wagon. This, in *Topos*, became the Juggler's wagon; and the little girl walks into it to find the Juggler with the wife he accidentally killed on their wedding night.

RW – I think, then, that you should tell us about the genesis of your films: your inspirations and references and how you worked on them, but also the processes before filming, your approach to the script as a musical score, as you have often said, and your co-writing collaborations.

AA – From the beginning, I conceived the script as a complicated serial collage of images and speeches. This, I later cultivated and refined further, as I consciously realised that all the elements of the cinematic medium narrate. So, my 'scripts' are closer to musical scores or multi-level storyboards. They may contain my drawings or fragments of paintings, images conceived from scratch or manipulated pre-existing images from the history of art, images and speeches I found in my dreams or my experiences, fragments of poems or advertisements. I could say that the raw material for my films has three sources: nuggets of art history, nuggets of autobiography and nuggets of dreams.

For *Idées Fixes*, I worked a lot with art books and contemporary art journals, such as *Art Vivant*. I was studying them systematically, almost as if I were indexing them. With regard to the overall composition of the film, I was in an intimate dialogue with Jean Thibaudeau, whom IDHEC had proposed as my advisor. Thibaudeau was in the editing team of the *Tel Quel* journal and was very interested in the *nouveau roman*. He didn't want to direct or orient me. He just spoke to me about freedom in the use of speech, which came from his study of the *nouveau roman*, and from the history of linguistics in the twentieth century, and from music.

After *Idées Fixes*, I experienced my return to Greece as a violent disappointment. Greek society was still very conservative, despite the progressive enthusiasm that followed the fall of the junta. The way I worked appeared mostly incomprehensible, while I had thought it was crystal clear: I used my unconscious but I structured it very consciously. This discontinuity was intensified by my family and the political environment – I was still very involved with political activism at the time. I made several attempts at artistic expression. Decisive was the disappointment of a particular rejection. I did a project for the women's pavilion for the festival of the political youth group to which I belonged. It was a series of photographs of a pregnant comrade, whom I asked to pose naked while performing domestic chores. I think that it was very much to the point. The organisers were shocked and prohibited its exhibition. I felt betrayed. A bit later, I filmed myself pregnant and naked, but I did it in secret, and then hid and forgot the material for the next twenty-eight years. I had the experiences of a second childbirth and a divorce.

After the divorce, in a twirl of intense energy, I was constructing the *Vipers*, big sculptures made of plastic bags and glue. Then, I left again for Paris, with my good friend Claire Mitsotaki. We found a new narrativity together, through long conversations, mingled with thoughts and dreams and readings. I remember clearly that my liberation after the divorce was expressed as an immersion in Gaston Bachelard and *Alice in Wonderland*, and a return to the era of painting I had loved since my adolescence, early Renaissance. I remember clearly discussing with Claire the way gardens were painted in the early Renaissance, gardens with a little gate far in the background... We were immersed in the Renaissance. Before co-writing *Topos*, we co-wrote thirteen short scripts, which we named *The 13 Terrors*. We proposed them to ERT (Hellenic Broadcasting Corporation) for a series but they were rejected. In *Topos*, we tried to juxtapose the temporalities of suddenness and repetitiveness. And light would come and create sound. Indeed, in making this film, I felt the visuality of sound and the sonority of image.

The main reference in *Topos* is Renaissance painting: Carpaccio, Fra Angelico, Pontormo... For example, the bodies of the actresses and actors are painted following the logic of Pontormo. The textile that clothes a body is continued in the colour of the skin; if the textile is light blue so is the human skin. So, I see the acting bodies as fragments of paintings. Then, there is kinesiology, of which I have already spoken; bare soles and sudden steps that tear the space around them. Another reference, as I mentioned earlier, is De Chirico; not only

Mystery and Melancholy of a Street but also his 'Swimmers' [*The Mysterious Swimmer*, 1934] swimming in solid ground.

The space was conceived as a co-existence of the industrial spaces of my childhood and the spaces from the paintings. Paintings as spaces, places, topoi. So, there were the real, existing industrial locations, such as the Gazi factory in Athens and the glue factory, in which I shot *Topos*, and then, the constructions that I made in them, in collaboration with the architect and good friend Kostas Angelidakis. We re-created entire excerpts from paintings. Most significant was a construction inspired by *The Dream of St Ursula* by Carpaccio. I drew a cross-section of St Ursula's room, which I completed with a garden; and then we constructed it on set. In another case, we painted a wide area of the floor, imitating the solid water in which De Chirico's swimmers bathed.

Immediately after *Topos*, Pavlos Zannas left the Greek Film Centre and two film proposals of mine were refused funding. So, I couldn't make films, despite being full of ideas and creativity. I channelled my efforts into other visual art creations instead. I designed the environment *Boat–Matrix*, which wasn't materialised; and then *Screen–Matrix*, which was. I worked in great detail, manually, creating huge metal surfaces covered with nails pointing upward. It was a very creative period for me, through which I conceived my next film. After *Topos*, I began writing down my dreams systematically in notebooks. I had realised by then that dreams are interesting as structures. I understood that what Freud said about displacement and condensation in the dream-mechanism describes in fact the way I composed images and sounds. It is not what the Surrealists called automatic writing; it is a conscious approach to the unconscious. I aim at a condition of wakefulness while dreaming and a dream-structured reality.

In *Topos*, I tried to enter inside the world of paintings; there is this intense idea of entering paintings and, at the same time, entire parts of these paintings are taken out of them. In *The Hours*, this intensity regards my own life experiences. I took my own experiences and I worked on them as if they were paintings. The structure was provided by the bipolar couples. There was also this provocative thought of square, where 'square' was what I called the rigour of dream structure. In *The Hours*, there is a sharp, acute, stinging connection of real moments from my life. These moments were, in a way, preserved in my memory, as if enclosed in a membrane, and they had kept all the intensity of their initial existence. They were memories in membranes, kept untouched by time. The dream-bet of *The Hours* was how to burst these time bubbles and create a time flow, finally including and accepting the frozen moments of the past. So, this film is the closest I have made to autobiography, yet it is a fiction; a fiction made from bubbles containing real moments of my life.

In *The Hours*, places in the industrial zone of Laurium in Attica were used as shooting locations. There was also a very significant construction, initially the interior of a bedroom, which was gradually transformed during the film. All the experience of the central character was materialised in the room. The room gradually froze, the walls, the furniture, the bed drapes, everything became earth, like a dug grave. At the time, I had a desire to make clothes out of earth. I drew clothes that stood erect like statues, made of soil and thorns. It was as if I extended the logic of *Screen–Matrix*, where I worked with nails, and turned it into human bodies. The body became earth. I saw the body as earth, and simultaneously as a dress that you can take off. In *The Hours*, I included an experience that I had, where I saw my own body from the outside. So, in the film this room made of earth appears, which in the end is immersed, drowned in water, to wash away this feeling of malice, enmity that I felt from my environment. And I arrive to pronounce the motto of the film – where the loving and the hating ones become one.

RW – It is not that they become one, I think; it is more of a dedication to them all.

AA – It is a Christian phrase, which also incorporates the end of my psychoanalysis, and my readings on shamanism, on what the Native American shamans call 'small tyrants'.

RW – Yes, I remember. I think that it particularly has a sense of forgiveness. The archaic syntax of the phrase resonates with the words of the mass. Most Greeks would recognise that the first, missing, part of the phrase is: 'We pray' – so, 'We pray for those who love us and for those who hate us'. After all, in the film, the central character says, 'I forgive you'.

AA – Yes, yes, 'I forgive you', yes, yes, in the end. When the room collapses and everything has become mud, and I am there, in the mud, and by myself, at last. Throughout the film I am always in relation to other people, but there I am found by myself and I find myself at last, and I say to all the ghosts of the past: 'I forgive you. *Go away!*', I release them. After I made this film, I felt hugely relieved, liberated. And yet, this film was not realised completely the way I wanted it; in recent years, I have been thinking that it would be interesting to make a film called *The Hours – After*.

RW – I would like to ask you about the relationship between how you imagined situations and dreams and schemata, and how these were realised in the films; for example, I remember the 'standing-vertical water'. . .

AA – The standing-vertical water, I initially conceived for *Topos*; I was even drawing it. As is known, I am an architect; it does not elude me that water cannot be vertically cut and stand alone. Yet, I was obsessed with it at the time.

And I am grateful that Claire (Mitsotaki), to whom I described my vision, did not correct me, did not tell me that this thing is impossible. She just quietly listened to what I said. And I kept drawing this standing-vertical water, which I wanted to appear in the last part of *Topos*, the Game, where all the elements of the previous parts were reversed. The game was an inversion of the laws of nature.

RW – Let us come now, to a genesis that we shared . . .

AA – Our creative collaboration started in reality a short time before *The Hours*. It is true that I wrote *The Hours* by myself . . . I had a collection of dreams, fragments of reality, pieces of paintings that were pouring themselves out of themselves, and notes, notes, notes, notes, notes. So, I sat in front of Rea, you, and I asked her to listen to me. And I told her all that as a continuous piece of speech and images, and I recorded it. It had been impossible for me to turn my parallel scores into a script that could be proposed for funding. I kept making new scores and drawings, and I couldn't turn them into a continuous text. I must say that, initially, I had tried to tell the film to my psychoanalyst but he refused.

RW – It was maybe good that you got out of the space of psychoanalysis. The film became something different from the narration of your analysis; it became an independent work addressed to the outside world.

AA – Precisely. I had understood that I was using psychoanalysis to channel my need for creation, and that I was wasting my efforts, and I wanted to get out of this situation. So, I found this adolescent girl, Rea, who sat there and listened to me, and my speech materialised and became the script of *The Hours*. So, you may not be a part of the creation of *The Hours*, but our collaboration starts then. After that, you left for Thessaloniki, to study architecture, and you didn't have a telephone, so we started an immense correspondence, which amounts to volumes of hand-written letters. I wrote freely. I knew that what we wrote to each other would be the material for a new film. So, I kept both sides of the correspondence.

RW – So did I. We both knew that our letters were part of a creative process. We started writing this film the year before I left for Thessaloniki, working on ideas about the Underworld and Antigone.

AA – Yes. And this is what we continued to do for the following years. We wrote letters to each other, and met on vacations, from 1995 to 2000, and wrote the script, and its variations. We did several proposals that were rejected before the one that was accepted. In the same way that the proposal of *The 13 Terrors* with Claire (Mitsotaki) was rejected before *Topos* and two scripts before *The Hours*, two scripts before *Thief or Reality* were rejected too. We had given them different titles: *The Hanging* and *Fragments*. The initial title of the final version was *On the Visible and the Invisible*.

The Thief, the character of the Thief as someone who comes and traverses the film, was your idea. So was the word 'reality' and the disjunction between them. While we wrote the script, we wrote down our thoughts about it, and at some moment we had this ingenious idea to use all this material to make a fourth meta-linguistic level, where all the characters of the film would meet around a table, dead and alive together.

RW – It was my inspiration, I was reading Words and Things *by Michel Foucault at the time, and it was I who made the composition. The words, however, come from both of us.*

On speech and death

AA – In composing this film, the different kinds of speech were important, and how these were expressed by different characters.

RW – Around the time that we were finishing the script, I was obsessed with linguistic functions. I was in an in-between phase of my life, finishing my first studies and just before I changed discipline to work on a PhD in philosophy. The structure of the film, the triple viewpoint, is a testimony to my turn to philosophical inquiry. On the other hand, a part of my linguistic readings was centred on Roman Jakobson and his theories on aphasia and the way toddlers learn to speak. I was thrilled, less with their scientific input and more with their poetic potential. It was from there that I found inspiration for a series of techniques regarding the structuring of discourse, and the processes of losing and re-finding the ability to speak. The speech of the characters of the Sculptress and the Scientist are based on the two kinds of aphasia, which was a way to stress their complementarity. Both you and I were preoccupied with the notion of losing and re-finding the ability to speak. After all, this is a repeated theme in your films. So, in this script, we worked on losing and re-finding speech, in many different ways. Even more so, this is the structuring principle of the 'Water Libretto'. In its construction, it follows the process of a toddler's learning to speak, that is why it starts with 'mama'; from a narrative point of view, it is the moment that the character of the Scientist manages to mourn her loss and thus to speak again.

AA – My story, which as you said always appears in my films, has to do with my own experience of losing and re-discovering the ability to speak, and of silence. After a violation in my childhood, I fell silent. I wouldn't speak and I couldn't understand what words meant. It was then that my father helped me, without fully knowing how and why. He started drawing pictures for me, a kind of primitive storyboard, which helped me to understand words again. This is what I allude to in the monologue of the short *Tears Sins*, which is included in my installation *Organic Games*. In a way this is the beginning of my conception of visual scores. Early in my life, I had the experiences of both losing speech and visualising words.

RW – For my part, I have always expressed myself well with both words and images, and I was convinced of their equivalence and communication. In my studies and research, I attempted to defend this position theoretically, which is still central to my research. About the time that we wrote Thief or Reality, *I came across the concept of synaesthesia, as well as Freud's visualisation, and soon after, I started studying Jacques Derrida. In* Thief or Reality, *apart from the structure, which was mostly mine, there was a rich material from multiple sources. The starting point was the story of the suicide of the actor, which was your preoccupation, as was interweaving it with* Antigone *and Bernhard. You invited me into this story. However, there was a meeting point for us both: we were at in-between phases in our lives. I was on the edge of adulthood and you were entering a different age of your life, and we spoke a lot of death. The film may be an invitation to live; the Thief is death.*

AA – I would say that I was always preoccupied with death. The first shot of *Idées Fixes* is a cemetery; in *Topos*, a woman gives birth and dies; in *The Hours*, a woman attempts suicide and re-evaluates her life; and the earth bodies I drew were tombs in a way, as were many of the environments and objects I created. Simultaneously, my real life had a relationship with death from a very early age. A particularly repulsive person to me, my governess Miss Sophia, represented a distorted, deathly religiosity; and then, the violation by my violin teacher took away my speech. Death was always there. So, the fact that we spoke openly about death in *Thief or Reality* was liberating for me. The suicide of Skylodimos didn't make sense to me though. He committed suicide while playing Antigone, in the way that Antigone did. I was shaken. It became an obsession of mine. I couldn't understand why he would do such a thing, precisely because I had had near-death experiences. I put in his mouth my thoughts in the post-mortem monologue: 'There has never been a paradise.' Death in *Thief or Reality* is a precondition – you said this – for us humans recognising our limits, becoming citizens. Being mortal makes us alive.

RW – Yes, all humans have this in common; and it can be the basis for solidarity between us all, despite us seeing the world in very different ways. This idea was central for me: being mortal and knowing it, as a condition of possibility for humanity. Moreover, this awareness may be liberating; it becomes a summons to live.

AA – For me, this film is simultaneously about playing with death and how playing conquers death. In a way, we include death in our being human. Darkness is not necessarily an enemy of light.

RW – This intimacy, this familiarity, is your perception. For me, death is a limit. That is why the character of Thief in the film can function as a screen for the other characters' desires – the phrasing that Thief is a screen was yours, by the way. The Thief is death, and reality as well. The Thief is there and unites us all; but each sees something different there. So, this non-being there, I am not sure if it is a synthesis of light and darkness, as you say.

AA – For me, it is a synthesis. From early on in our lives, we understand that we play with it. The strange thing is that this game begins in childhood. Already inside the concept of play, death is inscribed. By repeating death, we diminish its reality. It reminds us that reality always evades us and we never know the Real until the moment of death. Play as a fundamental principle of existence includes death and our acceptance of leaving behind the sources that defined us at birth. We diverge and converge, constructing a bridge, which prepares us during our entire life for the moment of death. The non-representable is represented at the moment of passage. What we look for in art, and this is crucial for me, is to transform death into existence, through children's play.

To play the game of art, we put in it our entire existence. And what is decisive for the success of a work, is that after it is finished, we understand ourselves better.

Appendix

Visual material selected by Antoinetta Angelidi

Figure A.1 Angelidi directing. From the shooting of the film *Topos* at the Gazi Factory, 1984.

APPENDIX 223

Figure A.2 Still, Angelidi, *Topos* (1985).

Figure A.3 Still, Angelidi, *Topos* (1985).

Figure A.4 Still, Angelidi, *Topos* (1985).

Figure A.5 Angelidi at the Gazi Factory. Portrait by Maria Stefosi, 1988.

APPENDIX   225

Figure A.6 Angelidi, preparatory sketch for the film *The Hours – A Square Film*, 1989.

Figure A.7 Angelidi, preparatory sketch for the installation *Boat–Matrix*, 1990.

Figure A.8 Angelidi, *Screen–Matrix*, installation (Epikentro, Patras, 1991).

Figure A.9 Still, Angelidi, *The Hours – A Square Film* (1995).

APPENDIX 227

Figure A.10 Still, Angelidi, *The Hours – A Square Film* (1995).

Figure A.11 Still, Angelidi, *The Hours – A Square Film* (1995).

Figure A.12 Still, Angelidi, *Thief or Reality* (2001).

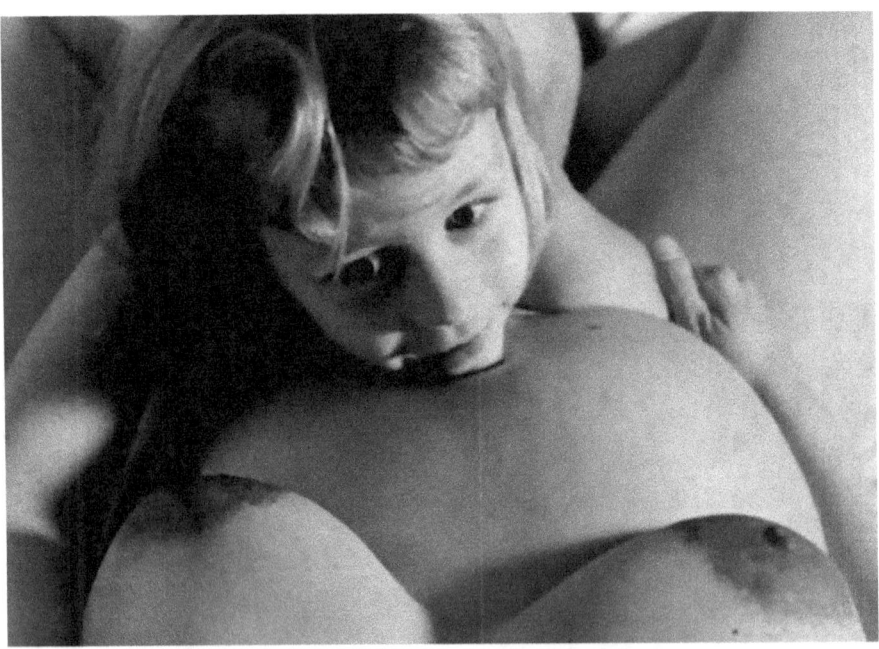

Figure A.13 Still, Angelidi and Walldén, *121280 Ritual* (2008). Original material shot in 1980.

APPENDIX 229

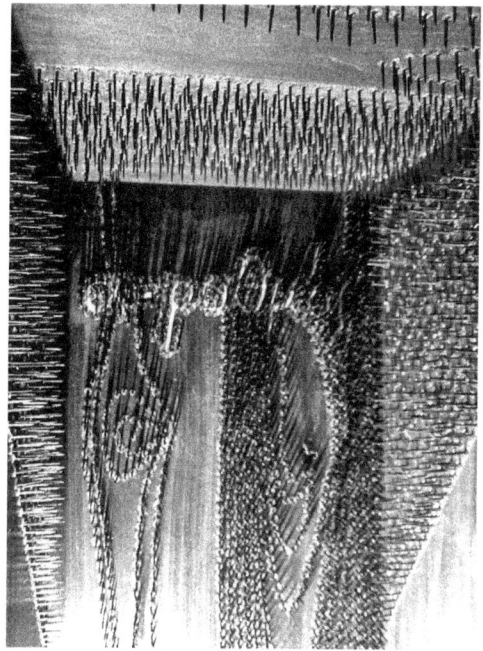

Figure A.14 Angelidi, *Father, Chair*, installation ('Stranger in a Strange Land', ReMap 3, Athens, 2011).

Figure A.15 Angelidi, 'Stitches Without Thread', environment (Choros 18, Thessaloniki, 2012).

Filmography

FEATURE-LENGTH FILMS

Εμμονες Ωρες Στον Τοπο Της Πραγματικοτητας (2022)
[*Obsessive Hours at the Topos of Reality*]
co-direction with Rea Walldén
166 min, digital, colour

Μηδεια / Κορη (in progress since 2008)
[*Medea / Kore*]

Κλεφτης h h Πραγματικοτητα (2001)
[*Thief or Reality*]
80 min, 35mm, colour

Οι Ωρες: Μια Τετραγωνη Ταινια (1995)
[*The Hours – A Square Film*]
80 min, 35mm, colour

Τοπος (1985)
[*Topos*]
80 min, 35mm, colour

Idées Fixes / Dies Irae (παραλλαγες στο ιδιο θεμα) (1977)
[*Idées Fixes / Dies Irae* (*Variations on the Same Subject*)]
62 min, 16mm, b/w with one coloured shot

SHORT AND MEDIUM-LENGTH FILMS

Encore – Το Τανισμα (2013)
[*Encore – Stretching*]
3 min 13 sec, digital, b/w

Tears Sins (2013)
21 min 15 sec, digital, colour

121280 Ritual (2008/1980)
co-direction with Rea Walldén
16 min, 16mm/digital, b/w

Knot – Not – Knot (2007)
co-direction with Rea Walldén
4 min, digital, colour

Metamorphosis Of/by AA (2007)
47 min, digital, colour

Ωρα Μεσημεριου (2006)
[*Noon Hour*]
co-direction with Rea Walldén
31 min, digital, colour

Το Δωρο (1981)
[*The Gift*]
30 min, 16mm, b/w

L'eau (1976)
[*The Water*]
7 min, 35mm, colour

L'histoirécrite (1975)
7 min, video, b/w

EXHIBITED ARTWORK

Οργανικα Παιχνιδια Ii (2013)
[*Organic Games Ii*]
installation

Ραβοντασ Χωρισ Κλωστη (2012)
[*Stitches Without Thread*]
multi-screen installation

Πατέρας, η Καρέκλα (2011)
[*Father, Chair*]
installation

Μαυρα Νερα (2001)
[*Black Waters*]
installation

Σελιδα Απο Το Βιβλιο Των Ωρων (1994)
[*Page from the Book of Hours*]
installation

Οθονη–Matrix (1990)
[*Screen–Matrix*]
installation

Πτωσεις (1989)
[*Falls*]
paintings

Εχιδνες (1982)
[*Vipers*]
multi-material objects

Index

abject, abjected, abjection, 23, 28, 99
abstract, abstraction, 3, 4, 28, 50, 54, 93, 128–31, 133, 134, 146, 167, 187
actor, 4, 9, 80, 96, 146, 157, 167, 171, 199, 200–2, 204, 207, 209, 215, 220
actress, 97, 99, 153, 167, 177, 199, 200, 201, 202, 204, 205, 209, 210, 215
affect, 68, 71, 77, 79, 83, 144, 146, 177
aggression, 68, 73, 96, 174, 181n21
Akerman, Chantal, 145, 184n47
Althusser, Louis Pierre, 18
ambient sound, 145, 154–6
androgyne, 178
Angelico, Fra, 29, 191, 192, 215
apparatus
    film, 19, 49, 151
    mental, 70, 78
    muscular, 88n71
    psychical, 71, 72, 75
Artman, Gilbert, 155, 208
audible, 114, 119, 151
audiovisual, audiovisuality, 10, 40, 53, 106, 114, 143, 144, 146, 149, 154
auditorium, 53, 148

auditory, 147, 149–53
    perception, 144
    cinema, 144
autoeroticism, 179

Balthus, Balthasar Klossowski de Rola, 29, 30, 191, 192, 201
Baroque, 132
Barthes, Roland, 147
Baudry, Jean-Louis, 19, 91–3
Beckett, Samuel, 100
Bellour, Raymond, 19, 37n21
Bergman, Ingmar, 135
Bordwell, David, 109, 110, 154
bound/unbound energy, 71, 72, 78, 79, 81, 126, 181n27
Brakhage, Stan, 46, 48, 50, 51, 54, 60n48
Brecht, Berthold, 26, 39n65, 49, 109
Breuer, Josef, 71
Burch, Noël, 4, 10n1
Burke, Edmund, 8, 125–9, 132, 134
byzantine, 80, 131, 132

Cage, John, 156, 158, 200
camera obscura, 18, 29
Carpaccio, Vittore, 29, 191, 215, 216

cathexis, 71, 79, 81
Chion, Michel, 145, 148, 152, 153, 159
Chirico, Giorgio, 9, 190, 191, 214–16
choreography, 134, 135, 155, 156
Cinema 16, 51, 54
cinema theatre, 92, 156
cogito, 20
commercial
　film/cinema, 46, 47, 91, 146
communist, 3, 39n58, 55, 56, 94
compulsion, 68, 70, 71, 76–8, 82–4, 86n29, 86n44, 108
condensation, 26, 83, 175, 204, 216
constancy principle, 70
contextualisation, 8, 51, 144, 158
Corday, Charlotte, 175–9, 182n33
corporeality, 130, 167
Courbet, Gustave, 28

Da Vinci, Leonardo, 153
Dada, 46, 58, 187
Dante, Alighieri, 33, 35, 153, 206, 209
David, Louis, 175
death drive, 68, 72, 79, 80, 81, 86n20, 182n29
death instinct, 67–9, 71–4, 78–82, 84, 85n2, 85n9, 86n44
defamiliarisation, 4, 8, 17, 24, 26, 106–10, 113, 124
Deleuze, Gilles, 128, 129, 131, 134, 151
Deren, Maya, 51, 52
Derrida, Jacques, 8, 28, 107, 110–13, 116, 119, 125, 220
dialectic, dialectical, 4, 23, 55, 58, 114, 121, 122, 128, 175
dictatorship, 1, 3, 94
différance, 110
displacement, 23, 26, 28, 73, 80, 83, 178, 179, 216
distribution, 144
Doane, Ann Marie, 20

documenta exhibition, Kassel, 3, 147, 200, 213
dolby digital, 143–5, 152, 155–7, 159n3
doublage, 152
dream
　mechanism, 24, 124, 154, 216
　work, 4, 5, 26, 83
Dreyer, Carl, 25, 129, 130, 165–8, 172, 173, 177, 179, 180n4, 183n38, 183n44, 183n45, 205
dubbing, 152
Dulac, Germaine, 50

editing, 55, 128, 143, 145, 146, 173, 203, 204, 208, 214
Eikhenbaum, Boris, 53, 109
Eisenstein, Sergei, 46, 54, 55, 208
electro-acoustic, 155
ellipse, 114, 116, 121, 173, 178, 179
elliptical narrative, 130
empathy, 129, 130, 134
Enlightenment, 16, 18, 20
epistemological revolution, 20
Ernst, Max, 189, 194n8, 204, 213
Eros, 67, 69, 70, 79, 80
expanded cinema, 53, 60n49
experimental cinema, 1, 9, 45–7, 56, 57, 113, 145
experimentation, 1, 7, 24, 26
　artistic, 136
　form, 17

femininity, 4, 115–19, 151, 204
feminism, 2, 6, 7, 17, 18, 25, 36, 152
feminist, 2, 5–7, 9, 15, 16, 18–21, 24, 25, 26, 28, 33, 39n58, 46, 55, 58, 99, 144, 145, 160n27, 186
film
　lyrical, 47, 48, 54
　novel, 46
　poem, 46, 52, 53
　structural, 4, 47–9, 56–8, 59 n16

filmic event, 148, 149
formalism, 106, 108, 110, 113, 122
Francesca, Pierro Della, 191, 192
French Impressionism, 128, 129
French Revolution, 16, 183n35
Freud, Sigmund, 4, 7, 18, 20–4, 38n29, 38n31 67–84, 85n2, 85n9, 85n10, 85n11, 86n19, 86n20, 86n29, 86n44, 92, 94, 106–11, 113, 171, 181n21, 188, 190, 192, 216, 220
Futurism, futurist, 46, 158, 187

Gance, Abel, 128
gaze, 29, 33, 36, 75, 79, 95, 101, 118, 135, 150, 173, 186, 193, 205, 209
Gehr, Ernie, 48, 49
German expressionism, 128, 129, 131, 132
gestalt, 158
Giotto, di Bordone, 131, 192
Gombrich, Ernst Hans, 131
gothic, 4, 130, 131, 213
Goya, Francisco, 187
Greek Film Centre, 5, 6, 146, 216
Greek Weird Wave cinema, 9, 11n29, 12, 36

heterogeneity, 24, 26, 39n55, 46, 47, 52, 124, 130, 149, 199, 200
heterosexual 20, 38n33
Hoffmann, E. T. A., 108

identification, 19, 26, 27, 94, 98, 101, 110, 134
  primary, 91, 100
  secondary, 92, 100
identity, 7, 8, 36, 91, 93–5, 97–101, 103, 164, 173
IDHEC, 3, 10n15, 39n58, 200, 205, 214
imaginary, 19, 23, 92, 98, 106, 121, 131, 133–5
imaginative, 96, 97, 125, 136
impulse, 22, 72, 75, 77, 83, 86n29, 171
inanimate, 32, 67, 72, 79, 149

industrial
  cinema, 47
  society, 179
  sound, 144, 155
  space, 2, 32, 158, 212, 213, 216, 217
infantile
  complex, 23
  neurosis, 181n21
instinctual, 76, 84, 84n1
  force, 7, 70, 71, 80
  impulse, 72, 75, 86n29
  theory, 69, 79, 81, 84
instrument, instrumental, instrumentality, 19, 52, 53, 113, 129, 147, 153, 154, 161n50, 208
Irigaray, Luce, 21–3, 25, 33, 38n36, 102, 172, 178
isotopy, 164
Isou, Isidore, 53, 60n48

Jones, Ernest, 69
jouissance, 21, 23, 172, 177, 182n29–n30

Kant, Immanuel, 8, 16, 125–9, 131, 133, 138n25
Karalis, Vrasidas, 3, 4, 73, 96, 130, 147
Klein, Melanie, 98
Kristeva, Julia, 17, 99, 102
Kuntzel, Thierry, 4, 5, 19

landscape, 145, 154, 156, 166, 177, 192, 200
Lang, Fritz, 192
language, 4, 21, 28, 48, 51, 52, 54, 57, 58, 68, 83, 110, 111, 120, 144, 146, 150, 152, 153, 167, 173, 182n29, 210
  cinematic, 1, 46, 124, 125, 136, 137
  poetic, 17, 102, 108, 109
Laplanche, Jean, 69, 82, 85n11, 87n56, 181n21, 181n27
Laurentis, Teresa de, 20
Le Grice, Malcolm, 19, 48, 56, 59n16, 93
Lemaître, Maurice, 53, 60n48

INDEX 235

lettrist, 53, 58, 60n48
Lévi-Strauss, Claude, 111
libidinal, non-libidinal, 68–71, 73, 79, 81, 97, 98, 102, 181
libido, 69, 72, 79, 80, 81, 98
locus, 27, 164, 186, 191
Lyotard, Jean-François, 126, 136, 167, 183n40
lyrical, 47, 48, 54

Magritte, René, 3, 114, 147, 170–2, 174–6, 181n25, 183n37, 184n46, 188, 194n8, 200, 213, 214
mantra, 149, 150
Marat, 49, 56, 120, 121, 175–9, 183n35
Marxist, 2, 55, 56
masochism, masochist, masochistic, 68, 70, 71, 73, 76, 77, 79, 88n67, 88n72, 181n21
materialist, materiality, materialistic, 7, 19, 26, 28, 92, 93, 135, 146, 147
Mayakovski, Vladimir, 55, 181n25
Mekas, Jonas, 59
materialist, materiality, materialistic, 7, 19, 26, 73, 81
metaglotism, 152
metaphysics, metaphysical, 20, 23, 36, 68, 77, 85n11, 111, 112, 129, 138n25
metapsychology, metapsychological, 19, 20, 68, 85n11, 85n12
Metz, Christian, 4, 18, 19, 91–3, 109, 200
mimesis, 116, 117, 129, 130, 134, 173, 178, 179
mirror stage, 20, 92–4
mise-en-scène, 11n26, 81, 130, 165, 171
Möbius strip, 34
modern, modernist, modernism, 25, 46, 47, 50, 51, 53, 125, 191
Modleski, Tania, 20
mono-
    cinema, 156
    film, 144, 157
    phonic, 143, 146, 148, 155
montage, 55, 183 n43

moviola, 143, 151, 155
multi-
    channel, 145, 159n3, 159n4
    track, 145
Mulvey, Laura, 20, 95, 145
Murnau, Friedrich Wilhelm, 4, 205
musical, 4, 40n90, 154–7, 200, 208, 209, 212, 214
musicality, 149, 150, 153–6, 208, 209

name of the father, 23, 98, 104n23
narcissism, narcissistic, 69, 79, 80, 102
Narcissus, 160n31, 190
negative therapeutic reaction, 70, 71, 82
Nietzsche, Friedrich, 81
nirvana, 70
non-binary, 169

object relation, 79, 88n82, 172, 181n27
objectification, 118, 179
objet petit a, 28, 173, 182n30
Oedipal, 20, 21, 33, 169, 171, 182n29
ontogenetic, 137
ontological, 8, 137
optical sound, 143, 156
oral stage, 98, 172, 181n27
ostranenie, 109

paradox, paradoxical, 8, 52, 67, 68, 81, 127, 131, 136, 137, 164, 182
patriarchal, 15, 18, 20–3, 27–9, 35, 57, 98, 102, 190, 205
patriarchy, 24, 98–100, 119, 178
phallus, 23, 99, 179
phenomenology, 110
pietà, 175, 183n40
pleasure principle, 67–71, 76, 78, 80, 82–4, 86n29, 182n29, 183n40
Poetika Kino, 109
poetry, 46, 48, 51–4, 127
Pontalis, Jean-Bertrand, 82
Pontormo, Jacopo, 29, 40n86, 191, 215
Potamianou, Anna, 72, 80, 85n2, 85n17

primal scene, 170–2, 174, 175, 181n21
psychedelic, 193
psychoanalytic theory, 20, 33

Rank, Otto, 108
Ray, Man, 46
realism, 17
reality principle, 69, 70, 98
reconstruction, 34
religion, religious, 33, 41n100, 67, 75–77, 101, 127, 129, 138n25, 191, 193
Renaissance, 18, 29, 30, 132, 135, 176, 190, 191, 215
repress, repression, repressed, 15, 23, 24, 27, 28, 35, 68, 75, 77, 81–4, 86n29, 102, 108, 175, 190, 206
rhythm, rhythmic, rhythmically, 30, 32, 34, 80, 114, 119, 146, 147, 149, 150, 153, 156, 193
Richter, Hans, 46
ritual, ritualistic, 29, 34, 67, 80, 111, 130, 132, 135, 149, 166, 172, 183n45, 187, 190, 191, 192
Romanticism, romantic, 17, 31, 32, 50, 171
Rousseau, Jean-Jacques, 111
Russolo, Luigi, 158

sadistic, 171, 182
Saussure, Ferdinand de, 18, 21, 109–12
semantic, 8, 16, 17, 48, 55, 102, 103, 146
semiotic, semiotically, 4, 18, 25, 49, 102, 106, 107, 112, 114–16, 118, 122
sexuality, 2, 4, 20–2, 38n31, 83 150
Shklovsky, Victor, 4, 17, 108, 109
signifier, 17, 19, 22, 28, 92, 108, 110–12, 114, 116, 118, 120, 124, 132, 135, 165, 168, 176, 182n27, 182n30
  cinematic, 93
  imaginary, 92
silent cinema, 130
Sitney, Adams P., 7, 47–9, 59n16
situatedness, 149
Snow, Michael, 49, 50

soma (body), 94
somatic, somatically, 158, 188
sonification, 146
sound
  marks, 154
  effects, 154
soundscape, 8, 144–9, 154, 156, 157
soundtrack, 5, 30, 116, 132, 143–8, 151, 152, 154–9, 179, 180, 183n43, 211
sous rature, 8, 112–15, 120
soviet
  avant-garde, 46, 51
  filmmaker, 55
  theorist, 53
spatiality, 27, 36, 115, 132, 135, 136, 152, 167
spectatorship 26, 92
spectre, spectral, spectrality, 8, 107, 112–15, 118–22, 178, 180
stillness, 55, 74, 92, 183n40
strangeness, 24, 26, 29, 36, 40n67, 124, 125
structural, 7, 17, 18, 19, 25, 27, 32, 36, 45, 50, 51, 110, 165, 200, 207
  feminism, 6
  film, 4, 47–9, 59n16
  filmmakers, filmmaking, 56–8
  poetics, 26
sublime, sublimity, 68, 125–37
super ego, 71, 74, 75, 77, 80, 81, 85n9
supernatural, 171
supplement, supplementarity, 20, 38n32, 111, 114, 116, 179
surrealism, surrealist, 29, 46, 58, 114, 171, 187, 188, 216
symbolic, symbolical, symbolically, 23, 35, 75, 81, 84, 87, 88n67, 96, 98, 100–2, 106, 111, 133, 165, 173, 182n27, n29, n30, n40, 183n42, 209
symbolism, 75, 189
synaesthesia, 26, 32, 220
synchronisation, 146, 148, 152, 153
syntagme, 109, 164, 167, 178

tableau vivant, 74
Thessaloniki Film Festival (International), 5, 6, 9, 146, 159n12
Thibaudeau, Jean, 5, 12, 49, 214
Thompson, Kristin, 109
tonal, tonalities, 149, 152, 153
Tornes, Stavros, 32
transcendence, 125, 127, 129, 134, 136, 137, 138n25
transcendental, 28, 54, 129, 132, 137, 174, 179
traumatic, 68, 70, 77, 78, 80, 83, 111, 170

unconscious, 19–21, 27, 33, 34, 68, 71, 75, 77, 80–3, 93, 103, 109, 122, 143, 146, 171, 187, 216
  collective, 25, 36

unheimlich, heimlich, 107, 109, 188
Urban Sax, 155, 208
uterus, 193
utopia, utopian, 16, 56, 176, 187

verbalisation 167
Vertov, Dziga 46, 51, 55
visual poem 173, 178
visualisation 26, 83, 205, 220
Vogel, Amos 54

Wees, C. William, 47, 50, 53, 54
wish fulfilment, 69, 70, 78
Wollen, Peter, 46
writing-under-erasure, 8, 107, 113, 116, 117, 119, 121, 122

EU representative:
Easy Access System Europe
Mustamäe tee 50, 10621 Tallinn, Estonia
Gpsr.requests@easproject.com